W9-AEF-067

WITHDRAWN

WILLIAM FAULKNER: THE YOKNAPATAWPHA WORLD AND BLACK BEING

PS
3511
.A86
Z94615
1983

WILLIAM FAULKNER: THE YOKNAPATAWPHA WORLD AND BLACK BEING

by

Erskine Peters, Ph.D.
(UNIVERSITY OF CALIFORNIA, BERKELEY)

NORWOOD EDITIONS
Darby, Pennsylvania
1983

Salem Academy and College
Gramley Library
Winston-Salem, N.C. 27108

Copyright © 1983 by Erskine Peters

LIBRARY OF CONGRESS CATALOGING IN PUBLICATION DATA

Peters, Erskine.
William Faulkner, The Yoknapatawpha world and black being.

Bibliography: p.
Includes index.
1. Faulkner, William, 1897-1962–Criticism and interpretation. 2. Faulkner, William, 1897-1962–Characters–Afro-American. 3. Race relations in literature. 4. Afro-Americans in literature. I. Title. II. Title: Yoknapatawpha world and black being.
PS3511.A86Z94615 1983 813'52 82-24657
ISBN 0-8482-5675-1 (Lib. Bdg.)

Design and Typesetting by
Mark Weiman

Manufactured in the United States of America
NORWOOD EDITIONS
Darby, Pennsylvania 19023

Dedicated to:

Paine College

Mama and Daddy

and
Miss Sarah and Mr. Doyle

Table of Contents

Preface

In my efforts to write a critical and speculative study, but also a useful and comprehensive one, I am indebted to many people. I especially want to thank Professors Carlos Baker and A. Walton Litz who guided the manuscript during its earliest stages, and who made me aware of the work to be done before I would have a worthwhile book. I am also very grateful for the suggestions and time given about and to various portions or all of the manuscript by Professors Barbara Christian and Marjorie Pryse. I am equally indebted, however, to about a half dozen or more anonymous but highly knowledgeable experts in the field who read and commented upon the whole or parts of this manuscript over the past six years when evaulations were requested by them by publishers or my senior colleagues at Berkeley.

None of the efforts of myself, my readers and evaulators would have come to fruition so soon though without the support of my research and teaching assistants: Resa Perlsten Sussner, Anthony Lemelle, Faith Mitchell, and Elfreda Chatman. For their fine typing services I wish to thank Susan Tiller, Mary Clarke, and Cynthia Sharp. Additional gratitude is owed to Elfreda Chatman, Cynthia Sharp and Sala Ajaniku for their extraordinary persistence and industry as we worked to bring the manuscript into its final form. Wendy Jester has given very good assistance as an editor. Thanks also to Herb Highstone for editorial assistance. Claire Burch and Mark Weiman have given support in so many areas.

For the cordial and generally splendid services of the library staffs at the United States Military Academy at West Point, where I was permitted by Colonel Jack L. Capps to use unpublished parts of the Faulkner concordances; the William Faulkner Collections, University of Virginia Library, where I was able to examine many of Faulkner's original manuscripts; and the Mississippi Collection, University of Mississippi Library, where I was able to search through many kinds of materials, I extend sincere appreciation.

For financial support I am grateful for the various amounts in grants received through the Rockefeller Fellowships in Afro-American Studies at Princeton University, the Faculty Development Program and the Department of Afro-American Studies at the University of California/Berkeley.

Obviously, I am indebted to numerous scholars such as Joseph Blotner, Jean Fagan Yellin, Cleanth Brooks–and others. Finally, I am particularly grateful to Agnes Moreland for supplying the phrase "black being" in her Ph.D. dissertation on Faulkner.

June, 1982
E. P.

Acknowledgements

Grateful acknowledgment is made to the following for permission to reprint material from previously published works:

The Memphis *Commercial Appeal:* For excerpts from "To the Editor of the Memphis *Commercial Appeal*" by William Faulkner, published in The Memphis *Commercial Appeal*, March 26, 1950.

The Dial Press: For excerpts from NO NAME IN THE STREET by James Baldwin. Copyright 1972 by James Baldwin.

Farrar, Straus & Giroux, Inc.: For excerpts from MYSTERY AND MANNERS by Flannery O'Connor, edited by Robert and Sally Fitzgerald. Copyright 1969.

Liveright Publishing Company: For excerpts from SOLDIER'S PAY by William Faulkner. Copyright 1926 by William Faulkner.

Louisiana State University Press: For excerpts from THE NOVELS OF WILLIAM FAULKNER by Olga Vickery. Copyright 1964 by Olga Vickery.

New American Library, Inc.: For excerpts from PÈRE GORIOT by Honoré de Balzac. Copyright by Signet Classics, 1962.

New York University Press: For excerpts from THE INTRICATE KNOT: BLACK FIGURES IN AMERICAN LITERATURE, 1776-1863 by Jean Fagan Yellin. Copyright 1972 by New York University.

Salem Academy and College
Gramley Library
Winston-Salem, N.C. 27108

Oxford University Press, Inc.: For excerpts from THE STRANGE CAREER OF JIM CROW by C. Vann Woodward. Copyright 1974.

Random House, Inc., Alfred A. Knopf, Inc.: For excerpts from ABSALOM, ABSALOM, by William Faulkner. Copyright 1972 by Vintage Books.

For excerpts from A FABLE by William Faulkner. Copyright 1954 by William Faulkner.

For excerpts from ALL GOD'S DANGERS: THE LIFE OF NATE SHAW by Theodore Rosengarten. Copyright 1974 by Theodore Rosengarten.

For excerpts from "The Bear" in GO DOWN, MOSES by William Faulkner. Copyright 1955 by William Faulkner.

For excerpts from ESSAYS, SPEECHES AND PUBLIC LETTERS by William Faulkner, edited by James B. Meriwether. Copyright 1965 by James B. Meriwether.

For excerpts from FAULKNER: A BIOGRAPHY by Joseph Blotner. Copyright 1974 by Joseph Blotner.

For excerpts from "The Fire and the Hearth" in GO DOWN, MOSES by William Faulkner. Copyright 1955 by William Faulkner.

For excerpts from FLAGS IN THE DUST by William Faulkner, edited by Douglas Day. Copyright 1973.

For excerpts from THE HAMLET by William Faulkner. Copyright 1973 by William Faulkner.

For excerpts from LIGHT IN AUGUST by William Faulkner. Copyright 1967 by William Faulkner.

For excerpts from INTRUDER IN THE DUST by William Faulkner. Copyright 1967 by William Faulkner.

For excerpts from THE REIVERS by William Faulkner. Copyright 1966 by William Faulkner.

For excerpts from THE SOUND AND THE FURY by William Faulkner. Copyright 1963 by William Faulkner.

For excerpts from "That Evening Sun" in COLLECTED STORIES OF WILLIAM FAULKNER by William Faulkner. Copyright 1950 by William Faulkner.

For excerpts from THE TOWN by William Faulkner. Copyright 1961 by William Faulkner.

For excerpts from THE UNVANQUISHED by William Faulkner. Copyright 1966 by William Faulkner.

Times-Picayune Publishing Corp.: For excerpts from "Yo Ho and Two Bottles of Rum," by William Faulkner. Originally published in The Times-Picayune of

September 27, 1925.

University Press of Virginia: For excerpts from FAULKNER IN THE UNIVERSITY: CLASS CONFERENCES AT THE UNIVERSITY OF VIRGINIA 1957-1958 by William Faulkner, Frederick L. Gwynn and Joseph Blotner, editors. Copyright 1959.

The Viking Press: For excerpts from A PORTRAIT OF THE ARTIST AS A YOUNG MAN by James Joyce. Copyright 1964.

For excerpts from WRITERS AT WORK: THE PARIS REVIEW INTERVIEWS, interview with Jean Stein (1956). Malcolm Cowley, editor. Copyright 1959.

W. W. Northon and Company, Inc.: for excerpts from KILLERS OF THE DREAM by Lillian Smith. Copyright 1949.

I.

The Cultural Legacy

If we are to undertake a thorough investigation of black being, that is, the realm and essence of black life as it is filtered through the thoughts of whites in William Faulkner's Yoknapatawpha world, we must first establish a historical and cultural context. This is necessary not only because the presence of black people in the Yoknapatawpha world is the direct result of a particular historical act—the African slave trade, which generated a troubled racial legacy for the New World; but also because a significant part of the making of this history is directly related to the cultural assumptions and points of view by which black existence itself would be perceived. The specific historical context is therefore germane to an understanding of how a concept of black existence was shaped as a result of black people's peculiar social contact with the American and the European mind.[1] Indeed, such a context establishes that the distorted, racist ideas about blacks with which we have become familiar today were formulated long before there was a William Faulkner. We find, moreover, that many of these ideas were crystallized by some of our world's most influential egalitarian thinkers.

As he reflected upon his visit to the Colony of Long Island from 1728-1730, Bishop Berkley wrote in 1731 that a "main obstacle of conversion" of the Africans and Indians to Christianity was the attitude of the first new world settlers. Berkley saw in these settlers "an ancient antipathy to the Indians . . . together with an irrational contempt of the Blacks, as creatures of another species . . . ."[2] Indications of this attitude as the Bishop observed it had been set down in writing some two centuries earlier by the Portuguese, the first European dealers of the African slave trade. Gomes Eannes De Azurara wrote paternalistically, ethnocentrically, and naively in his fifteenth century *Chronicle*, that the lot of the African since his contact with the European through enslavement had become very much "the contrary of what it had been," suggesting that before their contact with Europeans the Africans "had lived in perdition of soul and body." They had

> lived like beasts, without any custom of reasonable beings—for they had no knowledge of bread or wine, and they were without the covering of clothes, or the lodgement of houses; and worse than all, they had no understanding of good, but only knew how to live in bestial sloth.[3]

As an indication of the deep historical entrenchment of this attitude and its cultural legacy, we find William Faulkner five hundred years later uttering nearly the same words before the Southern Historical Association. Giving what he considered a great affirmation of the gift of Western civilization to black people in America, Faulkner described blacks as "the people who only three hundred years ago were eating rotten elephant and hippo meat in African rain-forests, who lived beside one of the biggest bodies of water without thinking of a sail . . . ."[4]

This pervasive European attitude of the African's otherness is also what characterized the speculations of Thomas Jefferson when he attempted to define the African in his *Notes on the State of Virginia* (1784). Jefferson used these speculations to defend his assertion that black people could never be incorporated into the state. Like Berkley, he wrote that the whites entertained deep-rooted prejudices against the blacks; that the blacks must have had ten thousand memories of the injuries they had sustained at the hands of the whites; that there would be new provocations; and that nature had made "real distinctions." Moreover, he wrote that the confusion created by these divisive circumstances would probably never end until one race had exterminated the other. Moving beyond the observations of Berkley, however, Jefferson further sought to elaborate upon what he labeled the physical and moral objections of whites to blacks. To Jefferson himself, the African's color was objectionable, for its distinction or oppositeness to whiteness seemed to him to have been an aberration of the true likeness of humanity. The result of this color for the Africans was that they had an inferior beauty compared to that of the whites, and the blackness made the Africans suffer from an eternal monotony.

Jefferson proposed, too, that the blacks, whose physical distinctions supposedly marked them as belonging to a lower species, had an inherent desire to mate with the whites "as uniformly as is the preference of the Oranootan for the black woman over those of his own species." Blacks supposedly possessed "a very strong and disagreeable odour" because, contrary to whites, they secreted more by the glands of the skin than by the kidneys and also, probably, because there was "a difference of structure in the pulmonary apparatus." That these freelaboring blacks could be induced to partake in amusements after a hard day's labor, knowing they had to work the next day, was evidence that blacks needed less sleep than whites.

If the blacks had brave and adventuresome characteristics, Jefferson stated, this proceeded more from the natural lack of forethought than from any true sense of courage. Sex for the black mates was more the result of passion and impulse "than a tender delicate mixture of sentiment and sensation." Grief and suffering were soon forgotten and the general existence of the blacks was characterized more by sensation than reflection. Blacks had a "disposition to sleep when abstracted from their diversions, and unemployed in labour." They shared in memory equally with the whites but were distinctly inferior in reason and quite dull in the imagination. Jefferson concluded that to protect or maintain the distinctions in the department of man against these "suspicions" of black inferiority, when emancipated the blacks had to be "removed beyond the reach of mixture." While this was unprecedented in history, he argued, it was necessary.[5]

Within Jefferson's framework lie the racist stereotypes of black being which would have their evolution in the pages of American literature for the next century and beyond. Almost any type from the black as brute beast to the childlike "Sambo" has a resemblance therein. As Jean Yellin has pointed out, Jefferson's delineation is evidence of the fact that the Sambo stereotype was alive in the culture prior to a native literature. Yellin also points out that the plantation novels that began to appear in America during the succeeding generation used this Sambo figure with very little variation. For the next eighty years "the black man was presented in minor roles . . . providing humor and local color, the only development being an increasing insistence on his grotesqueness, his hilarity, and love of servitude."[6] Such, then, is the essence of that thought which history highlights regarding the insidious attitudes held by the European toward the African, and which would duly touch the lives of all Americans.

Racist stereotyping–that is, the codification of the black race as an inferior species of humanity, the archetype of servility, ignorance, passion, and brute strength needing the paternalism of the white race for guidance and survival–which thwarts the early development of Faulkner's artistry and perspective, has its major literary roots in the plantation school writing of the Old South. The reasoning of the plantation fiction advances the conclusion that slavery was beneficial both to the superior whites and the inferior blacks, thus leading to the related premise, more implicitly dramatized in the fiction of later decades, that the blacks should have been content with what the whites deemed appropriate for them.[7]

In contrast are the abolitionist novels which are distinguished most from the plantation school fiction by their perspective and tone. The nostalgia of the plantation tradition is absent and is replaced by a characteristic confrontation with the ominous present. Characters are compelled to act under the sense of an impending doom brought on by the judgement of God or the fundamental working out of history. In the abolitionist novels the bondmen are given more significant roles in the plots, thus being brought more in line with the classical functions of character as have been delineated by critics like Northrop

Frye. But although the abolitionist novelists are much more critical of the system of slavery itself, the racist stereotypes do not always disappear. Some of these works contain as many or more sterotypes as the works of the plantation school. The abolitionist writers are especially inclined to portray the black character as a passive victim of injustices.[8]

The position most antithetical to that of the plantation tradition is found in the slave narratives. The fact that fugitives wrote most of these books as a result of having escaped from slavery is itself the greatest contradiction to the notion of the inherent servility of the black man espoused by the plantation writers. Although these narratives are sometimes remarkably different, each recognizes at some point that slavery was a state of war in which the enslaved victims took on a mask as part of their armor. That is, the bondmen generally saw the nature of their existence as something to resist, not to accept servilely. They struggled to attain self-realization which necessitated a fundamental opposition to authority.

Although Jean Toomer's *Cane* (1923) offers the first compendium of first rate portraits of black being in American prose fiction, Charles Waddell Chesnutt, Paul Laurence Dunbar, and a host of other black writers set out, somewhat as successors to the writers of the slave narratives, to challenge the conventional portraits of black being in American literature which had become even more reinforced by the great currency of the black-faced stage minstrelsy. A good example of this effort is Chesnutt's novel *The Marrow of Tradition* (1901). Types in this work range from that of the extremely dedicated and loyal Mammy to the "bad" or "crazy nigger" figure, to the well-educated, and the ignorant but curious. Chesnutt attempted to re-orient or kill off the stereotyped images for all time.

But like Dunbar, his contemporary, Chesnutt was not always successful at repossessing or reappropriating what he considered to be the true black character behind the mask. This is partly owing to the fact that the humor and pathos of black culture, which Chesnutt, Dunbar, and others appreciated profoundly, had been so abused by the stereotypes of the traditionalist Southern writers and the minstrelsy. Dunbar was sorrow-stricken over the fact that, rather than praise what he considered his more literary pieces, the general audience praised mostly his pieces in the black dialect. And Chesnutt eventually left the world of fiction writing entirely and returned to the practice of law because of the resistance to his point of view from the white American readership.

Among Faulkner's Southern white forerunners, it was George Washington Cable who stood at greatest odds with the plantation school. Like Faulkner, though, Cable was not totally free of racist attitudes. He believed that blacks were inferior to whites in the same way that most Anglo-Saxons believed that they were superior to the Celtics.[9] He saw inequality (which he did not equate with injustice) as a principle of nature relative to the individual and the group. As with Faulkner, there was often a great discrepancy between what Cable communicated in his fictional and his extra-fictional statements. Cable, however, regardless of his biases, had more ideological clarity than Faulkner.

He broke with the Southern fictional tradition by presenting the unequivocal view that justice in the law belongs to every man. He did not find it necessary in his fiction to have the blacks submit to the white man's dictum. In fact, all of the blacks in his novel *The Grandissimes* (1880) demonstrate some form of resistance to their situation. They range from the staunchly defiant Bras-Coupé to the subtle, linguistically adept Clemence. There are no mammies and no Uncle Remuses.

In his works, Cable's indictments are not only clear, but poignant and biting. In concluding the narrative of the runaway Bras-Coupé, for example, there is a sardonic indictment against society. Bras-Coupé is delivered "to the law to suffer only the penalties of the crime he had committed against society by attempting to be a free man." And regarding the punishment by death measured out to Clemence on account of her involvement with sorcery, the narrative reads that the South's fear of her black population "has always been met by the same one antidote—terrific cruelty to the tyrant's victim." Cable was not content simply to illuminate the more blatant injustices, but felt it necessary also to unveil the "sham freedom" granted to the freemen of color in pre-emancipation days. In so doing, he also attacked the fundamentally laissez-faire and more entrenched racist attitudes of the post-Reconstruction period. He wrote that *The Grandissimes* "contained as plain a protest against the times in which it was written as against the earlier times in which its scenes were set."[10]

While Faulkner did not exactly pick up where Cable left off, Hamilton Basso is correct when he calls Cable the "spiritual godfather" of Faulkner and a number of other Southern fiction writers including Ellen Glasgow and Thomas Wolfe.[11] Cable's words about the nature of the artist reverberated even through the next four or five decades down to Faulkner's Nobel prize message on the conflicts of the human heart. Cable, too, stated that it is "the haunted heart" that "makes the true artist of every sort."[12] This chronicling of the ways of the human heart is the underlying concern of this study.

So complexly rooted in the culture was the negative regard for blacks that not even the black writers themselves were totally exempt. As black novelist Paule Marshall has written,

> The Negro writer, instead of being primarily concerned with capturing Negro life in all its richness and complexity, instead of seeking to explore character in the full, which is a writer's main responsibility, was largely responding to the myth, reacting to it.[13]

Seymour Gross points out that when one really considers the history of the black person in the United States, one is hardly surprised to find that the concept of the stereotype dominates the criticism of the black man's image in the literature. The black man was a figure of moral debate and historical controversy from the country's inception. As an anomaly in a purported democracy from whose indicting presence the nation actually "could not flee except through chromatic fantasies, the Negro has always been more of a formula than a human being."[14]

Gross' "chromatic fantasies" points to stock figures used systematically to espouse notions of inferiority about black being. Alain Locke[15] and Sterling Brown[16] have classified these types as the comic peasant and comic Negro, the scapegoat, the bogey, pariah, savage stranger, and brute nigger, the tragic mulatto, and the exotic primitive. In attempting to define black being in such terms, many writers have inescapably and inadvertently left records of their own peculiar psychological condition. The study of the image of the black person in American literature becomes, then, also a study of aspects and manners of the white American mind and in particular, this mind as it is shaped by its own ethnocentrism, ignorance, naivete, insecurities, hate, fear, and guilt.

Literary history shows that before the advent of the plantation school Western literature is replete with stereotypic and stock characters which have little if anything to do with African being. Before Europe's contact with the African, there is the vice type character of the morality play and the vengeance-seeking hero, the avenging ghost, and the scheming murder villain of the revenge tragedy. From the Elizabethan tradition come the disguised heroine, the melancholy man, the loquacious old counsellor, the female servant-confidante, the court fool, the witty clownish servant. There are the cruel stepmother and charming prince of the fairy tales, the fainting heroine of the sentimental novel, the quest figure of the romance, and so on.[17] Nevertheless, as Northrop Frye has pointed out in his *Anatomy of Criticism:* to be a stock character does not mean that the being of the character is not capable of being individualized, rounded, and dynamic.[18] An excellent illustration of this point is found in Ralph Ellison's *Invisible Man*. Here, almost every character is akin to some historical stock figure out of African and black American and European lores and literatures. Yet they are all memorable persons in their own right.

Frye discusses four categories of characters with their subtypes according to their artistic function. There is the blocking agent or imposter who impedes the movement toward the desired goal and who stands in conflict with the self-deprecator, entrusted with advancing the schemes which bring about a victory. There is the buffoon who functions to increase the festive mood and who stands in conflict with the churlish or rustic figure who is often characterized by a sense of solemnity. Unlike the impostor and the self-deprecator, these latter two contribute mainly to the mood rather than to the plot.[19] Yet when we analyze the racist stereotypes of American fiction, we find confirmation of the more insidious reasons for their existence. The bogey, the pariah, savage stranger, and the brute nigger block the progression and threaten to spoil the society because the whites do not want them to reach outside of the established order. The contented slave is more self-denigrating than self-deprecating. The tragic mulatto is churlish because he is confused about his social and biological station as a result of sharing a portion of the so-called passionate and inferior blood of the black race and the supposedly superior, more rationally inclined blood of the white race. And the comic, happy Negro is so because, by not possessing the sense of responsibility inherent to the white race, there is little else that he can actually be except a buffoon.

In general then, we see that these racist types are not so much used as abused, which distinguishes them from their classical counterparts. Their pathetic and comic attributes are all meant to point fundamentally toward one notion—the inferiority of the black race, a corrupt as well as brutal legacy.

Not only were the black and white races brought into basic opposition through the enterprise of slavery, but the relationship between the two groups was crucially complicated by the fact that the imagery of light and dark, which exists in most cultures with both positive and negative connotations, had been developed by the Western world, especially through Christianity, into a dualistic schema which carried overwhelming philosophical and social implications. Among these, the ethical implications became some of the most notable and the most exploited, although a lot of this usage, too, was coincidental, having more to do with the general historical significance of the imagery of light and dark in the European cultures than with African humanity.

It seems, for example, a matter of fate that the word *Ethiops*, by which the black man in the Bible and in America was sometimes designated, and which derives from the Greek word meaning black, was also the symbol used as a complement to the Latin *nigredo*. In the European Middle Ages *nigredo* was used as a label for the first state of the soul before setting out upon its road of development toward self-perfection.[20] This suggests the concept of primitive which the Europeans eventually attributed to almost all of the darker races once they made historical contact. Considering the actual density or degree of saturation of this imagery within the European culture, it was a matter of course that African humanity, given the low status it was accorded in the social structure, became an instrument in the promulgation of this legacy and tradition.[21]

According to the Bible, sin is black. Also according to the Bible, which was believed by Europeans to be the fundamental account of history as well as the sole source of moral and ethical standards, the black man is the descendant of Ham who was made black and designated to till the soil unto perpetuity because he had committed the heinous sin of looking with laughter upon the nakedness of his drunken father. The great Cotton Mather instructed the colonial masters to tell their black slaves: "*That by their sin against God, they are fallen into a dreadful condition.*"[22] Thus, the black man was felt by many to be inherently degenerate, among the lowest ranks of the depraved. There was not much other than the African and the more dastardly acts of man which could be classified as "black as sin." Since blackness was the inherent symbol of depravity, to belong to or have any affinity with black humanity was something to be dreaded.

Negative connotations of blackness were so deeply ingrained in the Christian cultural experience that it did not take very long for even the blacks themselves to imbibe them to some degree once the imagery and symbolism of Christianity became a functional part of their own self-expression. Already in the eighteenth century we see the Long Island born, enslaved, religious poet Jupiter Hammon writing, ". . . and we should pray that God would give us grace to love and to fear him, for if we love God, black as we be, and despised as we be, God will love us."[23] Blackness of skin, then, was perceived as an extra liability for the aspirant of God's grace.

The influence of this legacy upon the developing thought of William Faulkner is significant. It is out of this same legacy, of course, that Dilsey speaks when she tells Jason in *The Sound and the Fury* that her heart is more sympathetic than his although her own may be black. It is also the cause of the terror and gothic effect at the end of *Absalom, Absalom!* when Shreve McCannon conjectures that "in time the Jim Bonds are going to conquer the western hemisphere . . . and so in a few thousand years, I who regard you will also have sprung from the loins of African kings."[24]

As a thorough-bred Southerner, Faulkner could not escape the influence that light and dark imagery had made upon his immediate cultural and racial context.[25] By looking at the extent of his engagement with the imagery of light and dark, which is found in his writing mostly prior to *The Sound and the Fury*, we find evidence of his early involvement with racial stereotypes as well as his eventual struggle to move away from them. In Faulkner's earliest writings the imagery of light and dark holds a prominent place, evidenced through the manner in which he perceives and recreates his world. This holds true even though the world of his earliest compositions is very much a mythical world in which there are no black people. The black characters begin to appear during the later stages of this early period when Faulkner moves from writing myth to writing history. At the point of this transformation the symbolic implications of light and dark are often cast onto black humanity. When not subjected to a more insidious form of racist stereotyping, Faulkner's black characters frequently carry a special mystique of sublimity which seems to point the way, in his evolution, toward the development of more individualized and complex renderings of black being.

Faulkner makes considerable use of the imagery of whiteness in his poetry. However, for some reason, after he begins to write fiction he abandons the explicit use of white as a predominant image. It may be that he realized that his early use of the imagery of whiteness to an often hypnotic extent involved the most superficial aspect of a cult of purity bound to the idea of the white woman as the overpowering object of desire. Speakers in his early poems make constant reference to the whiteness of the ladies they pursue. Even then, however, his use of whiteness is most compelling when he challenges its conventionality. This early, slightly Melvillian tendency toward the ironic use of the white image indicates his youthful urge to challenge conventions, and becomes more apparent later during his maturity. In the pastoral poem, "Sapphics," for example, we are presented with the typical "white Aphrodite."[26] The speaker in the poem "Portrait," on the other hand, appears to be more enchanted by the imaginative tension which envelops the young girl who is "young and white and strange" with a "dim white face."[27] In the poem "After the Concert," the "spring of certainties" is "whitely shattered about us/To a troubling music oft refrained."[28] Similarly, in the puppet play *The Marionettes*, the central character Marietta gains in life when she loses her white garb and wins the colored garments, or power of imagination.[29]

The allegorical uses of the image of whiteness also chronicle a young man's waning innocence. For in another early poem which was published eventually as the title poem for *A Green Bough*,[30] the assumed absolute beneficence of whiteness is forthrightly called into question. The speaker in the poem reports a May morning vision of a nymph whom he describes as "a white woman, a white wanton" in the lake. But he intends for us to see that this phenomenon of whiteness, as a concept, is greater than the woman herself. Instead of its being used as the woman's particular attribute, whiteness is made to appear to have its own inherent and potent meaning. The nymph is only the lure, the pursuit of which leads to the nearly fatal wounding of her pursuer, not by the nymph herself but by the illusion of whiteness, the same type of illusion which lures and destroys Melville's Ahab in his pursuit of Moby Dick. The speaker is explicit, too, in identifying the ominous aspects of this whiteness, since, for him, knowledge of this whiteness "is a dangerous mouth to kiss." The yearning to chase, to possess, and to know whiteness, then, has taken the protagonist into forbidden boundaries where another reality has been revealed and for which, ironically, he has had to pay with his innocence.

The imagery of blackness or darkness occurs more frequently in Faulkner's works.[31] It appears often in the context of the young poet yearning for the primordial womb of darkness and security. In his writings following his youthful and idyllic stage, the dominant image of the secure womb is transferred to the figure of the black mammy, whom George Kent has called "the symbol of an indestructible childhood Eden in a world in which time erodes."[32] Such is the role given to Mammy Callie in Faulkner's first novel, *Soldier's Pay,* and, in the same novel, to the balloon-like breasts of the black cook which enfold the young Saunders boy in his sorrow. This image of darkness, associated, too, with fecundity, is one of the most pronounced of Faulkner's early images. The sense of eternal time also later becomes specifically linked with black being. Yet, except for a few passages in the story "That Evening Sun" (1930), the image of darkness rarely conveys a strong sense of portentousness.

Faulkner was reported to have been so captivated by the quiet sublimity of darkness in his youth that he once said to his friend Ben Wasson, while listening to Beethoven on the victrola: "Even light can be too much distraction when music is being played. . . . Listen to those horns of triumph and joy crying their golden sounds in a great twilight of sorrow."[33] This special sensitivity to darkness, nevertheless, has its own particular pitfalls for the characterization of black being. While it does not connote violence, it often moves toward the other extreme of passivity, and Faulkner had trouble himself, as we shall see, in acknowledging and giving life to the more disgruntled blacks who sought to emerge out of the passive unconscious into the real world. In many instances, then, Faulkner's imagery of darkness is associated with pathos. And as with his use of whiteness, when his sense of darkness implies negativity it generally does so in an ambiguous or unconventional way.

The shadow image is another means by which Faulkner works with darkness. His fascination with the shadow runs throughout much of his work, and the potentialities he finds through its use have a number of ramifications for the way in which black being is seen in the eyes of the Yoknapatawpha world. Shadow signifies for Faulkner an extension as well as a reflection of a thing. A shadow is not totally representative of the object that casts it, neither is it fully integrated with, nor totally separate from it. Faulkner makes the meanings of the shadow, later associated with black characters, quite clear in some of his earliest writings. In the poem "Marriage," the idea of the malleable nature of the shadow is emphasized. It has no existence without the reality of the concrete object from which it is cast.[34] The black boy Ringo and the white boy Bayard are often portrayed in *The Unvanquished* as shades or extensions of one being; the horse-trader in *The Hamlet* has no identity without his ingenious black assistant; Roth Edmonds in "The Fire and the Hearth" desires to use Lucas Beauchamp's family as an extension of his privileges. A similar relationship exists between Mrs. Caroline Compson and Dilsey, and between Nancy Mannigoe and Temple Drake.

This is essentially the kind of relationship that the white world would prefer to have exist between itself and the black world. In his preoccupation with shadows in *The Sound and the Fury*, Quentin postulates a theoretical relationship that he believes exists between black and white being, that the blacks are obverse reflections of the whites. In *Soldier's Pay*, the black community stands in the shadow and serves as a chorus to the disillusionments of the white world.

Faulkner contributed a drawing called "A Jazz Band with Dancers"[35] to the 1920-21 issue of *Ole Miss* which makes an interesting aside for the discussion of his light and dark images. This particular sketch was highly representational and was, without doubt, designed to play up the cultural contrasts between black and white people on the one hand and their complementary relationship on the other. The blacks comprise the band in the picture and are obviously hired to perform the music of their culture for the whites. But the drawing is overall a comic rendering. White dancers, with sleek, swift, stylized and debonair facial expressions and body movements, are in the foreground. They contrast markedly with the black-faced band standing in the background, providing the impulse for the dance, not just through their music, but also through the minstrelsy-like hilarity of their gestures and facial contortions. Their heads are distorted to the point where they bear a closer resemblance to animals than to the faces of black humanity.

In his early years Faulkner also had thematic interests in the symbolic possibilities of the shadow, as is evident in a passage from *Flags in the Dust* in which the artist Horace Benbow describes the glass-blowing technique. The description is significant even though the image around which the passage is built is simply a vase. In describing the manner by which a vase comes into being through the glass-blowing process, Horace says: "At first they're just shapeless things hunching about. Antic, with shadows on the wet walls, red shadows; a dull red gleam, and black shapes like cardboard cut-outs rising and falling like painted balloons."[36] We are reminded of the antic gestures of the shadow-like world of the jazz band drawing and Quentin's theoretical definition of the relationship between the black and white races. But also, Faulkner was long under the spell of Keats' "Ode on a Grecian Urn," and the desire to mold something commensurate with the Keatsian urn, something as timeless, was among the young artist's definite yearnings. Keats had brought into being the true symbol of that primordial innocence and peace with which Faulkner was so enchanted and which he projected into the images of darkness in many of his earliest writings. Black being was often the chosen vehicle for this fulfillment.

The imagery of light and dark as it is represented by non-white and white cultures gets its broadest and most explicit thematic treatment during Faulkner's early period in a relatively unsuccessful story called "Yo Ho and Two Bottles of Rum" (1925),[37] about the accidental death of a Chinese messboy Yo Ho on board the Orient destined ship, *Diana.* Racial hierarchy is apparent by the organization of the ship's crew: the workmen are Chinese and the officers are white, though they are described as "the scum of the riffraff of the United Kingdom, a scum which even the catholic scum of the dominions beyond the sea refuses at intervals, vomiting it over the face of the globe. . . ."[38]

There is a Eurasian officer with "a sacred drop or two of British blood," who is described as saddled "with the white man's responsibilities while at the same time his lesser strain denied him the white man's pleasures."[39] It is clear from this description that Faulkner is well aware of the racial terms upon which his world is based. He even states as a matter of discrimination, demonstrating his early insight into the subtle aspects of racial casting, that the Chinese messboy Yo Ho served the officers "efficiently with remote yellow tolerance of the vagaries of the white man."[40] Obviously, then, the young Faulkner has the insight to create characters beyond mere stereotypes. His early perceptions are themselves standards enough, to use in judging his later difficulties in representing black humanity. The fact that Faulkner has these perceptions makes his own stereotyping of black characters the more inexcusable. Yet these same perceptions are an indication of the potential he developed in some of his black characterizations as he grew older.

More insight of this nature is demonstrated, too, by the method Faulkner chooses to reveal the deep and intricate nature of racism in this story. Ayers, the murderer of Yo Ho is described as "coarsened, surfeited with undisputed domination, with his blank conviction regarding his racial superiority."[41] After killing Yo Ho he can still protest that there are "plenty more of the fellers; one Chinee like another."[42] His final response is that of an exasperated man who deems that license is the prerogative of his station and power:

> Ain't I a white man? Can't I kill a native if I want to? I ain't the first man that ever made a mistake. I never meant to do the chap in; it was the bosun I was looking for. He had no business popping out on me so suddenly, before I had time to recognize him. His own bloody fault.[43]

That the narrator regards this arrogance of Ayers as fundamentally British, but also specifically racial, reveals that the young Faulkner did have insight into matters of race, enough to discredit the suggestion that his failure with black characterization was defensible from the point of view that he was simply a young and undeveloped artist. Of course, most of his early portraits of black being reflect his undeveloped artistry, but they also reflect his racist point of view. The racial paternalism Faulkner exposed aboard the *Diana* was not different from the racial paternalism in which his own life was rooted in the South. Even in his most mature years, he was not able to divorce himself from the paternalistic role he inherited as a son of the Southern gentry.

In "Yo Ho and Two Bottles of Rum," the darker culture of the East stands in direct contrast to the lighter one of the West. What the Orient represents here is akin to the imagery of passivity and timelessness sometimes associated with black being in the Yoknapatawpha world. Faulkner described the East as a "wall of contemplative Oriental calm," compared to the West which is a "mushroom civilization of a short yesterday."[44] Some of the pronouncements intended mostly as criticism of the West actually turn out to be ambiguous or unconscious statements about the East. The narrator says, for example, "And here again the East raised its implacability bodiless as mist against the West and civilization and discipline."[45] This is spoken with the implication that the words "civilization" and "discipline" do not have any connection with non-Western cultures, and that civilization and discipline *are* the West instead of being notions and concepts valued by the West.

This early writing of Faulkners illustrates such good potential for a developing artist fulfilling the role of seer, that it provides an invaluable measure of his later, though often less courageous, efforts to portray the truth. It also points toward the sometimes ambivalent relationship he held with the world of the abstract and the actual, which became a pitfall for him with many of his public pronouncements in later years. Although some of his racial statements were quite insidious, from the beginning there was apparently a struggle within his own human heart. Even his own interest in this ambivalence becomes apparent.

The simple, one-dimensional study, as has often been attempted of racial issues in Faulkner, does little justice to this subject or the reader. Every aspect, from his use of imagery to his use of character, must be considered in order to apprehend the whole. It is for this reason that the scope of this book has been designed to be comprehensive.

ENDNOTES

1. For a very scholarly and copious treatment of this subject, see Professor Winthrop Jordan's *White Over Black: American Attitudes Toward the Negro, 1550-1812*, Chapter I (Chapel Hill: University of North Carolina Press, 1968).
2. See Charles Colcock Jones, *The Religious Instruction of the Negroes in the United States* (Freeport, N.Y.: Books for Libraries, 1971), pp. 27-28. Originally published in Savannah, Ga.: Thomas Purse, 1842.
3. Cited in Albert J. Raboteau, *Slave Religion: The "Invisible Institution" in the Antebellum South* (N.Y.: Oxford University Press, 1978), p. 97.
4. William Faulkner, "Address to the Southern Historical Association (1955)," in *Essays, Speeches, and Public Letters*, ed. James Meriwether (N.Y.: Random House, 1965), p.149.
5. Thomas Jefferson, *Notes on the State of Virginia* (Philadelphia: H. C. Carey and I. Lea, 1825), pp. 189-198. Originally published in 1784.
6. Jean Fagan Yellin, *The Intricate Knot: Black Figures in American Literature 1776-1863* (N.Y.: New York University Press, 1972), pp. 3-11, 18.
7. Ibid., p. vii.
8. For the full discussion, see Ibid., pp. 84-147.
9. George Washington Cable, *The Negro Question: A Selection of Writings on Civil Rights in the South*, ed. Arlin Turner (N.Y.: W.W. Norton, 1968), pp. 28-29.
10. George Washington Cable, *The Grandissimes*, ed. Newton Arwin (N.Y.: Sagamore Press, Inc., 1957), p. viii. Originally published by Scribner's in 1880.
11. Ibid., pp. v-vi.
12. Ibid., p. x.
13. Paule Marshall, "A Panel Discussion: The Negro Woman in American Literature," in *Keeping the Faith: Writings by Contemporary Black American Women*, ed. Pat Crutchfield Exum (Greenwich: Fawcett Publications, Inc. 1974), p. 35.
14. Seymour Gross and J. Hardy eds. *Images of the Negro in American Literature* (Chicago: University of Chicago Press, 1966), p. 2.
15. Alain Locke, "American Literary Tradition and the Negro," *Modern Quarterly*, 3 (1926), pp. 215-22.
16. Sterling Brown, "A Century of Negro Portraiture in American Literature." *Massachusetts Review* 7, Winter 1966, pp. 89-90.
17. C. H. Holman, et al., *A Handbook to Literature* (N.Y.: The Odyssey Press, 1960), p. 470.
18. Northrop Frye, *Anatomy of Criticism* (Princeton University Press, 1957), pp. 171 ff.
19. Ibid., p. 171-176.
20. J. E. Circlot, *A Dictionary of Symbols* (London: Routledge and Kegan Paul, 1962, 1971), pp. 98-99.
21. Jordan, *op. cit*.
22. Cotton Mather, *The Negro Christianized, An Essay to Excite and Assist the Good Work, the Instruction of Negro Servants in Christianity* (Boston: B. Green, 1706; Evans American Imprints). Also, for a more expansive treatment of this theme as it made an impact through American literature, see Margaret Pryse's *The Mark and the Knowledge:*

Social Stigma in Classic American Fiction (Ohio State, 1979).

23. Stanley A. Ransom ed., *Jupiter Hammon: America's First Negro Poet* (Port Washington: Kennikat Press, 1970), p. 99.
24. William Faulkner, *Absalom, Absalom!* (N.Y.: Vintage Books, 1972), p. 378. Originally published by Random House, 1936.
25. The impact of this light and dark imagery upon the American literary imagination has been so potent that it has merited book-length treatment in Harry Levin's *The Power of Blackness* (N.Y.: Vintage Books, 1958). Levin demonstrates how Hawthorne, Poe, and Melville were "obsessed by the power of blackness," (pp. xi-xii). He discusses how blackness easily became a central metaphor for the American outlook because the American is constantly searching for the union of opposites between "the old and new worlds, the past and present, the self and society, the supernatural and nature" (pp. xi-xii).
26. William Faulkner, "Sapphics." Published in *The Mississippian*, 26 November 1919, p. 3. Reprinted in Carvel Collins, *William Faulkner: Early Prose and Poetry* (Boston: Little, Brown and Company, 1962), p. 51.
27. William Faulkner, "Portrait." Published in *The Double Dealer*, vol. III June 1922, p. 337. Reprinted in *Early Prose and Poetry*, p. 99.
28. William Faulkner, "After the Concert." Written in summer 1921; printed in Joseph Blotner, *Faulkner: A Biography* (N.Y.: Random House, 1974), vol. I, p. 308.
29. William Faulkner, *The Marionettes* (Charlottesville: Bibliographical Society of the University of Virginia, 1975).
30. William Faulkner, *A Green Bough* (N.Y.: Harrison Smith and Robert Haas, 1933), p. 7. Reissued by Random House in a combined volume with *The Marble Faun*, 1960.
31. The word "black" actually occurs infrequently in the Faulkner canon. When it does occur it is used to denote the rather conventional inherited meanings. It appears more in the novel *Sanctuary* than it does in all of Faulkner's other works combined.
32. George Kent, "The Black Woman in Faulkner's Work, with the Exclusion of Dilsey, Part II," *Phylon Quarterly*, vol. 36, no. 1, Spring 1975, p. 58.
33. Joseph Blotner, *Faulkner: A Biography* (N.Y.: Random House, 1974), vol. I, p. 183.
34. William Faulkner, "Marriage." This poem was written in the summer of 1921 and published in *A Green Bough* in 1932.
35. William Faulkner, Jazz Band and Dancers Drawing. Published in *Ole Miss*, 1920-21, vol. XXV, p. 137. Reprinted in *Early Prose and Poetry*, p. 81.
36. William Faulkner, *Flags in the Dust* (N.Y.: Random House, 1973), p. 180. In two prefaces Faulkner wrote for *The Sound and the Fury*, he specifically spoke of the vase as an emblem of true art's immortality. (See J. B. Meriwether, ed., William Faulkner, "An Introduction for *The Sound and the Fury*," *Southern Review*, 8, (Autumn,1972), pp. 705-10; and "An Introduction to *The Sound and the Fury*," *Mississippi Quarterly*, 26, (Summer, 1973), pp, 410-15.
37. William Faulkner, "Yo Ho and Two Bottles of Rum," in *William Faulkner: New Orleans Sketches*, (New Brunswick: Rutgers University Press, 1958), p. 121. Originally published in the New Orleans *Times Picayune*, September 27, 1925.
38. Ibid., p. 212.
39. Ibid., p. 213.
40. Ibid., p. 214.
41. Ibid., p. 217.
42. Ibid., p. 215.
43. Ibid.
44. Ibid., p. 218.
45. Ibid., p. 219.

II.

Early Characterizations

Faulkner's early characterizations of black existence fall into the categories set forth by writer Ralph Ellison in his analysis of the presence and absence of blacks in American fiction. Ellison writes that while blacks in much of twentieth century American fiction are billed as images of reality, they are really counterfeits. In truth, says Ellison, they represent a psychological process by which their creators work themselves into a frenzy as preparation for a social role which they feel compelled to play. Thus, the resulting stereotypes often serve as justification for their creators' own emotional needs and economic interests. The stereotype, then, is a social instrument, the major figure in the ritual of fiction which aids the white American in resolving his personal dilemma originating with his involvement in conflicting democratic ideals and anti-democratic practices.[1]

By the end of 1930, when he was thirty three years old, Faulkner had already published four novels and a number of stories and sketches. In none of these, however, except perhaps "The Longshoreman" and

The Sound and the Fury, are Faulkner's perspectives or characterizations of black existence artistically distinct from that of his Southern white forerunners. In "The Longshoreman," a New Orleans sketch of 1925, the characterization is significant because the image of sunbeams falling over the black longshoreman serves as a metaphor for the bars of segregation that imprison the blacks. And in *The Sound and the Fury* the authorial point of view is generally distinguishable from the more blatant Southern racist notions. Nevertheless, Faulkner had trouble throughout much of his career with his perspective on black existence and his characterization of it. Often he attempted to move forward only to fall back again into stereotype and prejudice. Indeed his inconsistency and timidity, rooted in the socio-cultural biases of his native South, often prevented him from growing as an individual. As a result his artistic achievement is uneven and his status as a true humanist is controversial. A saving grace, however, is that he became conscious of his own contradictions. This consciousness became germane to his racial sensibility in many of his later works. It is, of course, this sensibility as much as anything else that gives Faulkner the degree of heroic proportion as an author that he managed to garner for his time.

Faulkner's attempt in "Yo Ho and Two Bottles of Rum" to speak from a point of view antithetical to the traditional Southern racist viewpoint is overshadowed by his lower estimate of black being presented in his first novel *Soldier's Pay* (1926) and his third novel *Sartoris* (1929) (re-published in its original manuscript form with its original title in 1973 as *Flags in the Dust*[2]). Examples of this type of callous and inept racial portraiture can be traced through succeeding years of Faulkner's career up to his troublesome characterization of Lucas Beauchamp in "The Fire and the Hearth" (1942). Other intermittent examples are found in "Mountain Victory" (1920) and *The Unvanquished* (1938).

The focal concern of Faulkner's first novel, *Soldier's Pay*, is with Lieutenant Donald Mahon, the young World War I veteran who returns from the war fatally wounded to his hometown in Georgia. Except for some of the local figures, especially blacks, one might not associate this story, which is saturated with mythological allusions and English manners, with the American South. Cleanth Brooks suggests that one misreads Faulkner, even in this early novel, if one sees in his treatment of the blacks a "mere unsympathetic stereotyping," adding that if Faulkner's depiction "departs from reality, it is in the direction of a kind of black mystique. . . . "[3] Almost all of the characters in the novel, black and white, are in some form or another expressions of the early poetic sentiments of the young Faulkner. And the blacks here as a group definitely serve as a kind of classical chorus or backdrop to the white community. Yet the old stereotypes of black humanity are still present and are often rather crudely so. Some of these black images remind us that no matter how far we might have gone off into mythic Arcadia or a very stylized and conventional world with young Faulkner, we are clearly still within the boundaries of a very Southern mind.

No more appropriate figure could be used to set the old Southern racial tone for this novel than an overly indulgent black mammy. Mammy Callie Nelson enters the Mahons' yard in the fourth chapter, against the protestations of her grandson, Loosh, who is embarassed by her obsequious ways of interacting with white people. Loosh, like the wounded white man his grandmother is rushing to see, is also a veteran of World War I. In his years away fighting to save the world for democracy he has obviously grown more into his manhood, returning home with a greater consciousness of his status as a black man in society. But Mammy Callie ignores him and pushes toward the center of the action. Indeed she moves with a sense of that peculiar privilege granted to her as mammy by white society for her loyalty and compassion to the white household. Barely able to do anything other than to lope along, she must make her way to her "baby" and she scolds the reluctant Loosh accordingly, assured that it would certainly have to be a day of great reckoning when her "baby don't wanter see his old Cal'line";[4] for, after all, it is his mammy, as she refers to herself, the bourne of his innocence and childhood, who has come to see him. She is also the familial mainstay who brings the flavor of home back to the quickly deteriorating mind of the wounded veteran. As mammy, she operates as part of the institutionalized strategy to bring comfort to her white children and to brandish her more obstreperous black children like Loosh. Because she has a favored position, although possessing no legal rights of arbitration, she can make pronouncements with the most indicting implications for the whites. But because her pronouncements are generally taken by her audience to be mere spoutings, and are generally considered to be of little import, she is free from reproach. "Lawd, de white folks done ruint you,"[5] she exclaims with a sense of deep suffering when she puts her hand on Mahon's fatal wound.

Employed by the narrator to enforce a stereotypic image of the black male, Mammy Callie expresses disdain for her grandson, Loosh, as "dis triflin' nigger"[6] and mocks him for being in a soldier's uniform. What is actually carried out as the old woman subscribes to the role white society wishes her to play, is the emasculation of her own blood. Faulkner does not allow Loosh to project an individual identity, and he leaves Loosh buckled in this state throughout the novel. Loosh may be seen as a forerunner of the other youthful but emasculated black World War I veteran, Caspey, who appears in Faulkner's third published novel, *Sartoris* (*Flags in the Dust*).

Functioning to accommodate and compromise two diverging social realities, Mammy Callie accommodates the reality of her white master and compromises that of herself and her grandson. Perhaps she is thought to be acting according to the virtue of humility, but this kind of humility, devoid of personal integrity, only brings about humiliation. In her historical role as mammy her burdensome duty was that of nurturing the victimizers of her own children.

Loosh follows his grandmother's orders and approaches two higher ranking white soldiers with an attitude representative of his military training. Mammy Callie wants deference not protocol, however, and forces Loosh into his old state of racial subservience. From her point of view the old way of relating induces more warmth into the human relationship. It is in situations like these that the complexities of the black and white relationship in this culture begin to betray themselves. For, again, true ideals have become corrupted. Virtues such as humility and patience, all of which are ascribed to the mammy, have become entangled with their deformed reflections–subservience and obsequiousness–to the denigration and humiliation of the virtues themselves as well as humanity.

In another twist, Faulkner's narrator blames Loosh's attitudinal change from his original Southern upbringing on a world that went crazy during the war. Here Faulkner has to be appealing to a fraudulent and escapist type of reasoning. For he was in no way ignorant of the demeaning situation prescribed for black humanity in his world.

Neither was he unaware that black men who fought abroad for democracy became victims of riots and lynchings during the Red Summer of 1918 in the United States. During the next world war he made statements on precisely this type of mistreatment of black veterans, but in this early period of his characterizations, he was not comfortable enough with his own growing convictions about racial injustices to step clearly outside the behavior of Southern white culture.

The next black character to figure prominently in Faulkner's works is fundamentally the male counterpart of Mammy Callie. He is more complex than Mammy Callie and has a larger role, but he is very similar to her in that he is the old plantation retainer type. Simon, in *Flags in the Dust*, represents the black servant who was loyal before and after the Civil War. He functions to reinforce the superficial notions of the peaceful relations between the white master and black servant on the old plantation. In the tradition of the black characters of Thomas Nelson Page, he is a defender of the belief that the virtues of the Old South far outweighed the flaws. He, like his master, old Bayard Sartoris, desires to halt the onslaught of time. In fact, he is sometimes portrayed as being more bound by the past than his old master.

Faulkner's portrayal of Simon affirms his sentimental attachment to many of the attitudes of the Southern past, but it also reveals his growing ambivalence toward its values. The Yoknapatawpha world is a stage and the theatrical Simon knows that he plays a key role. When we first see him he is dressed in the aristocratic livery of the coachman and butler, in an old top hat and a linen duster. Self-conscious about his position, he sees himself as a privileged attendant and makes it known that he values his post. In Simon's point of view, it is the duty of the servant to serve as a just reflection of the master's traditions and manners. In public he projects himself as a servant having privileged contact with citizens of the first rank. Consequently, he is even sure that he can declare his station through his multisyllabic vocabulary of malapropisms. He presumes to assume responsibility for the maintenance of Sartoris dignity from which he seems to glean most of his own. He feels that it is his obligation to inform the master of the errant activities of the household, excepting, of course, his own.

Simon knows, however, that his liberties are granted by his master and that they, therefore, have limitations. Buffoon though he sometimes is, he knows that he is not supposed to engage in too much far-fetched speculation about the activities of the white fold, and he knows, especially, that he is not to prescribe their decisions or actions.

Presumably, one of Simon's attributes is his insight into the manners of both white folk and women. He is portrayed as comically lecherous and manipulative, although it is a combination of both of these characteristics that brings about his tragic and sudden death. His knowledge of white people's vagaries, while serving as the key to dealing with them, also becomes the means to his own ends. This is apparent, for example, in the comic scenes in which he plays upon the sympathies of his boss to repay the money which he has stolen from the church to finance his love affairs. Fundamentally, he thinks that people are to be dealt with in accordance with their sex, status, and race. As a bearer of the old Southern legacy, his conduct is more rooted in the chivalric than the democratic order.

Since the figure of Simon generally lapses in and out of the novel based on his comic function, it is not altogether surprising that before we have moved half-way through the work, his portrayal begins to vacillate between that of the vivacious, manipulative lecher and the doddering old man. He eventually becomes a feeble figure, aging and outmoded by mechanization. It is somewhat ironic that as a servant he should be the last proud vestige of the horse and buggy era. On the other hand, perhaps it is not wholly so; for in Faulkner's consciousness, no one—master, slave, or peon—is exempt from the inevitability of time's onslaught.

As Faulkner portrays him in his enfeebled years, Simon retreats into the past and converses with his original master, the dead John Sartoris, who was very much the exemplification of the age and period which stamped Simon and his race with what had appeared to be an unalterable status. Since Simon embodies the master-class values from that particular time, he chides the ghost of John Sartoris for not intervening to curtail the assault upon the historical identity of the Sartoris clan, the guardians of quality. Described by the narrator, at one point, as the caricature of himself, it is Simon more than anyone else who is overjoyed when the new heir is born, for it is a sign to him that the old times are returning. Exploiting him even into his senility for purposes of comic relief, the narrator proclaims at the end of the novel that it was Simon's death, not as Simon Strother, but as Simon Sartoris which made it most manifest that an era had ended.

Simon's son Caspey, the returned war veteran, is portrayed in a different stereotypic mode. Although he is introduced sympathetically and even somewhat nobly, Faulkner is much more uncomfortable in his attempts to create him as a character than he is in creating his doddering and comic father. The most sympathetic thing we hear from the narrator about Caspey is that everybody's work, from Simon's to Miss Jenny's had devolved upon the young Caspey before he went away to the war. But this is about as far as Faulkner's sympathy goes, for very abruptly his Southern racial condescension sets in and ironically instead of depicting Caspey's character, he implicates his own. Faulkner's narrator is irritated by what he interprets as the war's ruining of Caspey. He is discomfited by Caspey's newly acquired, irascible ways and resents his breaking away from the accommodating manner toward white people in which he had been raised. As a result, Caspey is thought to have been made a total societal loss for life in his native land. Here the narrator dares to state clearly the racist attitude which was generally implied in the earlier characterization of the veteran Loosh.

The narrator portrays Caspey as not having any personal accountability for his actions. In fact, he does not seem to recognize that Caspey is even capable of possessing any. Unlike the white soldier Young Bayard, who went off to the same war and returned with his own special sorrows, Caspey is not respected for the changes made in his character. This inept portrayal has more to do with Faulkner's racial antipathies than it has to do with Caspey's being a minor character. Caspey's change and his family's innocence are used as a point of ridicule and ploy for comic relief. This callousness by which he is portrayed stands out all the more clearly because the narrative is void of any historical perspective which might suggest that Caspey's altered worldview is a very obvious revolt against a status foisted deliberately upon generations of black being by the likes of the Sartorises.

The narrator's arrogance and disdain for the new Caspey are clearly grounded in his own set of illusions of what the war was all about. Caspey demanded the democratic rights that he expected would accrue naturally for himself and his own kind upon his return from helping to protect and establish those same rights abroad. Through the narrator's apparent animosity, Caspey is used to exploit the old taboo regarding the white woman and the black man, that incendiary myth articulated earlier by Thomas Jefferson that the ultimate aim of the black man is to have intercourse with the white woman. Thus Caspey is heard to proclaim, "I got my white in France, and I'm gwine get it here, too."[7] And, of course, there was no better way for the narrator to register the immediate and impending danger of the young man's transgression than through Caspey's own obsequious father, Simon. Horror-struck at this sense of violation, Simon warns him, ". . . nigger . . . de good Lawd done took keer of you fer a long time now, but He ain't gwine bother wid you always."[8]

On one level, the reprimand conveys the father's natural concern for his son, but on another it is also a statement about the narrator's inability to grant a genuine sense of integrity to black being. By projecting racial anxiety through the character of Simon the narrator seeks to sublimate his own fears. In his portrayal of Caspey, one cannot but link Faulkner with some of the most incendiary and insidious writers like Thomas Dixon who portrayed blacks as inherently antagonistic to civilized living. Other images of blacks in *Flags in the Dust*, however more subtly depicted, also suggest this association.

The old Sartoris matriarch, Miss Jenny, necessarily finds herself helpless and astonished in the face of the new Caspey and his "lazy insolence." Her unvarnished resentment pours forth when she demands: "Who was the fool anyway, who thought of putting niggers into the same uniform with white men?"[9] Eventually Caspey returns to the more agreeable disposition of Southern normality. But before he is broken of his new ways, the narrator seeks to justify his breaking by implying that a sense of one's responsibility for one's freedom of freedoms, which Caspey supposedly lacks, is the heart of the issue in his having to be so critical of him. Caspey's being knocked beside the head with a piece of firewood, as a way of helping him to resume his assigned role in the household and society, is an authorial twist which creates nothing more than low-level melodrama. It is clearly apparent that Faulkner lacks the narrative courage or developed sensitivity to delineate the integrity of black being. Consequently, we see that the motivations which lead to the physical confrontation between Old Bayard and Caspey are not at all sufficiently developed. The old man's pouncing upon the young veteran with a chunk of wood, suggesting a return to the old plantation order, is simply not convincing. It is not realistic that Caspey would so easily renege on his newly acquired, radical views. Somewhat aware of his own weakness, Faulkner tries unsatisfactorily to cover the scene with a touch of insincere humor.

There are similar instances in Faulkner's earlier and later writing in which we see the narrator's moral and political weaknesses causing distortions. In an early story, "Sunset" (1925), the key figure is a black man who runs a few miles away from a Southern plantation, gets into trouble, and soon thinks that he has arrived in Africa, his point of destination. He is awe-stricken by what he believes to be the barbarous actions of African bushmen, which in reality is a posse of white men chasing him. In the end he finds relief in being taken back into the secure fold of his old master's plantation. His obsequious counterparts appear in later works, too, for example, "Mountain Victory" (1930), in which the servile valet follows his master off to war and then returns after emancipation, loyally to the plantation. There is also Louvenia in *The Unvanquished* (1938) who, during an invasion by the Yankee soldiers, follows the directive of her old mistress to protect the plantation against the soldiers as well as the black defectors.

These extreme stereotypes mirror the images of black being that dominated American literature for nearly a hundred years, beginning with George Tucker's *The Valley of the Shenandoah* (1824) in which black characters are used to give testimony to the glorious past, and through the works of William Gilmore Simms whose fugitive slaves, once captured, are pleased to be returned to their masters. It is through exploitation like this that many of these writers fostered their own illusions and gave to their works an air of social comfort, which they wanted to project onto their own society.

Most of Faulkner's difficulty with black portraiture before and during his writing of *Flags in the Dust* originates from his belief that there had to be something in the Southern past worthy of preservation. It was hard for him to conceive that the legendary era of the American South could come into being and exist so long without having created some particular point of beauty that would hold through time. Joseph Blotner tells us that the romantic character of Chevalier de Bayard, the Sartoris namesake, known as the *chevalier sans peur et sans reproche*, was held as an ideal by the young Faulkner and his comrade Phil Stone.[10] The inculcation of this ideal was, of course, in no way unusual for the upper class Southerners of that particular era since chivalric lore had played a crucial role in the formation of their national character.

The narrator of Faulkner's *Mosquitoes* (1927) tries to celebrate and rationalize the past by focusing upon the black slaves. In his attempt to locate something that would not dissolve in time, he seeks to immortalize them. And in doing so, he uses generalizations which resemble in tone the paternalistic arguments of the Old South. For example, the descendants of the bondmen in the story are viewed as having "served with a kind of gracious dignity."[11] This is supposedly an unusual attribute since, in man's basic impulse toward self-reliance and self-preservation, it takes a very select group to "accept service with dignity."[12] It is, furthermore, the earnest illusion of the narrator that it is incumbent upon the servant himself to bring a sense of dignity to anything so unnatural. But such a point of view, devoid of personal courage and integrity, is ultimately what Quentin and Jason Compson inherit in *The Sound and the Fury*, a morally bankrupt legacy which keeps them in perpetual limbo beween the past and the present. Such percepts concerning the dispositions of the enslaved could achieve a truly worthy dignity and integrity only if they were uttered as the authentic moral urge of the enslaved themselves, out of their own compassion for the human lot, and not out of any sense of servility.

On occasion, too, Faulkner employs other types of racist and insidious extremes. His comfortable analogy of the black man's mentality to that of the mule in *Flags in the Dust* is a prime example. The passage is really a classical encomium on the mule, a literary accomplishment that is, at first, nothing less than entrancing. The mule is celebrated for all its abilities and limitations and is raised to symbolic and heroic proportions. It is garnished with laurels for its servile behavior which was fundamental to the rehabilitation of the South after the Civil War. The narrator proceeds to lavish sufficient sympathy and gratitude on the mule only to strike the final note: the mule is "misunderstood even by that creature (the nigger who drives him) whose impulses and mental processes most resemble his. . . ."[13] Here Faulkner endorses the racist notion of black inferiority which has been struggling to become and remain a fundamental tenet of American thought from the early moments of the country's inception. This passage is also a supreme example of Faulkner's sometimes tainted majesty. Ultimately, his grand gesture becomes self-defeating.

The stereotypic projections discussed here show a common relationship with the tradition of the black-faced minstrelsy. The minstrel show reflected a reality which was nothing more than a game of puppetry. It mirrored the essentially managerial relationship the whites sought to hold over the blacks. Faulkner understood the fundamental implications of puppetry as is evident from his youthful association with members of a student theatre group interested in marionettes. This awareness is illustrated in a poem Faulkner wrote later, probably during the autumn of 1921, while working at Elizabeth Prall's Doubleday Bookshop in New York and living in Greenwich Village.[14] The poem, "Two Puppets in a Fifth Avenue Window," is a study of the antic forms of shop mannikins. In the last stanza of the poem the mannikins reverse their roles and inform the passers-by that they are puppets in the hands of powers beyond their control. The same sense is set forth in the 1925 sketch, "The Longshoreman,"[15] in which a descriptive commentary on the focal character, a black worker, is explicitly concerned with the manipulation of the black American's life by the white American. We know, then, that even while Faulkner continued to produce the stereotypic images of Simon, Mammy Callie, Loosh, Caspey, and others, he was quite aware of the true nature of black reality. We see again that he somewhat inadvertently set standards by which we may measure his own kinship with the old conventions. Moreover, as Paul McPharlin has stated in his study on puppetry, the puppet, like Faulkner's stereotypic portraiture of black being, is "a projection or reflection of the human being who controls it."[16]

Often when depicting blacks as a group in writings as early as *Soldier's Pay*, Faulkner attempts to give them a more philosophical, though primitive, role. As his influential friend Sherwood Anderson does in his 1925 novel *Dark Laughter*, Faulkner also seeks to use the blacks as a moral backdrop to the activities of the whites who presumed themselves to be the superior and ongoing race, setting standards for the rest of mankind.[17] The young Faulkner's use of blacks in this role is not as sophisticated or ironic as that of Anderson. But in the works of both writers the whites have inadvertently, through their viewing of the blacks as a debased form of human nature by which they can rationalize their own moral laxity, set up a reflector for their own alternatingly comic and tragic predicaments. Because the white characters in these novels carry themselves with a sense of presumption, prerogative and privilege, not so unexpectedly are the blacks often ridiculed, even as victims of misfortune and oppression. In many instances, the blacks become objects upon which Faulkner's narrators and characters project personal conflicts triggered by their own inhibitions.

Faulkner's early characterizations of black humanity have their shortcomings, but they are also significant in that it is often through them that we see foreshadowings of the black characters with greater dimension like Dilsey Gibson in *The Sound and the Fury* and Lucas Beauchamp in *Intruder in the Dust*. The philosophical, yet primitive, roles of the blacks as a group are especially apparent in the world of *Soldier's Pay* where the whites suffer under the disillusionment brought on by their idealistic pursuits in World War I, and from a world becoming increasingly gripped by a hard skepticism about the nature of man and his destiny. Perhaps the blacks had already learned through the experience of slavery and its aftermath about as much as there was to know about the nature of man. They had no more innocence to lose.

The blacks in *Soldier's Pay* are portrayed as standing in contrast to much of the culture around them and which controls them. They have a different sense of time or they relate to time differently and are not caught up in industrial mechanization. They seem to the modernist man, frustrated by his inability to totally manipulate time, very much like the timeless images in John Keats' "Ode on a Grecian Urn." The narrator of *Soldier's Pay* presents us with images of

> Negroes humped with sleep, portentious upon each wagon and in the wagon bed itself sat other Negroes upon chairs; a pagan catafalgue under the afternoon. Rigid as though carved in Egypt ten thousand years ago. Slow dust rising veiled their passing , like time.[18]

Even though only passing attention is given to the black community in *Soldier's Pay*, the final chapter makes an attempt to use the black community as a figurative backdrop or contrasting reflector of the principal action taking place in the larger white community, the death of Lieutenant Mahon. The black community is very much like the chorus in the Greek drama, although it appears unaware that it is playing a role of any such significance. However, this insinuation of unawareness must surely be an underestimation of the black community's intelligence; for surely Mammy Callie and the Saunders' maid, who live in the black community and in and out of white people's houses, know of the nature of the death taking place. After all, it was Mammy Callie whom the narrator quoted as indicting the white world through its recent war for having destroyed young Mahon.

Despite the shortcomings in characterization, the black community does function as a touchstone as well as a reflector, and although it is not integrated into the dominant cultural reality, it is interlocked with it. Thus, we find,

> Under the moon, quavering with the passion of spring and flesh, among white washed walls papered inwardly with old newspapers, something pagan using the white man's conventions as it used his clothing, hushed and powerful, not knowing its own power: . . . 'Sweet chariot . . . comin' fer to ca'y me home. . . .'[19]

Black singing provides solace for the sorrows of that branch of humanity trying to endure the casualties of war, lost sons, and lost lovers. Similar significance is found in the quips made by the three young black men who pass the bereaved Parson Mahon and his dead son's friend Private Gilligan later on the road. Rather than passionate or sad there is a witty offbeat commentary: "You may be fas', but you can't las'; 'cause yo' mommer go' slow you down."[20] In the context of the greater world of the novel, the saying has a fundamental meaning for the white world whose fast leap into the chaos of war left it trudging under disillusionment and sorrow.

For the narrator, the "crooning submerged passion of the dark race," "a quivering chord of music wordless," rising out of the shabby little church from a collective voice which has taken "the white man's words as readily as it took his remote God and made a personal Father of Him," symbolizes a "longing of mankind for a Oneness with something, somewhere."[21] The blacks now function as a point of unification for the dissociated sensibility of the narrator.

This night scene is embellished with Faulkner's favorite imagery from the days of his poetry. The *a cappella* voices are compared to "a flight of gold and heavenly birds."[22] The shabby church is perceived as "beautiful with mellow longing, passionate and sad."[23] These were the same attributes that Faulkner yearned to see in a new American poetry. He asked at the end of a prose piece he once wrote, "Verse Old and Nascent: A Pilgrimmage," in which he attempted to summarize his own early involvement with poetry both as a reader and a poet: "Is not there among us someone who can write something beautiful and passionate and sad instead of saddening?"[24]

Although he continues to have some difficulty in his depiction of black being, as Faulkner grows he does not simply continue to deliver what parts of his audience and the general Southern community were calling for as representative portraits of black reality. He makes a major breakthrough for all Southern literature with his characterization of Dilsey in *The Sound and the Fury* in 1929, the same year in which *Sartoris* was published.

As we shall see in later sections of this book, where the emphasis is more thematic, the voice with the greatest integrity, and consequently, the greatest maturity and artistic accomplishment in Faulkner's canon is the one with the courage to probe deeply and to offer the phenomena and circumstances of culture and self up for scrutiny. This voice is more conscious, and reveals its awareness of its own relationship to the thought and actions of the Yoknapatawpha community. Faulker's ultimate achievement is that, unlike his narrative voice in earlier works like *Soldier's Pay* and *Flags in the Dust*, he dares to set forth the attitudes and assumptions of the Yoknapatawpha culture distinct from his own maturing consciousness. He begins the move away from many of the counterfeit productions of blacks which Ralph Ellison refers to as so pervasive in twentieth century American fiction.

ENDNOTES

1. Ralph Ellison, "Twentieth-Century Fiction and the Black Mask of Humanity," in *Shadow and Act* (New York: New American Library, 1966), pp. 42-60.
2. *Flags in the Dust* will be referred to throughout this book.
3. Cleanth Brooks, *William Faulkner: Toward Yoknapatawpha and Beyond* (New Haven: Yale University Press, 1978), p. 97.
4. William Faulkner, *Soldier's Pay* (New York: Boni and Liveright, 1926), p. 170.
5. Ibid.
6. Ibid., p. 171.
7. William Faulkner, *Flags in the Dust* (New York: Random House Vintage Edition, 1973), p. 67.
8. Ibid.
9. Ibid., p. 68.
10. Joseph Blotner, *Faulkner: A Biography* (New York: Random House, 1974), vol. I, p. 209.
11. William Faulkner, *Mosquitoes* (New York: Boni and Liveright, 1927), p. 11.
12. Ibid.
13. *Flags in the Dust*, p. 314.
14. William Faulkner, "Two Puppets in a Fifth Avenue Window." Summarized in Blotner's *Faulkner*, vol. I, pp. 319-20.
15. William Faulkner, "The Longshoreman," in *New Orleans Sketches* (New Brunswick: Rutgers University Press, 1958), p. 9. Originally published in *The Double Dealer*, Jan. - Feb., 1925.
16. Paul McPharlin, *The Puppet Theatre in America: A History* (New York: Harper and Row, 1949), p. 1.
17. Sherwood Anderson, *Dark Laughter* (New York: Liveright, 1970), p. 73. Originally published by Boni and Liveright, 1925.
18. *Soldier's Pay*, p. 151.
19. Ibid., pp. 312-313.
20. Ibid., p. 313.
21. Ibid., p. 319.
22. Ibid.
23. Ibid.
24. William Faulkner, "Verse Old and Nascent: A Pilgrimage." Originally published in *The Double Dealer*, vol. VII (April, 1925), p. 118. Reprinted in *Early Prose and Poetry*.

III.

Faulkner's Historical Context for Black Existence in the Yoknapatawpha World

The long experience of slavery in America left its mark on the posterity of both slave and master and influenced relations between them more than a century after the end of the old regime. Slavery was only one of several ways by which the white man has sought to define the Negro's status, his 'place,' and assure his subordination.

–C. Van Woodward,
THE STRANGE CAREER
OF JIM CROW[1]

The Yoknapatawpha world is one in which the past impinges heavily upon the present. The whites yearn to recapture the old life, to live down defeat and to grasp a new economic and political foothold after living under what they consider to be invasion and occupation by their Northern white brothers. The blacks, rendered powerless by the political chicanery and racism of both the Northern and Southern whites, maneuver to survive and endure the legacy of the Southern whites' frustration. The whites' disaffected, distorted, and often pathological relationship to the past is the major cause of the tragedies resulting in the distance in human and racial relationships that permeate this world. It is Faulkner's awareness of this distance and its sustained tragic note generated in his writings which help to give his work an overwhelming and profound sense of compassion for the society of which he held himself to be an inescapable part.

Faulkner did not set out specifically to write a history of the South, but rather to recreate some moments in that peculiar history. Yet, by the time he had finished his career as a writer, he had written, at various points throughout his canon, his own outline or sketch of Southern history. Even though this sketch is at times chauvinistic in its interpretation and selection of details, and there are conspicuous gaps and omissions, it is a history, often cast in an ironic vein, that highlights distortion, brigandage, callousness, illusion, paradox and contradiction. It is also a chronicle of how, through intimidation, black being was demoralized and made to suffer. And finally, it is an anticipatory history of a living South slowly gaining the fortitude at least to begin to acknowledge its past errors and thereby redeem itself from the curse of slavery.

Faulkner's use of chronology in *Go Down, Moses* (1942) is his single most conscious attempt to establish the historical development of black existence in Yoknapatawpha County. But there are numerous crucial details concerning the historicity of black being which are found in almost all of his works.[2] These are fundamental facts which contribute to Faulkner's portrait of his fictional county and to our sense of his view of black being. These details mark Faulkner's particular effort to delineate a region in which, according to his census, blacks outnumber whites three to two and in which race is not simply one aspect, but an underlying principle of life. As Faulkner developed his canon he consciously revised and modified some of his own attitudes toward racial issues and black being. He also made very notable attempts, especially in *Intruder in the Dust* (1948) and *Requiem for a Nun* (1951) to complete the chronicle of the blacks without being too apologetic.

In Faulkner's composite view of Yoknapatawpha history, the blacks were bound by the whites to tragedy and paradox from the inception. The courthouse described in *Requiem for a Nun* as the "protector of the weak, judiciate and curb of the passions and lusts, repository and guardian of . . . aspirations and . . . hopes,"[3] was also the repository of records which noted the sale of human beings and posted "rewards for escaped or stolen Negroes and other livestock. . . ."[4] Moreover, black slave labor was used in erecting these edifices, namely the jail and the courthouse, which would be used in succeeding generations to maintain black powerlessness. These democratic institutions would symbolize the extent to which the powerful whites would subject blacks to a humiliating and inferior status.

Also from his composite historical view, Faulkner saw that black humanity was cast from the beginning into a tragic relationship with the land. But he also viewed blacks as enduring that tragedy out of sheer will and ingenuity and out of an arresting passion and compassion for the land. Under tremendous psychological and physical duress, the blacks were a part of the white man's violent effort to conquer and subdue nature: clearing forests and diverting miles of rivers. Not least, the black man's tragic irony was also symbolized by the products arising from his sweat and blood upon the land. For even frail cotton had the power "to bind for life them who made the cotton to the land their sweat fell on."[5]

As he matured, Faulkner saw the South as tragically deluded with respect to slavery and just as deluded, therefore, in many of its dreams, ambitions and principles. In his later and more public years, he stated many times that anyone who thinks should be able to see that the condition the nation put itself into with respect to the blacks was not only unjust but also intolerable. It was all a basic human wrong. Thus, when speaking with firm and absolute indictment as he did in *Absalom, Absalom!* (1936), Faulkner attempted to pull the foundation from the Yoknapatawpha culture. Sorcerer that he could be and gothic genius that he was, he knew precisely that by magnifying the moral void present in Yoknapatawpha's history he could prick the community's imagination. This is one way by which he forced the Yoknapatawpha community to confront the basic reality of their existence. For the South would certainly be doomed, until in the words Quentin Compson repeats from his father in *Absalom, Absalom!*, it "would realize that it was now paying the price for having erected its economic edifice not on the rock of stern morality but on the shifting sands of opportunism and moral brigandage."[6]

Perhaps the greatest of ironies is that many of the white Yoknapatawphans displayed awe and amazement when they observed the wretchedness of many of the blacks whom they played a role in subjugating. As Faulkner often shows, wretchedness was thought by these citizens to be the natural state of black being. This is revealed through the passing comments delivered in the heavily biased and indiscriminate language of the whites of all classes. According to the general white Yoknapatawpha mind, black being was by nature relegated to the status of chattel and was unworthy of further recognition.

Surely the circumstances of bondage were created by the whites in league with one another, whose strength was based on the fact that they possessed the mechanisms and means to inflict violence, thus to terrorize. It is mainly through this that whites like old Carothers McCaslin in *Go Down, Moses*, acquired slaves over whom they held the power of life and death. Through the same means they stole land and had it cleared. What is apparent in this scheme, although Faulkner does not point it out precisely in these terms, is that the blacks in bondage were considered a natural part of the European conqueror's effort to seize dominion over nature. And since these enslavers considered blacks more a part of animal nature than human nature, blacks were naturally seen as a part of the challenge and the conquest. Ellen Coldfield Sutpen perceived her husband's bondmen as "beasts," and the community viewed them as animal extensions of Thomas Sutpen's brutality, "more deadly than any beast he could have started and slain"[7] in the Mississippi wilderness. In the years following slavery, Joe Christmas, Will Mayes, and Rider were bestially slain and Nancy Mannigoe was kicked into a gutter like an animal.

Faulkner's criticism of the Yoknapatawphans self-deceiving manner of regarding black humanity as chattel is expressed in a number of subtle ways. In "The Bear" we hear of Sam Fathers and his mother who are swapped by Carothers McCaslin to the Chickasaw chief Ikkemotubbe for "one underbred trotting gelding."[8] What Faulkner intends to show here is that slavery is really a reflexive phenomenon; that is, the being who poses as the superior human, who considers himself the most responsible among God's creations, is inadvertently revealing himself as the most debased. Just as they look upon and refer to their livestock, the descendants of the slavocracy still think of Sutpen's blacks as "wild" and those of his neighbors as "tame." Since blacks are thought of as commodities, the descendants of the slaveholders easily speak of them in terms of expendable items. Thus we hear the phrase "surplus negroes," for example. When blacks are not looked upon as chattel, they are often viewed as human aberrants. Thus, the white characters in Faulkner's world make numerous mocking references to the appearance of blacks in European clothes. Miss Rosa Coldfield is outraged that Sutpen, during his wedding to her sister Ellen, came "up to the very door to the church with that wild negro in his Christian clothes looking exactly like a performing tiger in a linen duster and a top hat."[9] Grandfather Compson believes that Sutpen's slaves were cannibals, who, after tracking down the French architect who had run away from Sutpen's evolving enterprise, were merry with anticipation that they would be allowed to eat him. Ironically, however, these same Yoknapatawphans who look upon the blacks as aberrants or beasts or chattel also see them as the requisite accoutrements of grandeur.

While slavery sought to strip Africans of their individuality and humanity, it also created the tragic dimension of namelessness and rootlessness. The names these Africans and their descendants came to assume did not designate their own blood association, but rather, like a cattle-brand, identification as someone's property or, in slavery's aftermath, as having been someone's property. Lucas Beauchamp reacted against this by changing the spelling of his Christian name from that of the white progenitor and master of his parents, Lucius Carrothers McCaslin, of whose kinship he was both proud and scornful. The deliberate act of changing his name was for him symbolic of a self-generative identity and autonomy.

An entirely new race was created in the Yoknapatawpha world whose paternity was not only sometimes anonymous, but dubious as well. It is a sure cause of much of the tension which stood constantly between the races. We learn in "The Bear," for instance, that Eunice's husband Thucydus might not have known that his owner, and not her, was the father of his and Eunice's only child. In "There Was a Queen," we also learn that Elnora's mother's husband might not have known that the master, and not he, was her father. More examples appear in the lengthy story of how Sam Fathers got his name, which originally was not Fathers but Had-Two-Fathers, and also in "The Fire and the Hearth" when Zack Edmonds wishes to keep Lucas' wife Molly at his house. Lucas Beauchamp's brother, James Beauchamp, feels deeply the crisis of namelessness and scorn for the name he carried. In leaving Yoknapatawpha County, "he had interposed latitude and geography too, shaking from his feet forever the very dust of the land where his white ancestor could acknowledge or repudiate him from one day to another, according to his whim, but where he dared not even repudiate the white ancestor save when it met the white man's humor of the moment."[10]

A bondman's tragedy is not just individual but also representative.

The old family records that Isaac McCaslin inherits relate his particular ancestory but carry larger meaning. As a boy of sixteen, he wonders, as he reads through the old plantation ledgers of his family, why the bondwoman Eunice had committed suicide by walking into the creek one Christmas day. He finds the answer by putting together what is told and not told in the records: that Eunice came to realize the agonizing fact that her daughter by her master (although passing for the daughter of her husband Thucydus and recorded as such), was unwittingly carrying the child of her own father and master, Lucius McCaslin. The young girl had been called into the old master's house to perform house work, then raped by him who knew that in the moment of his incestuous act he would become both father and grandfather to the child she bore, Tomey's Turl.

Faulkner intends for this tragedy to be all the more jarring by having Eunice's suicide take place in the cold season, chilling the intellect and stunning the heart with the allusion to Christ's nativity. Through Eunice's agonizing predicament he suggests that the fundamental situation of the bondman was *de facto* equivalent to a state deeper than grief. He further suggests that such a state necessarily creates a disposition of intense anguish which brings an individual to absolute repudiation of any form of belief or hope with regard to humankind.

Beyond the boy Isaac's initial astonishment lies his greater consternation arising from what he fears may be a horrible abyss in human relationships as is made evident by the very willful incest of old Man McCaslin. Isaac is bewildered by his ancestor's bequest of a thousand dollars to his son-grandson Turl, because he sees that the bequest had been used as a vehicle for the old man to avoid acknowledging his crime as well as his double-blooded progeny. The boy is even more awestricken that his kinsman represents the living proof that a man could know his own blood and still not love or respect it. The revealed activity of the old man makes more horrendous the human image for young Isaac and greater the human debt—passing on a burden to be assumed by succeeding generations.

As caustic as Faulkner could sometimes be in his indictment of slavery, there is amazingly no mention in his canon of slave uprisings in the United States, or of the many rumors of slave revolts which circulated during the era of the slavocracy. Perhaps to some extent he shared the belief of some of his characters in *Absalom Absalom!*, that American slaves were more "tame" or domesticated than those like Sutpen's "wild negros" from the West Indies. There is, however, a lengthy and graphic treatment of the slave revolt which Sutpen witnesses in Haiti. Faulkner compares it to a revolt of nature upon a land "where high mortality was concomitant with money and the sheen on the dollars was not from gold but blood."[11] That he may have wanted to feel that North America was somehow exempt from this type of upheaval is suggested in Quentin Compson's grandfather's belief that Haiti was "a spot of earth which might have been created and set aside by Heaven itself . . . as a theater for violence and injustice and bloodshed and all the satanic lusts of human greed and cruelty."[12] This treatment (or non-treatment) of this crucial aspect of slavery brings Faulkner close to supporting the notion of American innocence. For as grandfather Compson continues his discourse, he speaks of the West Indies as being the "halfway point between what we call the jungle and what we call civilization."[13] Africa is the "dark inscrutable continent from which the black blood . . . was ravished by violence," and North American is "the cold known land to which it was doomed, the civilized land."[14] Unlike the impassioned remarks of Quentin's father, his grandfather's comments are usually marked by greater conviction and discrimination, thus, making his pronouncements more significant. The total absence of revolt in the Yoknapatawpha saga is evidence of Faulkner's inability to portray truly rebellious blacks in his works. He makes major black characters tormented, confused, virtuous, stoic and humorous, but never rebellious like Jesus or Caspey or either of the Loosh characters, all of whom are minor characters.

Basic contempt between the black slave and the poor white is one of the most vivid aspects of the old regime that comes through in Faulkner's writing. This legacy of lower-class contempt passes on to succeeding generations. It is not easy to forget our uneasiness with the sinister white man and Ned at the mudhole in *The Reivers* (1962) nor the tension we feel for Lucas when he goes to Beat Four in *Intruder in the Dust*. This most notable example of this contempt in the Yoknapatawpha saga takes place, of course, when the white boy Thomas Sutpen is gruffly turned away from Mr. Pettibone's front door by one of the black house servants in *Absalom, Absalom!* Here, there is contempt based on the poor white's envy of the slave's material condition, the superficial aspect of the slave's life, which was usually only a step above the material indigence of the poor white, if that. But from this false notion of security there developed often intense hatred, with little recognition given to the fact that the slave was provided for only because he was property—an investment that had to be protected. The slaves were often vain about superficial aspects of their condition, which they considered better than poor whites, and consequently developed their own brand of hatred toward what they called "white trash."

Sutpen's slaves, for example, stop Wash Jones and jeer at him along the road after they hear that he told people that he "was looking after Kernel's place and niggers"[15] while Sutpen was away fighting in the war. Wash Jones attempts to create another station for himself because he thinks that he is suffering an injustice at the hands of men who act contrary to what he believes to be Christian doctrine: that the black man "had been created and cursed by God to be the brute and vassal to all men of white skin."[16] Thus, the slave and the poor white were in contention because neither wanted to be perceived as occupying the station of utmost disdain. Each wished to affirm that the other held the absolutely subordinate social position. This mutual contempt became a part of Southern history.

In *The Hamlet* (1940), Faulkner described slavery as "that single constant despotic undeviating will of the enslaved not only for possession, complete assimilation, but to coerce and reshape the enslaver into the seemliness of his victimization."[17] With this definition Faulkner avoided a comprehensive definition of slavery carrying implications like those which are so pronounced in his stringent indictment of ante-bellum culture in *Absalom Absalom!* (1936). This restrictive definition was, perhaps, a necessary part of that romanticism which lingered on in his writing while he was, to some degree, working his way out of the bondage of his own racial attitudes, or at least out of the attitudes of his culture. But one would be more inclined to think that, in this definition from *The Hamlet*, Faulkner was following his own favorite path of exploiting paradox. He saw in the master-slave relationship a reciprocal power struggle arising out of the general nature of human beings. In this struggle, which was for Faulkner always more psychological than physical, the master was not the absolute power that he thought he was or wished to be. The master's methods were often more blatantly dictatorial because he presumed that overt action was a prerogative of his power. The subjected blacks were not absolutely powerless, however, even though they certainly could not afford to be as forward as the master. They resorted to forms of subterfuge, as Ned and Simon did, or even to sabotage as Nancy did, and as Jesus, Caspey and Loosh would possibly be inclined to do. When the black characters are not thwarted by Faulkner's own racial prejudices, weaknesses and fears, the integrity which some of them hold over their presumed masters becomes quite evident. They especially demonstrate that the subject who could control the comic projection of himself would simultaneously illuminate the comic and also tragic circumstances of the master, who, in overestimating himself, inevitably underestimated the power of his subject.

Faulkner's fundamental conviction and sentiment about the Civil War was that each of the three peoples involved, the Northerner the Southerner, and the black, was characterized by their own peculiar mental state, ranging from euphoria to delusion and dejection. It was both the white Southerner and the black who were victims. The Civil War was the point at which time became blurred in the white Yoknapatawpha mind, the point from which time almost refused to proceed. It marked the entry of chaos into the white Southerner's world, the destruction of his dreams. Above all, it was a moment of surrender.

Miss Rosa Coldfield, as much as any other Faulkner character, has the peculiar voice of the white Southern victim. In *Absalom, Absalom!*, she presents an intense and stoic lamentation on how the world of the slavocracy, the world of her security and stability dissolved into fire and smoke around her. She feels the loss bitterly even though her Methodist father was a Southern emancipationist, who chose to nail himself in the attic and starve to death rather than fight in the war. Miss Rosa loses little materially in comparison to the great holders of land and slaves, but she is bitter along with the rest of the Yoknapatawpha white community because, like them, she has lost the historical sense of herself. Seeing herself as the epitome of the Southern victim, she levels her criticism toward the North with harsh intensity: "What creature in the South since 1861," she proclaims, "man woman nigger or mule, had had time or opportunity not only to have been young, but to have heard what being young was like from those who had."[18]

The dismantling of the South by the North was to Miss Rosa and most of her community very much like the slave Loosh's sweeping away with his hand the fabricated sand model of the battle area built by the white boy Bayard and his slave boy playmate Marengo in *The Unvanquished* (1938), Faulkner expressed the pain of the memory of the defeat of war through many of his characters, but also became critical of those who cultivated an obsession over it. He said in later years that it was important to know what the old illusions were, but they should not be taken too seriously. It is more important to cope with change and to work to free oneself from the old shackles. In *Flags in the Dust*, old man Falls, who remembers the war and his defeated comrades, thinks that the rest of the Yoknapatawphans were very much like he was–ignorant of the reasons for which they were actually fighting. Isaac McCaslin and his cousin Zack Edmonds present the South's stand as a rather quixotic adventure. Isaac comments:

> Who else could have declared war against a power with ten times the area and a hundred times the men and a hundred times the resources, except men who could believe that all that was necessary to conduct a successful war was not acumen nor shrewdness nor politics nor diplomacy nor money nor even integrity and simple arithmetic but just love of land and courage . . . ."[19]

Zack Edmonds adds to this his own understanding and assessment: "And an unblemished and gallant ancestry and the ability to ride a horse."[20] Overall, Faulkner viewed the Civil War as part of the general antics of mankind, tragic though it was. Perhaps it was not totally a conscious part of Faulkner's artistic design, but the Civil War in his works actually became a rather fitting, inevitable, cataclysmic outcome of that errant violence upon which the Yoknapatawpha world was originally established.

The tragedy of the blacks in the Civil War was the result of other men's folly. For the mature Faulkner, black being became the victim of a Northern adventure which proved to be about as irresponsible as its enslavement by the Southerner. If the South fought to preserve the status quo, then the North fought for a freedom to which it was uncommitted. But Faulkner's viewpoint is mainly ideological because his depictions of the blacks during this war are certainly among his worst. In *The Unvanquished*, he is nearly as deluded as the society he portrays because he romanticizes about Southern romance, in contrast to his greater works where he is a critical realist with regard to Yoknapatawpha culture. Granny Rosa Millard, for example, tells the dispersed, fleeing and disillusioned blacks to go back home to their masters. Moreover, she chides them as children: "I suppose you all want to cross some more rivers and run after the Yankee Army, don't you. . . . Then who are you going to mind from now on?"[21]

Being immersed in the romance himself, it is Faulkner who has the blacks cower and answer the old woman's admonition with: "You, missy."[22] He has them admit, without any sense of discrimination, that they must rely on the shelter of the old white woman for their survival. In truth, the old matriarch is acting out of a sense of her own needs and insecurity when she seizes the opportunity to lure the blacks back into her fold. She is establishing the pretext as well as the mechanism for the coming era of black peonage.

Much of what is said in *The Unvanquished* about the pathetic situation of the blacks loses its effectiveness and simply ridicules their situation. Loosh, for example, questions paternalism as the ultimate authority of the institution of slavery, but Faulkner himself often does not have the courage to develop along with the profundity of his characters. Thus, Loosh becomes the errant knave who is to be watched by his mother and grandmother. He is condemned because he has no sense of obligation or loyalty to the crumbling economic and social order. He is expected, like his mother, to assist the master unequivocally in his "will to endure." Bayard recalls: "Father said that Louvenia would have to watch him too, that even if he was her son, she would have to be white a little while longer."[23] Faulkner makes the situation even more ludicrous when Louvenia presumes to grant Granny the privilege of whipping the grown and married Loosh for having revealed to the Yankee Army where the family had buried the Sartoris family silver.

Loosh's wife, Philadelphy, epitomizes and illuminates the nature of the whole black predicament when she makes the decision to follow her husband against the arguments of Granny, her old mistress, who declares that she is headed for starvation. Philadelphy's situation epitomizes the black predicament because all that she can do is make a decision. She does not have an authentic opportunity to make a choice as the Yankee crusaders in their often shallow commitment would have her believe. This indicates the beginning of a new phase of tragedy, black peonage. It is therefore very conceivable that Cinthy, the old black woman ex-slave of Gail Hightower's childhood, could think that because her master had been killed and her husband had not returned all that the war had brought was turmoil. Stubbornly determined to stay on after she has been told that she is free, she asks with persistent scorn: "Free. What's freedom done except git Marse Gail killed and made a bigger fool outen Pawmp den even de Lawd Hisself could do? Free? Dont talk ter me erbout freedom."[24]

This old woman's point of view stands out because of the conviction with which it is expressed. In the democratic context it is an aberration, but from her point of view, against the background of hostility which the free blacks experienced before the war, it seems totally justified. Faulkner does not suggest that her point of view is representative, however. His main interest is to point up the fact that her notions carry great paradox and irony, of which he as a writer had a great fondness. The total nature of the predicament is probably best explained by the Alabama sharecropper and farmer, Ned Cobb, who was born in 1885:

> My grandmother and other people that I knowed grew up in slavery time, they wasn't satisfied with their freedom. They felt like motherless children—they wasn't satisfied but they had to live under the impression that they were. Had to act in a way just as though everything was all right. But they would open up every once in a while and talk about slavery time—they didn't know nothin about no freedom then, didn't know what it was but they wanted it. And when they got it they knew that what they got wasn't what they wanted, it wasn't freedom, really. Had to do whatever the white man directed em to do, couldn't voice their heart's desire.[25]

The era of Reconstruction is that time which Miss Rosa tells

Quentin he is lucky to have escaped. It was the period of "dark times . . . in Mississippi," according to Uncle Buddy McCaslin whose own slaves had run off with the Yankee troops. In the ludicrous mind of the defeated South, the blacks were conceived of as having "deserted" their enslavers. Because the blacks were looked upon as incapable of taking care of themselves under any circumstances, it was, of course, natural that the economically and culturally bankrupt Yoknapatawphans should hold this view. They are indeed outraged that the two women slaves whom Goodhue Coldfield, Miss Rosa's father, had "freed" and put on a weekly wage to discharge their market value, had been among the first to leave or "to desert and follow the Yankee troops."[26]

The men who perceived themselves as having been deserted by their slaves were among the most embittered of the defeated. Women like Miss Rosa, who fell to foraging along the garden fences of her neighbors before daybreak, thought that they had fallen from grace. Before the war, they had been deluded by their culture to believe that grace was their privilege. But with the South's defeat, their bitterness sometimes turned into a hostility toward their own people, including the women. For Miss Rosa, the period of the veterans' return was one of tremendous dread:

> It was winter soon and already soldiers were beginning to come back—the stragglers, not all of them tramps, ruffians, but men who had risked and lost everything, suffered beyond endurance and had returned now to a ruined land, not the same men who had marched away but transformed—and this was the worst, the ultimate degradation to which war brings the spirit, the soul—into the likeness of that man who abuses from very despair and pity the beloved wife or mistress who in his absence has been raped. We were afraid.[27]

Yet there were also the well-known outward manifestations of defeat and despair which culminated in violent intimidations and lynchings of whites and blacks by the armed men who rode out their desperation in the night dressed in hooded sheets and masks. This was the age of the fear of "negro uprisings" and the period of the emergence of a new character in Southern life: the Northern carpetbagger. It was for the white Yoknapatawphan an age of recalcitrance and outright resistance to cooperation with the men who had been their enemies in the war and the men who had been their slaves. According to Will Falls, Colonel Sartoris had a change for the worse in his life, "when he had to start killing folks. Them two carpetbaggers stirrin' up niggers to vote. . . ."[28] The embitterment in this period was so intense that Faulkner accounts for few times when the hardships of war even inadvertently bound its victims together for the common good.

Although there had been longstanding tensions between the North and the South, Faulkner's characters make no ante-bellum criticism of the North. For the Yoknapatawpha mind, antagonism was generated by the Civil War and crystallized with Reconstruction. What made the antagonism so entrenched was that the Southerner, who felt deeply that he imbibed the world's two greatest moral codes: chivalry and Christianity, and who thought that in his relationship with the black man he was undertaking a God-ordained task, found that his honor and courage did not have the fortitude he had come to believe they had. Consequently, it was necessary for him to consider that perhaps he did not have the affinity, the special relationship with God, he had assumed was his before his defeat by the North. For how else could a people of honor, courage and godliness be so miserably defeated except through God's favor for others?

The Yoknapatawphans came to believe that they were under a curse, that is, that they were in God's disfavor. Yet they were not prepared to acknowledge their sins. Cringing, they expressed their humiliation from the unbearable "iron heel of a tyrant oppressor" as Judge Hamblett termed it in *Absalom, Absalom!*[29]; but at the same time, characteristically, they not only oppressed, but sought to justify a perpetual oppression of the blacks.

Although Isaac McCaslin reveals no knowledge or evidence of any intentions on the part of the South to free the black man, he, too, is somewhat resentful that the slaves, for whom no date of freedom or death is entered into the commissary ledger, were freed by "a stranger in Washington." Isaac is indignant and humiliated because he feels, like the others in his milieu, that the moral responsibilities of the Yoknapatawpha whites were immorally and irresponsibly taken from them by the North. He shares the general presumption that "freedom and equality had been dumped overnight" upon the blacks "without warning or preparation or any training in how to employ it or even just endure it."[30] McCaslin attempts to universalize his criticism by saying blacks misused freedom not as children would nor yet because they had been so long in bondage and then so suddenly freed, but misused it as human beings always misuse freedom. . . ."[31] Isaac's attempt at universality fails, however, because his argument is based on the assumption that the whites who instituted and maintained the corruption were themselves capable of preparing or training anybody for freedom.

In *The Unvanquished*, Drusilla argues that the Yankees are alien to humanity, that they are pirates. Bayard counters that they are human beings. Before she ever sees a Yankee, Louvenia supposes that they are perhaps of another race. Miss Rosa Coldfield sees the Northerner as the agent of the South's everlasting dispossession; thus, she tells Quentin as he is preparing to go North to Harvard to study: "So I dont imagine you will ever come back here and settle down as a country lawyer in a little town like Jefferson, since Northern people have already seen to it that there is little left in the South for a young man."[32] One has little sympathy, however, for the victim Miss Rosa deems herself so appropriately as being, for it is of no moral consequence to her that the boot of the Southerner is yet upon the black person's neck.

Resentment for the North set the tone for succeeding generations. In *The Hamlet*, the loquacious sewing machine agent, V. K. Ratliff, characterizes the Northerner as someone who always carries out his aims with an organized syndicate. During World War I, Miss Jenny DuPre writes with all her self-possession to one of her young Sartoris nephews fighting in Europe: "We think it's about time you came home. Your grandfather is getting old, and it don't look like they will ever get done fighting over there. So you come on home. The Yankees are in it now. Let them fight it out if they want to. It's their war. It's not ours."[33] A generation after that, Charles Mallison would be told by his Uncle Gavin Stevens that "For every Southern boy fourteen years old, not once but whenever he wants it, there is the instant when it's still not yet two o'clock on that afternoon in 1863, the brigades are in position behind the rail fence, the guns are laid and ready in the woods. . . ."[34]

The black man's reality was the pressure point in this animosity which arose out of conflicting ideals, condescension and superiority and inferiority complexes of the North and South, respectively. Black being was in a tragic bind, but it was not necessarily the fundamental object of the sectional conflict. The sectional conflict had grown into more of an abstraction, a compounded state of belligerence for which black being seemed doomed to catch the boot heel as it attempted to live under the gaze of Confederate monuments like the one in the square of the Yoknapatawpha county seat at Jefferson.

The status of the blacks did not necessarily change after the war, but rather shifted with response to the conveniences they could provide in the world of Yoknapatawpha. Their freedom meant a change, but it did not mean liberty, independence, or autonomy. The reality was so ordered that all blacks were expected to adjust to the role of servants. When Colonel Sartoris was mayor of Jefferson after the war, he declared an edict "that no Negro woman should appear on the streets without an apron."[35] In the figurative language of the black longshoreman from Faulkner's early piece, "The Longshoreman," the black man wore a "jail suit." In passing reference throughout his works Faulkner contrasted the toil of the black laborers with the self-assuming role of the whiteman who looked on like Judge Dranke in *Sanctuary* who, from a leisurely and reclining posture, watched the black man mow the lawn. This symbolized the social hierarchy.

In *The Unvanquished*, the black youth Marengo is tragically prophetic in his malaprop used to express his revelation of his new identity after the Civil War. With the innocence of his youth he tells his white boyhood playmate Bayard, "I ain't a nigger any more. I done been abolished."[36] Indeed, the Yoknapatawpha world all but sought to wipe him out. The tragically ironic destiny of the black man following slavery is also foreshadowed in Loosh's response to Granny's questioning of his morality for giving the Sartoris silver to the Yankees:

> "I don't belong to John Sartoris now; I belongs to me and God."
>
> "But the silver belongs to John Sartoris," Granny said. "Who are you to give it away?"
>
> "You ax me that?" Loosh said. "Where John Sartoris? Whyn't

> he come and ax me that? Let God ax John Sartoris who the man name that give me to him. Let the man that buried me in the black dark ax that of the man what dug me free."[37]

The tragedy of Loosh's questioning is that it went fundamentally unanswered through all succeeding generations. Thus, when we hear Faulkner's definition of American freedom in the story "The Artist at Home," if we are aware of Faulkner's sense of the historical predicament of the blacks, we know that the black man stood far removed from this definition. That a man pays taxes was supposed to "indicate that he is free, twenty-one, and capable of taking care of himself in close competition."[38] In truth, the black man was given little opportunity to pay taxes and little respect if he was twenty-one or whatever age, since the Yoknapatawphans considers black men as boys and black women as girls, or as uncles and aunts when they are elderly. Moreover, legislation and violence were used to ensure that blacks did not participate, for the most part, in any kind of close competition. In *The Reivers*, the white boy Lucius reflects upon the probable intimidation of the blacks by the law officers in 1905, and is afraid for Uncle Parsham Hood and his home because of some basic contentions arising out of the affairs of the whites. In further self-illumination Lucius says, "But I was more than afraid, I was ashamed that such a reason for fearing for Uncle Parsham, who had to live here, existed."[39]

In one of his more perceptive moments, Isaac McCaslin, who is always sympathetic but is not always very discriminating in his analyses, reflects upon the black sharecropper's world as something working against him in return for nothing, not even a good risk. The sharecropper's compensations provided only the materials for bare subsistence, "the molasses and meal, the cheap durable shirts and jeans and shoes and now and then a coat against rain and cold."[40] The black man's general plight is symbolized even more by his once having had to bridle the mule at sunrise and follow him "through the plumb-straight monotony of identical furrows and back to the lot at sundown."[41]

As Faulkner portrays the McCaslin plantation commissary in "The Bear," he also reveals another aspect of the black tragedy in which blacks become pathetic participants. The building is wallpapered with advertisements which include those for patent formulas for bleaching the skin and straightening the hair of the blacks so that they "might resemble the race which for two hundred years had held them in bondage and from which for another hundred years not even a bloody civil war would have set them completely free."[42] From what we are told in *Requiem for a Nun*, we also understand that the black man's participation in the electoral process would, for a long time, serve to accentuate his plight as much as it would help to extricate him from it. The political arena was so filled with demagogues that the voting blacks would have no choice except to cast their ballots for a group who were almost always antagonistic to black interests and needs, who were, for the most part, antagonistic even to black existence.

The pervasive atmosphere of hostility toward the blacks, although some of its manifestations were so subtle or regulated that they seemed ordinary, created the need for overplay in social rituals. The white people had to be reminded that the blacks were supposed to be, and did indeed intend to be, in their service. In the Yoknapatawpha world corruption followed no line of consistency against which one could argue reasonably, and since the whole concept of "nigger" was a corruption of the entire scale of human values, one could not expect a fair encounter with anyone who saw the black man as nigger." Those who ignored the fact that corruption owes no allegiance usually became the victims of corruption's agents. Faulkner demonstrates this vividly in *The Reivers* with Boon Hogganbeck's attempt to use the mudfarmer's perception and treatment of Ned as a "nigger" to his, Ned's, and the boy Lucius' advantage. Boon assumes that the mudfarmer is at least consistent in his racial prejudices. If so, Ned, as a "nigger," is only three-fifths of a man and should not be charged the full price at the mudfarmer's crossing. Boon is assured that he is prepared to conquer the mudfarmer with the mudfarmer's own logic. But the mudfarmer is so deeply corrupted that he shifts the argument directed at his own person on to his mules, which he sarcastically implies are color-blind even to a nigger.

Distrust is a natural corollary of victimization and it underlies the manners of the Yoknapatawpha world. In one passing remark Faulkner highlights what he demonstrates on many occasions without explanation, that the approach of any strange white man toward a black home was almost certainly taken as some type of surveillance. As an example, in the story "Hand Upon the Waters," the lawyer, Gavin Stevens, dares to take himself into the hostilely inhabited backwoods to investigate the death of Lonnie Grinnup. Upon going with trepidation at night into the woods, he calls at the darkened house of a black man whom he knows as Nate. He shouts the name until Nate answers, but in answering, Nate does not open the door. Stevens informs him of where he is going, and Nate apparently knows why he is going there. He wants Nate to go to notify someone, some white person who can invoke authority, if he has not returned from the backwoods by daybreak. Nate is still reluctant to answer, and is called away from the door by an apprehensive wife. Nate's response to the situation is ostensibly contrary to his wife's, however, since he wants to respond with concern for Stevens' life. Nevertheless the wife's reply to her husband's concern is: "I can't help it! You come away and let them white folks alone!"[43]

Faulkner portrays the emotions of the woman as legitimate even though the courage of the man must surmount them. What the wife knows is that if her husband becomes involved in the situation, he faces extreme jeopardy to the extent that he could be killed for interfering with white folk's business. She knows that while he may help to uphold justice, historically, the world had shown little, if any justice towards him. She fears that his just act would prove meaningless to the white folk if she should need redress or defense for trouble arising from these same circumstances. What is revealed overall in this sense of distrust, which is naturally bred into the milieu, is again that the racial situation determined human response and thereby shaped the formation of the community's values. But such was the tragedy in a world made of so much human distance.

Similar forces are at work when Faulkner focuses on the white merchants who offer outcast food and other merchandise to blacks which they would never offer to white people, or in describing jobs designated as "nigger work." In time, there would be notable changes in the blacks' acquisition of improved educational facilities, or in the possession of electric lights and window screens which they had hitherto been denied by their poverty. Nevertheless, there was no unusual achievement in the Yoknapatawpha world as Faulkner finally saw it. There was hope, but no easy optimism. Faulkner feared the malicious potentialities of human nature. In the words of the elder John Sartoris:

Yoknapatawpha was a place "where only what a man takes and keeps has any significance, and where all of us have a common ancestry and the only house from which we can claim descent with any assurance, is the Old Bailey,"[44] the criminal court of London, that is. Black being was, of course, a major victim of this heritage and enterprise of Old Bailey's offspring who structured the tragic context of black existence in a new world.

ENDNOTES

1. C. Vann Woodward, *The Strange Career of Jim Crow* (New York: Oxford University Press, 1974), p. 11.
2. Blyden Jackson makes a very pertinent point regarding Faulkner's misuse of chronology in depicting Sutpen's "wild Negroes" from the West Indies. See Blyden Jackson, "Faulkner's Depiction of the Negro," *Studies in English*, 15 (University of Mississippi, 1978), pp. 33-48.
3. William Faulkner, *Requiem for a Nun* (New York: Random House, 1951), p. 40.
4. Ibid., p. 3.
5. William Faulkner, *Go Down, Moses* (New York: Modern Library, 1955), p. 256.
6. William Faulkner, *Absalom, Absalom!* (New York: Vintage Books, 1972), p. 260.
7. Ibid., p. 38.
8. William Faulkner, "The Bear" in *Go Down, Moses* (New York: Modern Library, 1942), p. 263.
9. *Absalom, Absalom!*, p. 24.
10. William Faulkner, "The Fire and the Hearth," in *Go Down, Moses*, p. 105.
11. *Absalom, Absalom!*, p. 250.
12. Ibid.
13. Ibid.
14. Ibid.
15. Ibid., p. 281.
16. Ibid., p. 282.
17. William Faulkner, *The Hamlet* (New York: Vintage Books, 1956), pp. 206-207.
18. *Absalom, Absalom!*, p. 19.
19. "The Bear," pp. 288-89.
20. Ibid., p. 289.
21. William Faulkner, *The Unvanquished* (New York: Vintage Books, 1966), p. 130.
22. Ibid.
23. Ibid., p. 23.
24. William Faulkner, *Light in August* (N.Y.: Modern Library, 1967), p. 418.
25. Theodore Rosengarten, *All God's Dangers: The Life of Nate Shaw* (N.Y.: Alfred A. Knopf, 1974), p. 8.
26. *Absalom, Absalom!*, p. 84.
27. Ibid., p. 157.
28. William Faulkner, *Flags in the Dust* (N.Y.: Vintage Books, 1974), p. 6.
29. *Absalom, Absalom!*, p. 203.
30. "The Bear," p. 289.
31. Ibid.

32. *Absalom, Absalom!*, p. 9.
33. William Faulkner, "All the Dead Pilots," in *Collected Stories of William Faulkner* (N.Y.: Random House, 1950), p. 531.
34. William Faulkner, *Intruder in the Dust* (N.Y.: Modern Library, 1964), p. 194.
35. William Faulkner, "A Rose for Emily," in *Collected Stories*, pp. 120-121.
36. *The Unvanquished*, p. 228.
37. Ibid., p. 85.
38. William Faulkner, "The Artist at Home," in *Collected Stories of William Faulkner* (N.Y.: Vintage Books, 1966), p. 174.
39. William Faulkner, *The Reivers* (N.Y.: Vintage Books, 1966), p. 174.
40. "The Bear," p. 266.
41. *Requiem For a Nun*, p. 245.
42. "The Bear," p. 255.
43. William Faulkner, "Hand Upon the Waters," in *Knight's Gambit* (N.Y.: Random House, 1949), p. 74.
44. *Flags in the Dust*, p. 96.

IV.

The Tragedy of Human Distance

". . . when I try sometimes to stand aside and look at it, I am ama-aze at the length, the blackness of that shadow. . . . It is the Nemesis w'ich, instead of coming afteh, glides along by the side of this morhal, political, commercial, social mistake! It blanches, my-de'-seh, ow whole civilization."

Honore' Grandissime, the Fairer,
in George Washington Cable's
THE GRANDISSIMES[1]

In the greatest fiction, the writer's moral sense coincides with his dramatic sense, and I see no way for it to do this unless his moral judgement is part of the very act of seeing, and he is free to use it.

–Flannery O'Connor,
MYSTERY AND MANNERS[2]

The Yoknapatawpha world is one in which black being lives in fear, in fear of the danger encountered when a black person attempts simply to live out the dignity of his being. The Yoknapatawpha world is one in which the relationship between black and white being is shrouded with myth, contradiction, and paradox. Black being is expected not only to suffer the white man's brigandage, treachery, corruption, humiliation, and deprivation, but is ironically also expected to benefit from it. Black being is a pawn used for fulfilling white people's desperate need to feel superior or simply, perhaps, just to establish an identity. For a black person to threaten this need of whites in any way is to risk his own life. The Yoknapatawpha culture itself is rigged to preclude the possibility of black being redeeming itself in respect to its own general welfare or, in effect, to deny it any claim to dignity. In Yoknapatawpha, black being is unacknowledged even to the extent that blacks often learn to deny many of the brutal aspects of their own existence. In many circumstances, blacks are expected to emphasize the ridiculousness of their existence. The racism in this world is a scheme of grand larceny designed to strip the blacks of their soul. And the degree to which this is successful provides for Yoknapatawpha what Faulkner comes to realize is a peculiar and tragic festivity.

Caught between the vagaries of the white man and chance, gripped by tension and terror, the black man knows that in this world the slightest provocation can mean disaster. He knows, too, as do Molly, Dilsey, Loosh, Old Job, Jesus, Lucas, and Nancy, that those white Yoknapatawphans who have the least awareness of themselves and of their peculiar identity in time and space, must experience horrible self-revelation when they finally see that they have been nurtured to act as agents of evil. The story of what the white Yoknapatawphan thinks and feels when he realizes himself to be fundamentally treacherous to human dignity and existence, has yet to be written.

In Faulkner's saga it is almost exclusively the young boys like Lucius Priest and Charles Mallison who are brought to the crossroads of that realization. The black man, from the vantage point of his struggles with deprivation, prejudice, and chance, looks upon it all from his own special angle. He knows that the Yoknapatawphan's perception of black being is inextricably tied to the wretched distortion of his own white identity, of who he thinks he is as white humanity, and who he thinks his fathers were. By viewing the Yoknapatawpha situation from this angle, what the black person sees is very much a tragic comedy in which he is only one of the victims. From his observation of his victimizer, the black man knows that what he is witnessing around him is one of the most pathetic cases of mistaken identity as has ever appeared on the world stage.

Walter White wrote that with the Civil War the South had been "defeated both in logic and in the test of armed strength,"[3] and that its inability to deal with this truth had not only kept it on the brink of hysteria but had also caused it to slip more deeply into a state of "mental inertia," and "moral, spiritual, and intellectual sterility and blindness."[4] He went on to say that "in creating a psychology of oppression of the Negro it . . . hamstrung itself."[5] The white Yoknapatawphans live on the defensive, projecting onto black being a hatred of something that is terribly wrong inside themselves. Confused because they can neither defend nor explain the old way, including the deep-seated and historical hatred of black being, they cannot tolerate criticism of their racial life. Thus, the white Yoknapatawphans harbor a seething tension stemming from embarassment of their few minor traces of heroism and their major sense of defeat. Sustained, too, by bitter hostility toward the North, Yoknapatawphans carry the indignant sense that they remain beyond reproach because the North violated the rules of the game concerning the white man's relationship to the black man: the Northern whites were so corrupt as to pretend that black humanity could be raised as the vital issue for their fighting each other. So the white Yoknapatawpha mind perceives itself as persecuted in the name of the "nigger." Black being becomes the resonator of the whiteman's internal vicissitudes.

The Yoknapatawpha world is designed to breed men to deny the fact that there is racial conflict. This paradox is representative of the communal complicity. To acknowledge that there is conflict in their relationship with black being would be comparable to raising black being above the place of insignificance designated by the white community. It would be acknowledging and affirming black being as a part of humanity.

On a deeper level, such an acknowledgement would mean that the white Yoknapatawphans would be challenging their own superiority, thus their identity. And as Faulkner sees it, human beings do not tamper readily with their identities. They are afraid to loosen old bonds, to shed old securities, no matter how terrifying and destructive these might sometimes be to their lives. People are afraid of their own fragility, their own transience. Change may bring them too close to their own death. They do not generally realize that while change often means the death of something, it is also the augur of life. Those who cannot transcend the literalness of that which shackles them will soon perish anyway; for if they cannot express transcendence, they cannot truly represent humanity.

Faulkner comes to think that there is something immoral about people who become so tied up in the personal moment that they overlook the need to deal with past and future.[6] Joe Christmas is tragic and is to be pitied because he could not know his past and thus his future was thrown into confusion. Faulkner argues, however, that a man who is capable of knowing his past but who will not attempt to cope with it, working uselessly rather to eradicate it, is just as doomed as Joe Christmas. He sees the Yoknapatawpha world as being caught between two destructive extremes. On the one hand there are too many callous Jason Compsons who could be successful and, on the other, too many Quentin Compsons who are too sensitive to face the reality of their lives. Such is Faulkner's basic view about the Yoknapatawpha world. He attempts to lay out this view with his acknowledgement that sometimes the writer even as truth-seeker, writes about himself only as he presumes himself to be, hopes to be, or hates himself for being.[7] Yoknapatawphans, so torn within themselves, can hardly help but strike out at the world, since they will not face the world within themselves.

In their own special way, each black person who passes through or seeks to inhabit this world signifies and illuminates some particular aspect of the Yoknapatawpha way of being. Some more than others, though, point to the ultimate distance, the tragedy which lies between the races. Their lives do not share in every common experience, but all of the lives of the blacks contribute to a common testament. Caspey Strother, for example, has been sent off to World War I to fight, and die if need be, but when he returns home, he must reassume his previous role of peon. His spark of life must be smothered. Molly Beauchamp has been the only mother that Roth Edmonds has ever known; she suckled him at her breast with her own son when his mother died at his birth. But it is the same Roth, whom Molly sees as one of the causes, or a symptom of the causes, that led to her grandson's death in the electric chair at age twenty-six. There is Nancy Mannigoe who has no protection from outright abuse and murder, who as Faulkner says, had dedicated herself in service to the white people who would not be there to give her assistance when she most needed them.[8] There is Charles Bon whose existence was denied by his father Sutpen, and there are his descendants who come into this world and suffer for related reasons. There are Lucas Beauchamp and Jesus who comprehend and bear witness to the black male's emasculation, just as Eunice has borne witness to and been the victim of rape. And, too, there are the comic manipulators like Ned and Old Het whose genius it is to know the manners and dangers of the Yoknapatawpha world so well that they not only know how to avert danger, but also how to wage their own small, but on-going battles with the whites who attempt to control the blacks. Moreover, some blacks become the official scapegoats by which all of the other blacks are made to remember that their existence and manner of being is proscribed. In the course of their tragic victimization blacks become exemplars of the harsh and stubborn depths of the community's tragedy.

The superbly written and very moving story of Rider, a twenty-six-year-old sawmill worker in "Pantaloon in Black" is an excellent expression of the cruel waste of human life brought on by the racial distance established by the whites in the community. "Pantaloon in Black" is one of Faulkner's best short stories and it contains one of his most successful and circumspect creations in which he is deeply involved with a black male character. Written in a passionate and patient prose style, this is the story of a young man who, after only six months of marriage, loses his wife to an untimely death. But in trying to endure his own isolated and misunderstood grief, he also loses his own life.

At the opening of the story, Rider stands at his young wife Mannie's burial site overcome with suffering as he watches the men fill in her grave. Faulkner accentuates the visual and auditory imagery at the gravesite and uses it to underscore the weight of the grief that this man suffers as he tries to understand this abrupt intrusion of death into his life. We hear the dirt clods as they strike the pine box separately and fatefully, suggestive of the tolling of the death bell itself except that the sound is hollow, flat, unlingering. This striking foreshadows Rider's imminent death. In his overpowering grief, this man looms larger in humane proportion than the generally uncomprehending world which surrounds him.

Faulkner highlights Rider's tragedy by making him of tremendous size and physical capacity. The shovel Rider seizes as he throws himself into helping to fill his wife's grave is like a child's toy in comparison to his size. When Faulkner brings this image into the narrative the great outpouring of Rider's grief is accentuated. His easy handling of the shovel only goes to point out the tragic and dramatic irony of any great man caught in a futile attempt to grapple with the ineffable nature of death. The imagery of the sea shore also foreshadows the washing in of Rider's own time for dying. Like the rising tide to which he is compared, his emotions are persistent and all-consuming. While friends and relatives may bury his wife, Rider knows they cannot bury certain contingencies of life. Rider's struggle is later symbolized in Faulkner's detailed description of his body during his contest with the gigantic log at the lumber mill on the Monday morning following the funeral. At one point, we are told that the sound of the rise and fall of his chest is like "someone engaged without arms in prolonged single combat."[9] He could not communicate his anguish, therefore, he could not evoke the requisite sympathy.

Although he comes to be portrayed as the community's victim, Rider holds what amounts on a philosophical level to be an erroneous and subsequently tragic conception of his own reality. He had thought that by marrying and settling down he would have a more beneficial and meaningful life. He had thought and believed that between man and nature, or even between nature and man and God, intercommunication and understanding was universally possible and could bring peace within one's grasp. He thought that his joy in marriage, and his relinquishment of drinking and gambling as testament to his love, were not only understood but also sanctioned by God, nature, and man. However, neither God, nature, or man seemed to understand.

So fully has Mannie symbolized for Rider the belief and meaning of life he thought he had found, that with her death he retreats into his erstwhile abandoned life of wastefulness. In doing so, he not only loses sight of the belief he thought he had found, but even more dangerously, he becomes very shortsighted in his judgement of the Yoknapatawpha racial reality. Feeling compelled to kill the white man who cheats him, he signs his own death warrant by touching off the deep-seated antagonism and hatred of black being existing in the Yoknapatawpha world. In cutting the white man's throat, Rider brings himself to a point with the whites that is analogous to his own state of frustration and blindness. Extremes of passion coalesce around Rider as a fearful racial symbol, and the passionate men take their black victim. When emotional response as this seethes in the Yoknapatawpha community as it does also in *Light in August*, "Dry September," *Intruder in the Dust*, Faulkner shows the tragedy and awesome horror of people living on the rawness of impulse and instinct. Consequently, efforts such as those of Old Miss Habersham, coupled with those of the two boys Aleck Sander and Charles in *Intruder in the Dust* are not to be seen simply as heroic gestures but more as a historic momentum hopefully leading the Yoknapatawpha world out of its peculiar state of moral chaos and damnation.

Rider cannot communicate with his social or moral universe, and all possibilities of comfort for him seem to be gone with the death of Mannie. Dislocated from the context of his own reality, the language of his grief sets him apart from the Yoknapatawpha community, black and white. The blacks feel the depth of his sorrow, but in their efforts to assist, they only make his sense of helplessness seem more acute. The black people's sensitivity to his grief leads them into overstatement regarding Rider's situation, which only disturbs him more. At the gravesite, for example, one of the men tries to relieve him of the shovel as he hurls the dirt into the grave but the offer is rebuffed. Another tries to prevent him from going back to his lonely house but with the very inappropriate suggestion that the wife's spirit had not yet settled down to rest. Rider's grief is so intense and extreme that he is beyond the total reach and comprehension of the blacks; yet the blacks respect that this predicament which they do not understand is still worthy of their sympathy.

Faulkner has used the peculiar markings, the makeshift tombstones on the black gravesites to signal the degree to which the white community has a disparaging and uncomprehending perception of black being. That the white community does not understand the reason for the use of all these odd markings is, for Faulkner, a sign not only of a lack of their sensitivity but is also indicative of a basic cultural ignorance of the blacks living among them. White sympathy and comprehension are so minimal that the whites grant little validity to black manners, whether in regard to black emblems or black suffering.

Faulkner strongly condemns the whites for their lack of compassion for those aspects of life which he believes that with the exertion of a little human effort whites might comprehend better. He sees those who make no effort to be more human as partly responsible for their own inadequacies, especially for their distorted perception and presumption. And particularly in this story, Faulkner is extremely critical of the smug presumption held by the white Yoknapatawphans in believing that they comprehend all that is worthy of being understood regarding black being. They hold a low estimate of the worth of black being and are consequently a treacherous element to black fate.

While Faulkner is not generally as caustically ironic or witty in his treatment of the subject of racial presumption as Herman Melville is, for example, in "Benito Cereno," one finds that both authors' perceptions of this flaw and its tragic implications are essentially the same. In Melville's story, Captain Delano and Don Benito are fatefully trapped and blinded by their presumption. In "Pantaloon in Black," it is racial presumption which often deprives the white citizens of a sense of compassion and pity. In violating all of the rules of decency, these whites make way, according to Faulkner, for the fates to take revenge upon them.[10] Consequently, Faulkner depicts the world of some of the whites in "Pantaloon in Black" as a vapid and vacuous one, a world in which the people are preoccupied with the shallower aspects of life, of politics and picture-shows.

To illustrate this, Faulkner has moulded his criticism of the deputy sheriff's household into a very poignant portrait. He juxtaposes insipidness with hysteria as the deputy sheriff tries to talk to his wife about the eventful day of Rider's lynching. The wife is not very responsive. Thus, she makes the deputy even more uneasy about his conviction that Rider's actions after his wife's death only point up the inhumanity of the blacks. The undercurrent of hysteria observed in the deputy is also used to reflect his uneasy conscience in knowing the one truth that his wife also takes time to assert in her own matter-of-fact way: that he and the other officers made no effort to defend the prisoner against the lynchers. The deputy is forced to admit that the law officers were negligent, and that by not defending the black man they were more concerned with saving votes than the life. What is as astonishing, however, is that the wife of the deputy is not really concerned with the lynching victim or her husband. She is irritated at having been obliged that same afternoon to give up the first prize at her club's rook-party when someone asked that the scores be recounted. Her preoccupation with this inconsequential game of chance stands as a cynical counterpoint to the fatal game of dice out of which Rider and the white gamester have both lost their lives.

In their domestic life, this couple, like the community and Rider, are separated by a tragic gulf in communication. As a result of domestic emptiness and adherence to the community's inhumane code of conduct, we sense that the deputy has been engulfed in a moral vacuum. His complicity in the manhunt for Rider should serve to make him more aware of the frigidity and death in his married life.

His frustrations have been compounded because his human values are constructed upon a shallow and simple-minded logic. For after all he has been through, he still has the need to believe that black being stands in the shadow of a superior and white form of humanity. Obviously, too, the picture-show which his wife is preparing to rush off to has probably little intrinsic worth since she shows such a limited capacity to respond to the horror of a lynching. We surmise then that she surely does not recognize that she is a part of a living and tragic theatre. Or maybe the picture-show and the rook parties are all part of the opiate she uses to keep from knowing.

In the Yoknapatawpha world we see again and again that to assume innocence when one is guilty only compounds the terror. The terror of the white victimizer is that his black victim can and does think, and that the black victim's thoughts could turn into vengeful action at any moment. The victimizer makes a tremendous intellectual effort to keep his own tragic deeds and his general tragic existence at a distance from himself. He feels compelled to create within himself the sense that his racial reality exists apart from his own being and therefore does not pertain to his conscience. Black being is posited as an alien reality, and not to believe in this causes turmoil in the white man's soul, pitting him against the power base of white society. For the victims, like Old Job in *The Sound and the Fury* and Jesus in "That Evening Sun," the tension and the terror, come in realizing that what the whites fear, that the black's feelings of humiliation and intimidation may not be so easily held below the thresholds of thought and action. The feelings of the blacks may become manifest. But the victimizer seeks to make this terrible reality pleasing to his own mind. Moreover, the ultimate paradox is that through the victimization of black being the Yoknapatawpha world seeks desperately to restore what it believes to be its lost innocence and thereby to purify itself of its own limitations by projecting them onto black being. Black being is seen as the manifestation of the evil that should be extricated from human culture.

The Yoknapatawpha community, taken as a collective character, is among the most contemptible of Faulkner's creations. It is often the reservoir of brute ignorance, frustration, and stubborn belief. Its tenacious clinging to the errors of its past gives it a characteristically negative posture. Working as a force of stasis, this posture is generally antithetical to the vision of Faulkner's best narrators. Thus, the major aura of suspense and tension in *Intruder in the Dust*, for example, is built around the conclusion of the community that Lucas Beauchamp, a black man, has murdered a white man. And in the mind of the community in *Light in August*, Joanna Burden is not murdered by the individual Joe Christmas, but by "Negro," a composite image of black being. The community is the provincial adherent to a clouded legacy of anger which it senses strongly, but can only vaguely define. It recharges itself through suspicion, rumor and vengeance.

The community grants white men latitude if they ally themselves with it. The undefinables, like Joe Christmas, are always threats. The community is the tragic residue of a historical legacy of ghosts and phantoms "of the old spilled blood and the old horror and anger and fear."[11] As Olga Vickery points out, "Society has myths not only of the hero but also the antagonist, and it has evolved its rituals to deal with each. Collectively, Jefferson is Southern, White, and Elect, qualities which have meaning only within a context which recognizes something or someone as Northern or Black or Damned."[12] And as Agnes Moreland has pointed out, "For Faulkner's Southern white man, especially, *being white* and *being* are equivalent. Consequently, any situation that can alter the whiteness also threatens to negate being. . . ."[13]

Though the Yoknapatawphans are obsessed with their racial beliefs and bewildered by their historical situation, Faulkner wants us to see that they nevertheless are not without the capacity for understanding their own evil; neither are they without free will. "Dry September," a story involving the lynching of a black man, Will Mayes, is important in this context. Mayes represents the qualities which community myths project upon black being. Accused by rumor of attacking a white woman, he is lynched by what Faulkner portrays as the mental processes of Yoknapatawpha. Through the murder of Mayes, the lynchers seek to affirm and reinstitute the racial myths of the culture. The collective black community, as represented by Mayes, is the scapegoat of a psychology which operates on the principles of "nice believing": what one wishes and needs to believe takes precedence over what is true.

As some of the white women in *Light In August* find a perverse thrill in the notion of a black rapist ranging free in the Jefferson area, so do these women in "Dry September" who associate with the accuser, Minnie Cooper. Whether or not anything has really happened, they are eager to take part in the atmosphere of excitement: "When you have had time to get over the shock, you must tell us what happened. What he said and did; everything," they coax Minnie.[14] The sighs of these women are like sirens for the sadistic men of the community urging them on to perform castration rituals upon black victims and to murder. In this instance, the black man is regarded as bestial. Any such suggestion of intimacy between the black male and white female is tantamount to an assault upon the realm of humanity, which is thought to be the white Yoknapatawpha community exclusively. This feeling of humanity as being exclusively white is surely wishful thinking which itself is rooted in a terrible inferiority complex. It must be an inferiority complex deeply rooted in frustration since such an heinous act as lynching was to become a major symbol of white presumption to superiority. Also, the sense of racial hatred could be, for the lyncher, not so much an antipathy for black being, as much as a distance he feels between himself and his idealized image of what it means to be white. The lynching of blacks is one of the prices he has to pay to maintain an affinity with his ideal.

As we see in the example of Hawkshaw, the white Jefferson citizen who offers his feeble defense of Mayes, any attempt to deny the racial allegations or any attempt to enlighten the community of its notions about black existence, is a betrayal of the sacred trust believed to have been given to the white man. It is "nigger-loving." Acceptance of rumor is a habit of the community. When it perceives a black threat to any aspect of its lifestyle, the community will go to any lengths to protect itself. Not many is this world have come to believe as Byron Bunch does in *Light in August*, while he ponders the stories he has heard about Gail Hightower's background, that "always . . . when anything gets to be a habit, it also manages to get a right good distance away from truth and fact."[15]

Faulkner reveals the depth of the perversity in the thought processes of this community within which the constantly intimidated blacks try to eke out an existence. One vivid example of this is shown when the community watches the burning house of the abolitionist descendant, Joanna Burden, the "lover of Negroes" who, in the minds of the whites, retained a so-called threatening aura "which they had reason (or thought they had) to hate and dread."[16] But as these same members of the community watch her burning house and want to "get a nigger" for her murder upon whom they may exact the white man's revenge, they nevertheless also become frustrated and outraged that Joanna's death has robbed them of a concrete focal point on which to project their vengeance and anger toward the North for its role in the Civil War and Reconstruction.

It is this mode of paradoxical behavior which Faulkner feels is the most fundamental element of the Yoknapatawpha tragedy. Too few people make an adequate effort to reflect upon their lives. More than recollections of time gone and knowledge ascertained and experienced pondered upon, the past is too frequently the intemperate resurgence of an old matrix of old emotions. Most members of the Yoknapatawpha community have no adequate understanding of their historical, psychological, or philosophical underpinnings. Perhaps for this reason there is an immense sense of aloneness and distance on the part of the narrators in stories like "Dry September," "Pantaloon in Black," and *Light In August* in which the community as a composite character plays a significant role.

The action of "Dry September," turns into an obscene and murderous ritual for venting frustrations against the natural conditions of sixty-two rainless days, and into a perverse action through which members of the community act to appease the gods of the social order and the rage within themselves. Much of this condition is symbolized by the image of dust, representing Yoknapatawpha as a near wasteland, an immoral zone. That the barber Hawkshaw attempts to make Will Mayes exempt from the aims of the lynchers does not, however, make the black community itself exempt. A nigger would still be wanted. Hawkshaw's plea does not even approach the heart of the problem. The taboo which restricts white women to white men only is a fantasy which belongs as much to the white man as to the white woman because of the white man's sexual fears and insecurities.

To examine the taboo involves examining the self, something which the white Yoknapatawphan is inclined to resist. In addition, there is the intuited fear that by examining the self one would begin to see that the abominable blackness characterized as "Negro" is a projection of his own being, his own identity. Identity, after all, is the sum of one's values, which, if viewed from the truest reflector, the self, might force one to see his own negativity.

On the one hand, these lynchers are individuals coming together as a group rather than as a community. They do fear public opinion to some degree as is intimated at one point by the apprehension of the soldier about having their intentions overheard. On the other hand, public opinion against the heinous practice of lynching most certainly has not crystallized in the community, for if it had, Hawkshaw would not feel compelled to act surreptitiously to save the victim when he could have appealed to officers of the law. Neither would Hawkshaw have had to suffer disgrace in the eyes of the victim who only perceived him as part of the mob. Moreover, Hawkshaw could see that the law itself might not have been any better than the opinion of the mob.

Even the portrayal of Minnie Cooper as a woman of slightly ill-repute does not really aid in illuminating the nature of the injustice of the sexual taboo. At most, this portrait suggests a fundamental bias toward spinsterhood and gives an additional dimension of stereotypic complexity to the story. Ironically, Minnie illuminates more about the nature of the community. When we first see Minnie, no man has had a sensuous thought about her in years. Yet after the lynching, when the idea of blackness, which they associate with some primal and potent form of sexuality, has kindled their emotions and imaginations, the same men look upon her with intimations of sexual desire. The black scapegoat was made into the source of perverse regeneration, that is, the black beast has made Minnie potent and the white men now wish to partake of her. The white community is again thought to be safe from fear and drought. But conversely, the core of the black community is stricken with fear and terror.

As in "Pantaloon in Black," one participant in this lynching takes his frustration home. Faulkner uses the home repeatedly as a point of reference because he views the structure of the community as psychologically interrelated rather than segmented, the fact of segregation notwithstanding. There is constant reverberation among all the parts including the home. In *Brother to Dragons*, Robert Penn Warren's long poem about the mutilation and murder of a black slave by Thomas Jefferson's nephews, the narrator says that "doom is always domestic."[17] Like Faulkner, Warren suggests that human distance makes for a kind of social fatalism out of which can come little that is fruitful.

This condition of life makes a poor showing for what Faulkner conceives of as *the trilogy of man's conscience*. As he constructs this schema: one man says, "This is dreadful, terrible, and I won't face it even at the cost of my life; the second says, "This is terrible but we can bear it"; the third says, "This is dreadful, I won't stand it, I'll do something about it."[18] Very few Yoknapatawphans ever reach the third, the ennobling stage.

Even though there are mutilators like Percy Grimm who, as individuals, feel cut off from the community, by taking on violent racist leadership roles they, too, become a fundamental part of the community. They reaffirm the value of a peculiar kind of racial violence in the Yoknapatawpha world. Flannery O'Connor says that in her fictional world "violence is strangely capable of returning . . . characters to reality and preparing them for their moment of grace."[19] Unfortunately, violence in the Yoknapatawpha world is not at all redemptive. In the manner of classical tragedy, the white Yoknapatawpha predisposition is founded upon pride, which may lead to still another tragic fall beyond that fall which came with the Civil War. To free themselves from their tragic limitations Yoknapatawphans have to come to the realization of Oedipus that they are their own curse. They may then be redeemed, in Christian terms, when they are capable of encompassing human brotherhood. "That the scapegoat pays for the sins of others is well known, but that is only legend, and a revealing one at that," James Baldwin writes. "In fact, however the scapegoat may be made to suffer, his suffering cannot purify the sinner; it merely incriminates him the more, and it seals his damnation. The scapegoat, eventually, is released, to death: his murderer continues to live."[20]

To be sought out as the lynch scapegoat is the ultimate form of abuse that black being must undergo and endure in the Yoknapatawpha world. Yet there is a complex of other rites and actions all of which are a part of the paternalistic structure in which the white man supposes that he has been appointed the superintendent of earthly life. In this role, he makes black being his pantaloon, the on-going butt of life's tragic jokes. Black existence is viewed as it is in the minstrel shows, its basic humanity and any pretension thereto are cast into the realm of the ridiculous or the absurd. Even more, in the deepest Yoknapatawpha sense, black being's assertion of its humanity is viewed with contempt. No integrity is assigned to its emotions since its emotions are taken as questionable and overindulgent. In consequence, for example, Rider's suffering cannot be real. As a matter of course, people who manage to exploit others sucessfully often do develop contempt for them.

Although the stories "Red Leaves" and "A Justice" take place in the old Choctaw and Chickasaw settlements on the fringes of the Yoknapatawpha world, upon close examination they reveal more about the Yoknapatawpha world proper and its relationship to black being than about Indian life per se.[21] Both of these stories, but especially "A Justice," border on parody and allegory and are profound and somewhat satiric analogues to the structure and development of Yoknapatawpha paternalism and its fundamental disregard for the African descendant's humanity. As exemplars of the tall tale, these stories are necessarily far-fetched, but the exaggeration only exists and functions in relation to a fictive norm. We are not to be deluded by the fact that Faulkner has used Choctaws and Chickasaws as the instruments of the action, and is simply appealing to the prejudices of the reading audience with their basic notions of the Native American as uncivilized in their customs.

The story "Red Leaves," for instance, takes place very early in Yoknapatawpha history. It is the tale of an African slave who tries to escape the eerie circumstance of having to be buried according to custom with his deceased Choctaw master. The plot of the story entails the trials of the slave as he runs off into the woods to escape death and the trials of the Choctaws who have to track him down and bring him back so that the sacred burial ceremony of the chief, Issetibbeha, can be accomplished. Although the central aspect of the plot has to do with what Faulkner represents as a sacred aspect of the rites for burying the dead, as the story develops its most appreciable dimensions begin to extend out of the realm of mere legend and into a rather off-hand and very unself-conscious parody on the historical situation of slavery and its aftermath. The Choctaws are conscious of having to become involved in a major historical phenomenon initiated by the white man. Since their general view of slave ownership is that it is troublesome, they perceive themselves as also having become entangled in the white man's enterprise of human exploitation; they have been robbed of some of their own vital cultural possessions, including their own peculiar sense of how time flows as well as their freedom from continuous and bothersome labor.

The system of slavery has affected the culture so profoundly that at times the entire hierarchy of ruling cousins in the clan have to gather in a conclave to ponder over what the narrator specifically calls "the Negro question." They discuss a number of options all of which seem to force them to "do as the white men do," to "raise Negroes and sell them to the white men for money."[22] While this procedure seems to them to be the most plausible initially, it does not prove totally satisfactory because it is still too troublesome. But as with the white man, it does not occur to the Choctaws to let the blacks go free.

It cannot be doubted that since Faulkner has been so explicit in his use of the phrase "the Negro question," he would expect us to overlook its very significant polemic reverberations. For what we have seen erecting itself here is nothing other than the structure of the black man's experience in America. The Guinea bodyservant, who flees into the wood to escape the fearful rites, is in touch not so much with Choctaw culture as he is with the basic and elemental principles of a bondman's existence. This particular bodyservant's plight is simply a shadow of a political scheme of a much more tremendous magnitude.

In the story, "A Justice," we find a much more illustrative example of the structure of the bondman's world. Written in an elliptical manner, the story is constructed so that the deeper implications might easily be overlooked. It is in the form of a parable which, like "Red Leaves," points to the complexities of a peculiar system of cuckoldry and the absence of true justice for the victims. While it is not without its humorous aspects, the story has a very elusive moral which the young boy Quentin, to whom the story is told, will have to unravel, or have revealed to him as he grows into manhood in his native Yoknapatawpha world. A more mature Quentin will be expected to move beyond the literalness of the story as a wilderness tale and on to an understanding of the special significance of these human relationships. This is not yet the Quentin of *The Sound and the Fury* for whom life has been soured by an intense internalizing of the experience of living in a culture he feels is so bankrupt in values that it can offer him no future. But it is the same alert and sensitive young boy, who, in "That Evening Sun," becomes privy to some special information which may serve later as a partial gloss for the initiation fable transmitted to him in "A Justice" by Sam Fathers. For surely he could never forget that most stringent articulation of black circumstance made by Jesus during Nancy's crisis in "That Evening Sun": "White man can come in my house, but I cant stop him. When white man want to come in my house, I aint got no house."[23]

Almost one hundred years old, Sam Fathers is responsible for keeping up the buildings on grandfather Compson's country estate. He is perceived and portrayed as being fundamental to the continued existence of the estate and, in his role as the blacksmith on the place, in accord with the old symbolism attached to his profession, he is the forger of great meanings as well as of things.

In telling the boy Quentin the story of how he got his name, Sam Fathers is preparing the foundation which will, in time, inform the boy about the complex social reality to which he is heir. Like Dilsey and Nancy, it seems somewhat ironic that Sam, the offspring and symbol of a crucial historical predicament, would be the man of composure who keeps things around him "whole and sound."[24] Born of a Choctaw father and an African mother, Sam Fathers lives among the blacks in the Compson quarters. We are told that although he has his own peculiar complexion distinct from that of the other blacks, and was raised in the Choctaw culture where he retained a sense of separateness, the blacks still look upon him as one of their own by virtue of his African mother. There is little doubt that the rest of the white society does so for the same reason. Yet he was not rejected by the Choctaws. Rather he was considered a young brave and was told that he could stay among them if he wished at the time his mother was sold.

But when Quentin contends that Sam Fathers is not a Negro, his major intention is to free the old man from the social stigma placed upon the African descendants by the Yoknapatawpha world. One discerns in Quentin the emotional need to have the old man stand above any racial limitations if he is to remain for him a symbol of creative power and retain his stature as his initiator into life's more adult mysteries. Quentin is enthralled by what he is told and by who is telling it, but both he and the old man show a great deal of emotional detachment from the main crisis in the story. Perhaps it is because of this detachment Sam Fathers is able to maintain while relating the story of his origins and how he got his name that the crucial historical import of the tale almost eludes us. Yet this story is especially representative of the insensitive manipulation of the plight of black humanity trapped in the predicament of American slavery and its aftermath.

Sam Fathers learned of his origins from the Choctaw, Herman Basket, who told how the power-hungry Choctaw, Doom, returned to the Choctaw plantation from New Orleans with a white wife and six black people to add to the group of bondmen already there. These six were won in a gambling game aboard the steamboat, and when Doom arrives home with them their fates are in question because the Choctaws to whom they are offered do not want them. Since the Choctaws feel that owning slaves complicates their existence and in surmising that Doom is using the bondmen to work his way to power, they do not simply reject the bondmen but move beyond that to hunt them sometimes with dogs for sport. This activity is of course reminiscent of what the whites put the runaway bondmen through when they chased after them with dogs.

In one act of resistance while living among the Choctaws, the blacks manage to run away and hide among some logs in the woods, but they are eventually tracked down by the dogs. The ownership of the blacks shifts from hand to hand. This trading and planning upon the lives of the enslaved is done without regard for, and quite in negation of, any personal or interpersonal affiliations among the bondmen. It is not surprising, then, that when one of the bondmen objects to the taking of his wife, and in so doing expresses a relationship with a bondwoman that runs deeper than a chance association of bondmen, that the story reaches an unexpected turn. The bondman asserts that the woman is his wife and that he wants to keep her with him. Reflected in this bondman's predicament is the beginning of that situation which Jesus sums up in "That Evening Sun" and which is brought out in the conflict between Zack Edmonds and Lucas Beauchamp in "The Fire and the Hearth." Of course, the claim to a wife by a bondman is seen by the captors as an act of defiance;

for in the ways of slavery, there are no social attachments as sacred as the one which orders the captive to yield to the captor.

Even when the chief lends his assistance to the bondman whose wife is being taken by Crawford-fish, one wonders whether the bondman has any actual recourse to gain compensation for his grievances or whether Chief Doom is simply contriving his own mechanism of defense upon Crawford-fish who believes that the chief has poisoned his way to power. When the bondman appeals to the chief five months later about the same problem, the reply is that the unprivileged man must adjust the matter for himself. At this point, one is inclined to believe that the bondman does have some leverage for his claims, but we soon learn that none of it really matters to Doom since he suggests that they settle the issue by a means not readily available to the bondman.

Even though the bondman manages to win the match to retain his wife, he is still left at the mercy of the free man who uses the license of his freedom to renege on the original agreement. Thus, the generally defenseless black man is told that he has to meet another challenge if he is to retain his wife. His crushing a clod of dirt and sifting it through his fingers and his repeated jumping upon Crawford-fish's dead cock used in the first gamble are symbolic gestures of his helplessness. When Crawford-fish's light-colored baby, who will grow up to be Sam Fathers, is born to the black man's wife, the bondman appeals to the chief a third time to see that justice is carried out. But the chief jokes indifferently about the bondman's adverse circumstances. He proclaims that the black man should be proud of a fine yellow man, sardonically adding that he did not see how the child could be darkened by justice.

The chief's final proposal becomes a ludicrous ordeal for the black man whose cabin is enclosed with a very high fence over which he has to leap with a pole. This supposedly gives him access while it acts as a deterrent to Crawford-fish. The deceptive form of the activity of this episode is reminiscent of the last major deception played upon Jim by Huck Finn and Tom Sawyer, in which Jim, not knowing he has received the freedom he has longed for, is held in temporary bondage for the selfish and whimsical fulfillment of the boys.

The child's name, Had-Two-Fathers, as given by Doom, symbolizes the mockery in the design upon the black man's existence, biologically and socially. In due course, with the birth of another son, this time a black one, the husband is supposed to be appeased. But, for all of that, the real structure of his social condition has not been changed. Indeed, the dubious paternity of the black American race is just beginninng.

This story has the effect of making us believe that we are really only experiencing another form of lynching, a psychological lynching in which the act of castration is not accompanied by bloody death but rather by a rather heartrending continuation of a struggle with and against life. The desires of the woman have been totally overlooked and the man has been cast into the role of history's buffoon. Like Eunice and her husband Thucydus, this couple, by fact of their defenselessness, is expected to suffer the outrage or make the best of it. Actually, these blacks seem to have little choice as we see in the case of Lucas Beauchamp some generations later making his way to the house of his white landlord, Zack Edmonds, to retrieve his wife and take her home. However, Lucas does return in anger to the landlord's house with the intention of challenging the white man to a duel. Others are treated very much like Nigger Jims, juggled back and forth by chance, fate, and the white man's whims. They have no recourse and no redress.

Similar implications are apparent in the ludicrous actions in Faulkner's story "Was." Here again the conjugal relationships between the blacks are dictated by the games of white men. "Was" is the story of Tomey's Turl who runs off from his master's plantation to a neighboring plantation whenever he can to court the bondwoman Tennie Beauchamp. The master's method for settling this problem is through a poker match, which is one of the things at which these members of the frontier aristocracy feel most adept. Thus, the matrimonial fate of Tennie and Turl are bound by their masters' wagers. As paternalists, these masters, of course, see their gesture as sympathetic.

So it is, too, with the seemingly benign rituals of the Christmas Gift and the Christmas Middle alluded to in several of Faulkner's works. Their functions as sympathetic gestures also point more to assist the attempts to control and manipulate black being than to express any real sympathy for it. In *Flags in the Dust* we hear the blacks along the side of the road calling to young Bayard Sartoris on Christmas Day for their Christmas gift, which the white man, if he is caught off guard, is supposed to be obliged to give in the form of a penny or so to the poor "darky," and which the white man perceives as a sign of his compassion.

In *The Reivers*, Ned William McCaslin, descendant of the McCaslin masters and their black slaves, talks about the annual grant called the Christmas Middle. Before the Civil War this "middle" was a special patch of cotton reserved in the field to be sold to provide a yuletide fund or reward for all the slaves. It was to be used for no other purpose, and this was the token for their year of toil. As Ned relates it, one of the McCaslin heirs had maintained the practice into the succeeding era of tenant farming and sharecropping. All of this is only representative of the heritage of paternalism carried by the whites toward the blacks in the Yoknapatawpha world.

This is the nature of the reality which the white boys like Quentin, Lucius Priest, and Chick Mallison will need to understand when they have passed through their initiations into adult life. They cannot remain innocent for long of the corrupt legacy in which they will certainly be asked to participate. Truly, unless these youths find the courage to usher in a new era of vision for the regeneration of their own spiritual well-being, they will bear witness perhaps to more occasions of the type in which we have seen Will Mayes juggled straight out of life into death by way of the rope and faggot.

Very significantly, there are pairs of blacks and whites, male and male or female and female, which appear on numerous occasions in Faulkner's depiction of Yoknapatawpha County. These associations, if sustained for a long period, however, are usually corrupted or distorted by the factor of human distance which the culture and the community dictate should be held between the races. These relationships, unless maintained from a distance, are not deemed viable in a region where white superiority and domination are the order of the age. Consequently, since these relationships often begin in childhood, sometimes infancy, if they are not completely broken off, they are necessarily compelled to pass through a rite of passage in order that all involved, especially the black, may know that there is no such thing as racial equality. They are to understand that what happened in childhood is to be attributed to a period of innocence to which they cannot return, and that those who may attempt to return do so at the risk of death. These relationships are not usually portrayed in depth, but through his interest in them, Faulkner momentarily highlights some significant aspects and principles of the racial complexity of Yoknapatawpha existence.

The most detailed account of a black and white pair is that of the black slave boy Marengo and his white playmate-companion, Bayard, in *The Unvanquished*. They make sand drawings of the Civil War battlefields together, run together, and even shoot at the Yankee troops together. Their relationship is portrayed as one of fundamental harmony, even in the midst of the turbulent Civil War. Both boys, one of the master class and one of the slave class, live harmoniously because supposedly neither has yet come into an awareness of his particular life situation and its dictates. The plantation romance convention has a great deal of influence over Faulkner's frame of mind in the writing of this novel, and in consequence, affects his depiction of the characters.

A major aim of the novel is to show that while some characters are attempting to discard impractical and outmoded traditions, others are either attempting to hold onto them or are plainly incapable of letting them go. The black characters, especially, are not as free as Faulkner and his narrator seem to think they are, or wish to think they are. Throughout the novel, for example, the narrator Bayard attempts to demonstrate that Marengo (Ringo) is actually the brighter of the pair. Yet, in numerous instances, Ringo's brightness is simultaneously diminished by the fact that he is cast as Bayard's shadow. Possibly the reason why Ringo is not given his full, postulated stature is that his childhood friend Bayard, now old and narrating the story, had imbibed the rites of passage which have carried him into white adulthood and now he, too, stands at the other side of the gulf of human distance which flows between the white and black world.

In *The Hamlet*, there is a clear example of a relationship based upon the principle of the racial double which exists between the white hostler Pat Stamper and his black associate. These two men function as if they are higher and lower extensions of the same organism much in the way that the Yoknapatawpha white world wishes to sustain its historical relationship with black being. Also in *The Hamlet* there is a related brief account of Hoake McCarron and his black bodyservant who have a similar relationship. Of Hoake McCarron we are told:

> He grew up with a Negro lad for his sole companion. They

> slept in the same room, the Negro on a pallet on the floor, until he was ten years old. The Negro was a year older. When they were six and seven, he conquered the Negro with his fists in a fair fight. Afterward, he would pay the Negro out of his pocket at a standard rate fixed between them, for the privilege of whipping the Negro, not severely, with a miniature riding crop.[25]

Moreover, Hoake McCarron's rivals sometimes take advantage of the black bodyservant as if he is the physical extension of McCarron, and the sadistic element associated with the racial linkage is all too obvious.

In *Absalom, Absalom!* there are interesting black-white relationships between the half-sisters and brothers Clytie and Judith Sutpen and Henry Sutpen and Charles Bon. But even though Clytie is the black daughter, by her own will she attempts to maintain a somewhat egalitarian co-existence with the white daughter Judith. The relationship between Henry and Bon is more one-sided than that of the sisters. In this instance the white brother falls more in the shadow of the black brother. Faulkner uses Molly Beauchamp and Miss Worshamp in "Go Down, Moses" and *Intruder in the Dust* to suggest that the women pairs maintain stronger bonds of sentiment. Miss Worshamp, known as Miss Habersham in *Intruder in the Dust*, and Molly have, at some point, undergone the rites of passage regarding their racial status, but seem to have managed to maintain some genuine level of affection for each other.

The most provacative and significant black-white relationship, however, takes place between Zack Edmond's son, Roth, and Lucas and Molly Beauchamp's first child, Henry, in "The Fire and the Hearth." It carries crucial implications for the human distance which Faulkner portrays in his Yoknapatawpha community. In his treatment of this relationship, Faulkner focuses on the rites of separation which reflect the tragic, irrational, and absurd chasm between two psychologically and physically related races. In this story of white and black cousins, lord and peon who nursed together in infancy from the same breasts, we have the archetypal experience of the black and white relationship as it emerges from early childhood.

According to Lillian Smith, not only do the peoples of the South have special relationships, but the word "relationship" itself has a special meaning. In its most literal sense, it signifies a bridge, a connection and interconnection. But the mythic mind of the South sees something quite different, "mongrelization, fusing, merging, melting . . . it is not restrained by barriers of time and space, or cause and effect, or facts that contradict, or logical categories."[26] Rigidity is the key to the South's sense of power and, more tragically, to its sense of its own place in the universe. Thus, black and white humanity should not relate too closely.

From Roth's and Henry's infancies, an intimate relationship develops. But in time, the young Roth begins to imbibe the biases and prejudices of his white elders, and the old deadly forces of pride and vanity intrude into his mind shattering the bond between him and his black foster-brother. Because of his innocence of the racial rites of passage, the young Henry does not comprehend that the white boy in his newly found arrogance is trying to reject him. Moreover, Henry does not see that Roth is trying to redefine and take control of Henry's being and his own. The most Henry can do in response to Roth's sudden change is to rationalize it, to explain the drastic change in their sleeping situations as dictated by Roth as a necessity of the hot weather. But Henry begins to know on a deeper level that his rationalizations and virgin efforts to maintain the old equilibrium do not stand up to Roth's caustic spurning. Racial heritage has interposed itself into the relationship and the world begins to be seen as much from the past as it is seen from the present. The tragedies of history begin to do their work upon the future.

Innocent of the subtler complications of black and white relationships in the Yoknapatawpha world, Henry is initiated at this crucial moment by his parents into that new world of division within which he must learn to live as he grows out of childhood. Thus, when Roth does become ashamed of having succumbed to vanity and begins to grieve because of it, he finds, to his amazement, that he has to prepare himself for a new Henry. The tragic gulf between himself and Henry has opened up, and Roth realizes and has to accept the fact that it is now too late to recover what is lost. That first quality of childhood will never be recaptured with his foster-brother. If it does become possible to cultivate a relationship with any integrity, Roth cannot presume so easily that it is his privilege to set the terms; for Roth is shocked into the recognition that the new Henry is prepared to leave him alone with his pride and vanity.

Henry is prepared to assert his own dignity with composure and with an apparent understanding of the racial presuppositions upon which Roth's vanity is founded. Now he can tell Roth,"I aint ashamed of nobody. . . . Not even me."[27] Henry has been made to see that the rites of passage that the white world has established are intended to develop in him a confused and deep sense of shame for being black. But the preparation given by Lucas and Molly shields their son from this terribly perplexing predicament. In fact, their interpretation of who he is and of what the prsesent circumstances of his life represent may even provide him with a sense of compassion for Roth's condition and, as a consequence, an even greater vantage point from which to view his world and the entire human predicament. It is that vision which will enable him to endure.

This crisis in the early lives of the sons is a reflection of the almost impregnable predicament of the fathers. Even more than their sons, Lucas Beauchamp and Zack Edmonds "had lived until they were grown almost as brothers lived. They had fished and hunted together, they had learned to swim in the same water, they had eaten at the same table in the white boy's kitchen and in the cabin of the negro's mother; they had slept under the same blanket before a fire in the woods."[28]

Since Lucas is the actual blood relative of his white landlord, Zack, his experience in early manhood is an excellent example of black American peonage, the structure of which is established in "A Justice" and further delineated by Jesus in "That Evening Sun." Because of his peculiar pride in being a direct, though illegitimate, descendant of the favored McCaslin male line in contrast to his landlord cousin, who is a descendant of the McCaslins on the female side, it does seem that at points Lucas' self-image is formed perhaps more by the fact that he is a McCaslin than that he is a black man in outrage because he has been cast into a condition of peonage. The tendency to see Lucas in this light is lessened, however, when we learn not only that he changed his Christian name to give himself a mark of distinction from the McCaslin patriarch, Lucius Quintus Carothers McCaslin, but when we learn as well of the intense nature of his personal struggle with Zack under racial peonage. As Cleanth Brooks points out, the account of this experience within the larger span of

Go Down, Moses and within the story "The Fire and the Hearth" itself "is one of the most moving that Faulkner ever wrote."[29]

Ironically, the situation in which Lucas finds himself is very much a result of a very humanitarian gesture made by Lucas and his wife Molly. But since the white man feels himself to be within a different zone of reality from his black peons, what Lucas and Molly perceive as compassion and human assistance, Zack views as the black man's necessity or obligation and the white man's prerogative. Furthermore, the fact that Lucas has to struggle through a flood to make the gesture to save Zack's wife and child is not simply a symbol of an ultimate sacrifice, but it also points out the terribly tragic and dramatic irony of what is actually sacrificed in relationships of this nature.

How long Zack would have expected to keep Molly in his house estranged from her husband is inestimable and Lucas realizes this as soon as he notices his altered domestic circumstances. Lucas knows that his own ideals stand little ground in this world with the white man's prerogative, and he meets the new change with justifiable and emotional incoherence. It is as if he has lost his grasp on reality or as if, perhaps, he had never really had it within his grasp: "it was as though on the luring and driving day he had crossed and recrossed a kind of Lethe, emerging, being permitted to escape, buying as the price of a life a world outwardly the same yet subtly and irrevocably altered."[30]

Bereft of his wife and child and therefore of his sense of dignity, Lucas is hurled into a kind of existential chasm. His reason for being is rather groundless. At this moment, he loses much of his particular claim as a black McCaslin and becomes a representative of the general black historical predicament. His new predicament is the ironic reward for his courageous but unsuccessful attempt to help save his landlord-cousin's wife in childbirth. Remembering the bondman who fought almost helplessly but continuously in "A Justice" to keep his wife, and hearing his words "And what am I to do?" reverberate and embrace our consciousness, we watch Lucas, disaffected, outraged, and confused. Now the fire on the hearth, which has burned since Lucas and Molly's wedding day, and which Lucas thought would be the living symbol of his family's warmth and unity, begins to magnify and illuminate his forlornness. In his anguish over his wife and child having been away from him for six months with no indication of when it will end, he is tempted to extinguish the symbolic fire which significantly was started by his cousin Roth as a wedding gift.

Instead of extinguishing the cherished symbol, however, Lucas resolves to struggle against Roth himself. As abruptly as his wife had been removed, Lucas stops his plowing one day while in the middle of a furrow and leaves the mule under a tree in the field. Walking staunchly up to the white man's house, he declares, "I wants my wife. I needs her at home. . . . I reckon you thought I wouldn't take her back, didn't you?"[31] He has made his stand but knows that in this world he cannot be sure of what price he might have to pay for having made it. But it seems that Lucas had made up his mind either to be or not be. If he braved the flood in which he nearly lost his life to save Zack's wife, he would do as much to save his marriage.

Although Zack is indignant and defensive about Lucas' insinuations that his wife may be held at the white man's house in adultery, he nevertheless feels that there is nothing inappropriate about keeping Molly and her child away from their husband and father to insure that his white child have the comforts and privileges the world is obliged to give. After all, in Zack's mind it is to his son that the world belongs. Lucas is somewhat startled that the white man is indignant, and, thus, finds that in addition to making his demands he also has to remind Zack of the privileges of power which he as a white man obviously takes for granted. He knows that the white man sees him as a "nigger." In fact, Lucas declares the white man's thoughts for him when he says, "I'm a nigger," then adds, "but I'm a man too."[32] And, since he knows that Zack sees him basically as a "nigger," Lucas dares to remind Zack of their blood kinship, almost mocking the white man's own existence by saying that "the same thing made my pappy that made your grandmaw."[33] It does not take much, however, for Lucas to see that his words have not really shaken the white man's assumptions of power and that the white man has no real intentions of reassessing those assumptions.

With Molly's return home, we see even more of the proud investment Lucas has in his manhood. It will take more than Molly's presence at home, however, to abate Lucas' outrage and humiliation for all he has undergone. He does not know whether what has happened can ever be erased and he deliberates on whether he should kill Zack or take his family and leave the Edmonds' place in order to preserve whatever dignity he has left. Upon consideration, he decides he really does not want to kill his landlord cousin, but he cannot be sure he might not be compelled to if he chooses to leave the place. He understands well that a peon does not have enough freedom to leave a white man's farm and crop when he gets ready. And neither is he sure he will not be compelled to kill Zack simply through the anger he may experience when he faces him to let him know he is leaving. Beyond that, Lucas is also apprehensive about killing Zack because to kill him when the man has sent his wife back might appear to the public very much a declaration that Zack had used Molly and had grown tired of her.

In addition, Lucas discovers that Molly has brought the white child back with her to continue breastfeeding with her own child. For Lucas this is like living with the symbol of his defeat and he makes his anger known to Molly, prompting her to decide to return the white child to its father. Molly's concern for the white child is supposed to be taken as typical of maternal affection and as the woman's way of intervening between the men to avert chaos. But even though Lucas is angry about the white child's presence he insists that his wife will not be the one to return the child, that Zack will have to come personally to ask for him. This is for Lucas the essential test of power and manhood. Naturally, though, Lucas cannot help but feel that he is being mocked all the more when the white man does not come. Now it is again Lucas who has to make the retaliatory move; thus, he goes into Zack's house in the night and stands over the sleeping man with an open razor.

But what we have unfolding before us is hardly a revenge tragedy. It is, instead, a melodramatic episode overwrought with passion and sentimentality. The reason for this could be that Faulkner simply did not intend that death be the end of all, not even of outrage, anger, anguish and humiliation which result from the chasm made by the distance between the races. If the outcome is determined by this reason, then Faulkner has to find a way to begin a rather formal reversal of the action and has to diminish the emotional pitch of the story without bringing too much into question the narrative effects he had already built around Lucas' very determined personality. Whether it is altogether convincing or not, it is the chivalric code of honor which becomes the vehicle for this reversal and for diminishing or diverting the emotional intensity. While Lucas is standing over the bed of the sleeping man, Zack awakens in fright and appeals to him to put the razor away in order that he may talk to him. Lucas does finally throw the razor out the window and the men decide that the most honorable way to settle the issue should be through a test of skill rather than outright murder. To settle the affair in this way would help to uphold the honor of their McCaslin heritage. Their struggle over the pistol leads, in the end, to a misfire while Lucas has the pistol in Zack's side but Lucas could possibly have shot Zack long before, as Zack believed he would.

The scene is handled with a lot of sentimentality. Yet it is ironically the sentiment which passes between the men during the critical moment of the misfire that increases the symbolic implications of what Faulkner evidently feels ought to be the better way of living in this world. For the imagery of the description of this final episode is nothing less that that of sexual passion, the pasion of creativity and life in the sight of death: "Lucas clasped the other with his left arm almost like an embrace and jammed the pistol against the white man's side and pulled the trigger and flung the white man from him all in one motion, hearing . . . the incredibly loud click of the misfire."[34]

Throughout all of this Molly must surely realize how sensitive the whole situation is and recognize as well what a difficult position she has been caught in herself. Still, she moves along submerging her anxiety. In trying not to provoke Lucas any more than he already is, she merely looks after the welfare of the two infants. Lucas returns to her and they resume what they can of the serenity of their earlier relationship. While Lucas believes that it was the strain of fortitude in the blood that he and Zack inherited from old Carothers McCaslin which graced both of them with the misfire, he is still determined that he will never fully bow to his white cousin landlord. Lucas realizes that neither fortune nor grace will totally eradicate that crucial point of disturbance in their racial association, and Lucas has articulated this as well as Jesus when, in confronting himself about his doubt of the use Zack might have made of Molly, he raises the powerfully proverbial and immensely burdensome proposition: " 'How to God,' he said, 'can a black man ask a white man to please not lay down with his black wife? And if he could ask it, how to God can the white man promise that he wont?' "[35]

Out of black existence in the Yoknapatawpha world we have Lucas Beauchamp communicating his frustration with the words: "I'm a nigger." And we have Nancy Mannigoe in "That Evening Sun" pronouncing both in frustration and horror: "I aint nothing but a nigger. . . . It aint none of my fault."[36] Her utterance expresses the nadir of social worth and dejection that surrounds black being. The pathetic truth about black existence as it has been manipulated and structured by the white Yoknapatawpha world is that it is a symbol of worthlessness and, therefore, vulnerable to anyone wishing to carry out worthless acts. By proclaiming that she "aint nothing but a nigger," Nancy means that her status in this world is so near emptiness that she is forced to live in constant anxiety, in a state of despair and dread. By creating this "nigger" image of black being in its treatment of Nancy, Lucas and others, the Yoknapatawpha world blinds itself to the fact that it is, by the same turn, casting a debased and wretched image of itself.

Writing of a world comparable to and regionally linked with Faulkner's, Flannery O'Connor illustrates this point of view very well in her story "The Artificial Nigger," a prime example of how in the imagination of whites, black being can be used to create a symbol and attitude of disparagement. "The Artificial Nigger" is the tale of an old man who, in hoping to give his young country-bred grandson a bad impression of city life, uses every means that he can, the most prominent of which is that the place is "full of niggers." This is a boy who, however, has never seen a "nigger" because before he was brought to the town as an infant, his grandfather and others had run the last remaining black person out of the area. When the boy does see his first black person while riding the train in route to Atlanta, he, to his grandfather's surprise and disappointment, identifies the black person as a man. O'Connor is, of course, consciously exploring the theme of prejudice by using the innocence of this young child, the ironic light of truth which the old grandfather has totally forgotten.

It is only a moment though before the comic irony of the situation takes on more tragic proportions. For the boy, having lost the game played with his grandfather because he did not even recognize his first "nigger," is compelled to find an object upon which he can project his mounting anxiety and self-hate. Black persons now become objects of his enmity because he associates them with his own humiliation. The boy in being initiated by his grandfather to the world outside of their little country town also acquires a tragic and burdensome emotion of race hatred and revenge. After their turbulent and distressing bout with each other in the city, it is, ironically, still black being, for which the grandfather has so much contempt, which becomes his and the boy Nelson's pawn for mercy and their agent of reconciliation. Just as in Faulkner's world, the personalities warped by racial prejudices are generally made like that by the people themselves.

Racial presumption does its job in numerous ways in Faulkner's Yoknapatawpha world, and, as in O'Connor's story, the result cannot help but be some terrible psychological and social confusion. It is probably largely this confusion that James Baldwin was responding to when he travelled into the South and reflected: "I was not struck by their wickedness, for the wickedness was but the spirit and the history of America. What struck me was the unbelievable dimension of their sorrow. I felt as though I had wandered into hell."[37] In much of his work Faulkner has sought to provide us with an index to the circumstances of human distance which create this hell. One cannot create hell for others without creating it for oneself as well we learn.

ENDNOTES

1. George Washington Cable, *The Grandissimes* (N.Y.: Sagamore Press, Inc., 1957), p. 156.
2. Flannery O'Connor, *Mystery and Manners*, ed. Robert and Sally Fitzgerald (N.Y.: Farrar, Strauss and Giroux, 1969), p. 31.
3. Walter White, *Rope and Faggot* (N.Y.: Alfred Knopf, 1929), p. 15.
4. Ibid., p. 17.
5. Ibid.
6. William Faulkner, *Faulkner in the University: Class Conferences at the University of Virginia 1957-58*, ed. Frederick L. Gwynn and Joseph L. Blotner (Charlottesville: University of Virginia Press, 1959), p. 36.
7. Ibid., p. 25.
8. Ibid., p. 21.
9. William Faulkner, "Pantaloon in Black," in *Go Down, Moses*, p. 142.
10. Faulkner in the University, p. 5.
11. William Faulkner, *Light in August* (N.Y.: Modern Library, 1967), p. 41.
12. Olga Vickery, *The Novels of William Faulkner* (Baton Rouge: Louisiana State University Press, 1964), p. 67.
13. Agnes Moreland, "A Study of Faulkner's Presentation of Some Problems that Relate to Negroes." Unpublished Ph.D. dissertation, Columbia University, 1960, pp. 50-51.

14. William Faulkner, "Dry September," in *Collected Stories* (N.Y.: Random House, 1950), p. 180.
15. *Light in August*, p. 64.
16. Ibid., p. 41.
17. Robert Penn Warren, *Brother to Dragons* (N.Y.: Random House, 1953), p. 10.
18. *Faulkner in the University*, p. 62.
19. Flannery O'Connor, *Mystery and Manners*, ed. Sally and Robert Fitzgerald (N.Y.: Farrar, Straus, and Giroux, 1961), p. 112.
20. James Baldwin, *No Name in the Street* (N.Y.: Dell Publishing, Inc., 1973), p. 54.
21. "Faulkner makes no pretensions to accuracy in his treatment of Indian life. He is careless with details, often confusing customs of the two Mississippi tribes and, in his early work, labeling his Indians indiscriminately as Chickasaws or Choctaws," Elmo Holwell in "William Faulkner and the Mississippi Indians," *Georgia Review*, 21 (Fall, 1962), p. 386; Lewis Dabney in *The Indians of Yoknapatawpha* (Baton Rouge: Louisiana State University Press, 1974) speaks of "the obscurity of Faulkner's historical basis"; A. A. Hill in "Three Examples of Unexpectedly Accurate Indian Lore," *Texas Studies in Literature and Language*, 6 (Spring 1964), p. 82, writes: "William Faulkner's use of Chickasaw history was not generally more accurate than was necessary for purposes of fiction. . . ."
22. William Faulkner, "Red Leaves," in *Collected Stories*, p. 319.
23. William Faulkner, "That Evening Sun," in *Collected Stories*, p. 292.
24. Elmo Howell in "Sam Fathers: A Note on Faulkner's 'A Justice,'" *Tennessee Studies in Literature*, 12 (1967), p. 149, has a contention about Sam Fathers' paternity different from my own. I find it plausible but not convincing, although it matters little regarding my general interpretation. Howell argues: "The paternity of Sam Fathers, who plays a central role in Faulkner's 'The Bear,' is clearly established: he is the son of Ikkemoutubbe, or Doom the Chickasaw chief, and a Negro slave woman. In 'A Justice,' however, Sam appears to be the son, not of Doom but of another Indian, Crawford. Nowhere does Faulkner use dramatic irony with more puzzling effect. In his Yoknapatawpha chronicles he is not always consistent in the handling of characters, sometimes changing the facts of birth or relationship from story to story, and readers have been led to take Sam's parentage in 'A Justice' as such a discrepancy. But Faulkner was very much aware of what he was doing in 'A Justice.' A cardinal point is that Sam is the son of Doom, the chief, and to read the story in any other way is to overlook the moral meaning that Faulkner was trying to establish."
25. William Faulkner, *The Hamlet* (N.Y.: Vintage Books, 1973), p. 135.
26. Lillian Smith, *Killers of the Dream* (N.Y.: Anchor Books, 1961), p. 219.
27. "The Fire and the Hearth " in *Go Down, Moses*, p. 114.
28. Ibid., p. 55.
29. Cleanth Brooks, *William Faulkner: The Yoknapatawpha Country* (New Haven: Yale University Press, 1963), p. 250.
30. "The Fire and the Hearth," p. 46.
31. Ibid.
32. Ibid.
33. Ibid.
34. Ibid., p. 57.
35. Ibid., p. 59.
36. "That Evening Sun," p. 293.
37. *No Name in the Street*, p. 55.

V.

Minds in Collusion: Miscegenation and Mulatto Crises

> *But eventhough people have these good feelings and desires, if they cannot handle their symbols, if they cannot keep the mythic mind out of the rational mind's business, there is inevitable trouble.*
>
> –*Lillian Smith*
>
> *KILLERS OF THE DREAM*[1]

The mulatto is a specific historical being born out of the mixing of the blood of the African and the European. The mulatto becomes the so-called "tragic mulatto" mainly as a result of human minds working in collusion with the creation of myths generally mandated by their own psychic needs. The tragedy of the mulatto arises, as Lillian Smith might state it, as a consequence of the inability of people to handle their symbols. As in the other dilemmas caused by issues of race, the tragedy is not simply that of the victim but also that of those who create the conditions and the circumstances for it.

In the Yoknapatawpha world the mulatto symbolizes the fear of black being touching white being, that is, a fear of defilement of a presumed European or white purity. This is the essence of the dread of miscegenation, and it takes on a gothic pitch in Yoknapatawpha culture. As one of Flannery O'Connor's characters says, miscegenation is "the ultimate horror."[2] It is very much a political fear arising out of the belief that whiteness, biological whiteness that is, is the principal axis of humanity, civilization, and culture. Therefore, the heirs must be purely white if the legacy, presumed to have been wrought more exclusively by the intelligence of the European, is to be entrusted to them.

With the subject of miscegenation, feelings predominate over reason. For the Yoknapatawphan these are dreaded feelings which overwhelm his being irresistibly. In the classical sense of the workings of the mythic mind, the Yoknapatawphan resists investigation of the object of his fear and resists logical association with it. This resistance has its own specific causes, primarily a fear of self and of the guilt and shame which may result from self-knowledge. The notion of blackness entering into the realm of whiteness suggests association with the tainted, the stained, the polluted. In the way of the human mind, displacement of the causes of the dilemma is easier than confrontation with the self and society. The mulatto's misfortunes and shortcomings, then, flow naturally from the stigma of black blood.

The story of the tragic mulatto is actually just another saga in the tragedy of the disesteemed. The theme surrounding most tragic mulattos in American literature has been that of the identity crisis. However, it is the denial of birthright as an extension of the denial of black humanity which is the true core of the problem. The often noticeable sympathy for the suffering mulatto character, more than for the suffering of the ordinary black character, because it is mere tokenism, is further substantiation of the existence of the myth in the white mind of black inferiority.

The issue of race in the Yoknapatawpha world has to do mostly with the notion of birthright. The tragic mulatto theme is only one aspect, but is also an accentuation of the issue. The mulatto may feel particular alienation, owing to his not being acknowledged by the white parent. Yet the entire population of black being also feels this alienation because its basic birthright of human participation in the brotherhood is not recognized.

The relationship between the races, especially pertaining to offspring, reveal some terrible and haunting truths. If, for example, the white man cannot love his black children because they are black, it is implied then, that he loves his white children, not because they are his offspring, but because they are white. Their relationship to him is determined by a superficial factor rather than by their essence. The revelations that arise in examining this subject of miscegenation as it affects the Yoknapatawpha world are painful at every turn.

The first mulatto heroine in American literature, Cora Munro of James Fenimore Cooper's *The Last of the Mohicans* (1826), is a prime illustration of the vast distinction there is between coming to a tragic end and in being conditioned to move toward a tragic end, as are most of the mulatto figures who succeed Cora Munro in American literary history. The tragic cases demonstrate repeatedly that the issue is one which revolves around the question of birthright. Even though Cora Munro dies tragically, her death is not tainted by racial circumstance, for unlike her literary successors, she is accorded her birthright by her father who loves, protects and acknowledges her.

In time, the depiction of the mulatto moves to the extreme of using death as the only possible solace for the mulatto. Death becomes the symbol of reprieve. In many instances only death provides "a logical escape from a world in which to be partly colored is considered an even worse disgrace than to be a full-blooded Negro."[3] Death might be avoided if at the last moment it is discovered that the hero or heroine is actually all white,[4] providing relief not for the suffering human being *per se*, but more precisely for the suffering of the white mistakenly trapped in this condition. The natural world of the literary mulatto becomes one in which he is unfulfilled as a human being and burdened with a sense of doom.[5]

Sterling Brown, perennial scholar on the subject of the black in American literature, has written that in the history of the mulatto figure in fiction, the authors themselves have created additional problems.[6] It is Brown's contention that black writers insist so much upon the mulatto's unhappiness in the white world, that these writers often have the mulatto run away from the white world back into the folds of a stereotyped, unfulfilling black fold life—its vibrant laughter, innocent ways, and music. The white writers insist upon the mulatto's unhappiness more from a biological standpoint. For them the problem arises out of the double inheritance of blood. The white authors portray intellect and discipline as supposedly coming from the white blood and emotional aspects with an inclination toward indolence and savagery as coming from the black.[7] The poor character is in a constant state of internal warfare over which, since it is supposedly biological, he has no real control. His condition is predetermined.

He is doomed.

This is the heart of the myth of miscegenation which Faulkner attempts to deracinate with regard to the circumstances of Joe Christmas' existence in *Light in August*. It is the heart of the same myth which he attempts to depict in various forms of realism in *Absalom, Absalom!*, "Delta Autumn," "Elly," "The Bear," and "The Fire and the Hearth."

When the physical appearance of a person who has some African blood is very much like that of the whites, the white Yoknapatawphans are often afraid of not being able to make concrete racial distinctions. Thus, they project their fear upon the person whose existence they believe generated it. As Melvin Seiden points out, it is not miscegenation itself that Faulkner is dealing with, "but the fear of miscegenation . . . its chimerical, hallucinating force."[8] Seiden states further that miscegenation is not only "a threat to Southern honor but also an obsession threatening the well-being and even the sanity of those who fear it."[9] Thomas Sutpen renounces his first wife and child in the West Indies because she, having a remnant of African blood, cannot serve his purpose in the white man's world. He cannot attain respectability if alien blood is suspected in his family. Because Sutpen's son, Henry, fears miscegenation more than incest, he kills his mulatto half brother, Charles Bon, who is engaged to his sister. He kills him also because he cannot tolerate Bon as the flesh and blood representation of his father's participation in the "sin" of miscegenation.[10]

In the Yoknapatawpha imagination, black blood and black flesh are an anathema. The Yoknapatawphan cannot express why; he is simply heir to a cultural myth. In "The Bear," Isaac McCaslin relates the myth of the children of Ham which maintains that a wrathful but just God, to whom the Yoknapatawphan in his delusion is convinced he is a true servant, has cursed these black descendants of Ham to be forever in servitude to the whites. The whites believe that their skin betokens Christian purity, thus superiority. Out of this Calvinist and Manichean amalgam, there arises in the Yoknapatawpha mind the frame of reference that black and white stand in polarity to one another in the same way as their supposed corollaries, sin and virtue.

The moment in which this is most dramatically illustrated in Faulkner's works is when Miss Rosa Coldfield convulsively reacts to Clytie's touch in *Absalom, Absalom!*, as the young mullata tries to bar Miss Rosa from climbing the stairs to the room where Judith is sitting with Charles Bon's murdered body. The significance of the moment lies not so much in the fact that Clytie has touched Miss Rosa's flesh, but that she has touched the spinster's insides. Also indignant that the black woman should overstep proprieties and address her by her first name, Miss Rosa experiences shock and a truly gothic shudder from mere contact of the coffee-colored woman's hand. She recalls the incident to Quentin Compson:

> I know only that my entire being seemed to run at blind full tilt into something monstrous and immobile, with a shocking impact too soon and too quick to be mere amazement and outrage at that black arresting and untimorous hand on my white woman's flesh.[11]

Miss Rosa's reaction to the touch of black flesh is similar to the reaction of the grandmother in Faulkner's story "Elly" when she is introduced to the suspected mulatto Paul de Montigny. Elly would have us believe that she cares nothing about the stories of Paul's "nigger blood," but it is actually his unusual features and the notion of his dubious identity which stimulate her romance with Paul. Elly's grandmother, who would protect Elly's purity, as well as that of her lineage, is the guardian of tradition, forbidding the breaking of racial taboos. When she is first introduced to Paul, with whose background she is familiar, she starts, "violently backward as a snake does to strike."[12] She cannot forgive Elly for bringing "a Negro into [her] son's house as a guest" and for "having [her] sit down to table with a Negro man."[13] Her unheeded injunction, an echo of Mrs. Compson's proclamation about Negroes sleeping in the bedrooms in "That Evening Sun," is that this man suspected of having black blood must not sleep under their roof.

Paul, the victim, is very much in the background. His existence, like that of Charles Bon, St. Velery Bon, Joe Christmas, and the idiot Jim Bond, is mostly a gothic abstraction tangled in the history of the white people's minds. Yet the abstraction is a profound determinant of Yoknapatawpha character and destiny. Thus, the world of the miscegenation myth is one of tragic fantasy. The psychological matrices are so complex that often romance stands at one end and tragedy at the other.

The story of the Bon lineage in *Absalom, Absalom!* which begins with the birth of Charles Bon in Haiti in 1829 and goes possibly beyond the year and the disappearance of his grandson, Jim Bond, in 1910 is illustrative. Charles Bon is the archetypal phantom, the intruder who provokes the macabre Yoknapatawpha imagination. His presence betrays the community's desires, preoccupations, and value system. It is through what Charles Bon represents in the country's imagination that the novel is able to achieve its truly gothic pitch.

The son of the young peasant born Virginian, Thomas Sutpen and a Haitian mulatta, Bon is a product of the past who emerges to confound Thomas Sutpen's ambition to place the capstone of honor and respectability upon his life efforts. With regard to the structure of the novel, Bon's resurgence into his father's life simultaneously interrupts and advances the movement of the saga. His appearance makes it vital that Sutpen's abandoned past be retrieved and accounted for; thus, the story has to move backward. By moving backward, advancements in the plot are made in the form of revelations which only the past can provide. The overall implication, for purposes of theme as well as plot, is that Charles Bon is an agent of fate, or, in a more specific sense, the agent acting in the design of his mother and her lawyer in retaliation for Sutpen's repudiation of her.

Charles Bon's whole being is bound by Yoknapatawpha myth. Miss Rosa Coldfield speaks of him with the intimacy of an acquaintance, but she never really saw him until after he had been murdered by his half brother, Henry. Neither did Mr. Compson who is totally infatuated with the myth, and who thinks that Bon "must have appeared almost phoenix-like, fullsprung from no childhood, born of no woman and impervious to time and vanished, leaving no bones nor dust anywhere. . . ."[14] Mr. Compson is fascinated by Bon as the exemplar of the pleasurable life. Bon and the myth and the delights of octoroon existence titillate Compson's imagination into extremes of fantasy and sensual speculation. Of especial interest are the idyllic forms Mr. Compson uses in speculating how Henry Sutpen first saw his half brother riding through a grove, crossing the campus in a French styled cloak, or even more to Mr. Compson's pleasure, Henry's formal introduction to Bon in the setting of the hedonist, reclining in delicate garments in a sunny, intimate chamber. Mr. Compson attributes to Bon such seductive powers that his passionate descriptions can be seen, rather obviously, as his own wishful thinking. Bon is the "cerebral Don Juan" whom Henry vicariously loved through his sister. Yet for all Mr. Compson's efforts to render his view of Bon into concrete form ,he cannot depict much more than a spectre hovering above the historical setting.

So potent is his fantasy that Mr. Compson is frustrated that he was not there to see Bon in person. The frustration leads him into making equivocal assessments about Bon, his esteemed creation. Mr. Compson never judges Sutpen for his bigamist acts, but he indicts Bon for his bigamist intentions. However, Bon is also portrayed as existing in a morally irreprehensible sphere with regard to the confusion emerging from his incursion into the Sutpen household. Even more paradoxical is the fact that Mr. Compson berates Bon for paying Judith the "dubious compliment of not even trying to ruin her."[15] In his attempt to create an image of Bon for his own satisfaction, Mr. Compson participates in the same denial and usurpation of Bon's being which he accuses Sutpen's wife Ellen of for having arranged the engagement between Bon and Judith. In addition to Mr. Compson's equivocation and paradox are his outright contradictions. If Henry was doomed to kill Bon, as Mr. Compson thinks, then also fate must have acted out a retribution upon Thomas Sutpen. On the other hand, when Mr. Compson indicts Bon's moral character, he disregards what he has already attributed to fate and insists that Bon must have been working premeditatively within a grand scheme for vengeance. Mr. Compson feels that if the hand of fate is not operating in the drama, there definitely must be some ulterior motive connected with Bon's emergence. He finds it especially unusual for this older, extremely good looking New Orleans gentleman with a cosmopolitan flair to have come to study at an unestablished, recently founded college in the backwoods of Mississippi where he meets his half brother who will take him to their father's house as a suitor for their sister. It is Henry, Bon's murderer, nevertheless, who is the one portrayed as the innocent victim.

Ironically, Bon is expected, as his name suggests, to be good for the Sutpens. Seized upon by Ellen Sutpen as a vehicle for helping their family attain social status, Bon becomes the new life spark for

Judith's heretofore stagnating existence. He would be fine clothing for daughter Judith in public. Bon is seen as a needed complement to the other furnishings of the estate. Since, in comparison to the clumsy social affectations of Henry and his father, gleaned from backwoods society and raw money, Bon's mannerisms are the exemplar of polish, he would be the perfect model for Henry's social grooming. Henry needs Bon as an image of identification beyond and in contradistinction to the harsh ruthless image provided by his father.

Bon is the ironic agent who does not act, but activates. Whereas Sutpen had been known to generate trouble, Bon brings trouble to his father, and thwarts the general course of his activity. On account of what Bon represents, we get a sense of the structure of the Yoknapatawpha psyche in its cultivation of a predisposition for what it considers moral and ethical scrupulousness and Protestant virtue. It has no qualms about the foundations of its peculiar culture having been established upon a barbarous and inhumane enterprise, which represents a flagrant travesty of true Christian virtues. Yet this is the psyche which revolts against the idea of legal marriage between the white and any other race.

The community's preoccupation with Bon's presence also brings the nature of the exploitation of both black and white women in the culture to the forefront. Both are victimized by white masculine designs and desires and are seen merely as objects. The black woman is reputed to be capable of animal sexuality, while the white woman, being used as an attendant vessel, is thought to exist ideally in a marginal void.

Henry's moment of decision to kill Bon to prevent the marriage to Judith, is the instant in which the ultimate sensibility of the culture and its truest values are exposed. It is the moment of horror in which the Southern ethos rises indomitably above Christian percept. Miscegenation is not seen at all as the mixing of the races, which the Southern fathers have carried out as a prerogative of their power over blacks, but becomes the abominable notion of introducing black blood into the white race. The double racial standard is apparent. Sex forced upon the black woman by the white man is tolerated and so is the offspring. But when occuring between a black man and a white woman it is all an abomination.

The comic irony of it all is that Bon, the man with some black blood, becomes eternally tied to the Sutpen family when Miss Rosa unwittingly enters the date of his death along with Ellen Sutpen's in the family Bible. In addition, Bon is buried next to Ellen Sutpen, who would certainly not endure her eternal rest if she knew she was spending it next to a corpse in which African blood once flowed. She could probably not endure it even though it had been her own doing to thrust Bon upon her daughter.

Bon is so entangled in the imaginations and passions of others that no one is even sure of just what Bon himself knew. No one is sure whether he knew that Sutpen was his father. The only opportunity one has for seeing Bon on his own is in a letter he wrote to Judith while he and Henry were serving in a Confederate regiment, which letter Judith gave to the grandmother of narrator Quentin Compson. One is not sure to what degree the letter reveals the total character of the man. It has a philosophic but bland prosaic opening, and is written without date, salutation, or signature. It is in no way an amorous letter. The tone is distinctly distanced and more nonchalant than contrived or pretentious. The language is generally circuitous, but amply direct when directness is intended. Bon does not speak of himself personally, nor does he speak to Judith in an involved way as one might expect in a letter from a fiancé to his betrothed when separated by war. He writes with more concern for fact than for any emotional connection. He has nothing fundamental to say about the two of them, and seems only to be performing a necessary and effortless gesture. The sense of his character comes over as easy, but as not giving, with no inclination of affection, not even through relish of style even though he uses a great deal of passionately fatalistic imagery in relating his thoughts about the war. One has the impression that he is an adept participant in the events of the war, but that he is not overwhelmed or weighted down by their implications. The ostensible absence of rhetorical flourish suggests that his intention is to debunk any notion of romance.

Charles Bon, like Cooper's Cora Munro, is the product of the marriage between a West Indian mulatta and a white father. The conditions of their lives, however, stand at great variance, mainly because one is accorded the birthright and the other is not. Racial fantasies have taken over in one world but not in the other. Owing to the reveries and daydreams of those who try to shape Bon's story, his life has been buried beneath others' notions and illusions, and the life quest of his son Charles Etienne de St. Velery Bon, who seems not to know where to search nor whom to look to for his birthright, becomes all the more inescapably tragic.

The crucial beginning of any so-called tragic mulatto is that he is a victim of someone else's imagination. St. Velery Bon's existence, like his father's, is bound up within the community's fantasies, as betrayed by Mr. Compson who harbors a tremendously romantic preoccupation with what he projects as the ceremony, splendor, and tragedy of the octoroon class. First presented in a bucolic scene in *Absalom, Absalom!*, St. Velery Bon is described as an ethereal being, and is imagined to have had an appearance which suggests that, like his father Charles Bon, he was born without human agents. He is a boy whose personal quality is more like light than human. That he looks three years younger than his actual age, when first seen, is supposed to render him an idyllic delicacy which, however, will prove more destructive than rewarding when the child becomes an orphan and has to accept the more shocking reality of life in its Yoknapatawpha form. The boy's emotional insecurity has already been made apparent in that he is portrayed as constantly clinging to the apron of his mother's duenna during their visit to his father's grave. Also, the fact that St. Velery is given a sexless face enhancing his delicacy only marks his potential vulnerability to tragedy. Although he is described as more like light than human, he is thought to be a child unused to sunlight who has grown up midst shadows and candles. Since St. Velery has had little contact with the earth, he is thought not to have breathed air but some soft radiance which emanated from his mother. Early looked upon as enigmatic and solitary he is destined for an alienated existence; for even during childhood he responds to those around him with "an aghast fatalistic terror."[16]

When he is orphaned at the age of twelve and sought out in New Orleans by the enigmatic Clytie, he is already descending from his comfortable ethereal existence. His stylish Fauntleroy clothes having gotten too small, Clytie dresses him in an oversized jumper coat, bundling his other belongings into a bandana handkerchief. Clytie's rustic mannerisms and the boy's new denim garments represent his transformation to peonage: he is now closer to the blacks who live under the imposed status as tillers of the earth.

St. Velery must adjust to the strangers, Clytie and Judith, who, on the one hand, sacrifice the pittance of food they have for him, but who, on the other hand, immerse him in water and scrub his body, not as if it were dirty, but as if there were something wrong with it, as if it were inherently stained. When he has the inclination to play with the neighboring black children he is drawn away by the coffee complexioned Clytie herself. Thus, he is cast between two categories of humanity out of which his basic life tension begins to emerge. Undoubtedly, he is being prepared for a peculiar rite of passage into what will be for him an ambiguous social domain.

St. Velery plunges into an appalling world of solitude and despair. Told that he is "negro," he soon also becomes acquainted with the meaning of "nigger," the condition of pariahship and degredation to which he is perfunctorily assigned. He comes to realize that he can accept but not control this condition, since it is enforced not simply by individuals, but by the collective community.

In time, St. Velery becomes as stoic and cynical as his surrogate mothers, accepting the denims and homemade garments and attic room without gratitude or comment. The child is left to examine the enigma of his skin color in the lonely company of a broken mirror which is later discovered hidden beneath his mattress.

That Mr. Compson is so witlessly concerned with why St. Velery needed to associate with the blacks in the community is a fundamental complicating factor in the particular victimization of blacks of this type. Mr. Compson is preoccupied with the need to justify what he perceives as the young mulatto's senseless mingling, although he must certainly be aware of the Yoknapatąwpha racial mores. His ability to ignore the sinister racial design affecting St. Velery's life is astounding; yet this inability functions to illustrate the deeprootedness of the contradictions existing within the Yoknapatawpha mind. Of course, Mr. Compson probably also suspects that it is the one-sixteenth of African blood that is acting as a biological determinant for St. Velery's social desires. This perverse imagination relishes its own obsessions, yet fears what it imagines, consequently creating potentialities for great racial tension and violence. It is this imagination which Faulkner most poignantly intends to indict. This type of mind victimizes the whole of humanity and defrauds the potential of the culture to take on the greater and more humane aspects of civilization.

St. Velery's first public encounter with trouble comes at age seventeen when he is handcuffed, bandaged, and taken to jail after a skirmish which some say he started at a black social event a short distance from Sutpen's Hundred. Since he is supposed to have started the fight for no apparent reason, Mr. Compson thinks that surely this combative nature that is coming out must originate from the abnormality of his racial mixture. St. Velery's sullenness and his refusal to deny the charges in court are taken as obvious signs that he is inherently disturbed. For, no man so white and unskilled with a knife, would attempt to use one on blacks, Mr. Compson thinks.

Mr. Compson and the community's imagination push St. Velery toward social dispossession and a pathetically stubborn attitude. The communal voice, as transmitted through Mr. Compson, is led ironically to say of its product: "Better that he were dead, better that he had never lived."[17] That he transgresses the racial hierarchy is disturbing to the social structure and the white imagination. Thus, the people in the courtroom bellow in dread: *"What are you? Who and where did you come from?"*[18] What they propose as an opportunity for him to leave the area is really an eviction.

The general course of the young man's travels out into the world appears to have been psychologically damaging since he is brought back to Sutpen's Hundred despondent and severely beaten. However, public opinion turns more against him. The community cannot tolerate the physical appearance of his dark skinned wife whom the community also perceives as mindless. As with Joe Christmas of *Light in August*, it is assumed that in the course of St. Velery's meanderings he probably sought out trouble. St. Velery is condemned by other men's desires and habits of belief rather than by rational thought. The more he denies being white, the more the blacks believe that he is a white man. The whites believe he lies out of plain fear or that he claims black identity as a vehicle for pursuing his sexual pleasures. The community imagines him as referring to his son, Jim Bond, as "inescapably negro."[19] This, ironically, is thought to be a means of freedom for the son from the peculiar predicament of his father, for it is deemed easier to be all black than mulatto.

Until he dies of yellow fever, St. Velery farms a part of Sutpen's Hundred and lives the life of a hermit with his wife and child. He is seen only three or four times in Jefferson and is at those times so beligerently drunk that he is held by authorities until retrieved by his wife. The society calls his despair invincible, but it cannot or will not recognize the role it has played in the undoing of this man.

Thrown into the world without any social anchoring or touchstones for their birthrights, St. Velery Bon and Joe Christmas, who appears in Yoknapatawpha a few generations later, are frustrated and restless. Their conditions are the natural outgrowth of communal myths which have worked in collusion to stifle their existence. Their lives are not much better off than that of Jim Bond the poor idiot son of St. Velery who spends many of his nights roaming and howling through the Yoknapatawpha countryside. For, in a sense, as we see them, St. Velery's and Christmas' existences are essentially howlings of their own agony. They agonize in their inability to give functional and generative meaning to their being.

Joe Christmas of *Light in August* is perhaps Faulkner's most compelling and problematic character. His existence is an example of the perplexities involved in the cultural life of modern Western man. He has been the subject of a large body of critical writings which range from the study of the tyranny of his childhood to the end product, Joe, the marginal man, the existential man, the pariah.[20] The notion of miscegenation is one of the critical complicating factors of his early existence. It triggers his first identity crisis when he is alienated by the children at the orphanage who call him "nigger." Soon his racial identity is surrounded by other complicating psychological problems which contribute to the total shaping of his character. The irony beyond the general tragic implications of the notion of miscegenation is that Joe almost certainly does not even have black blood. Yet he is crushed by rabid communal thought which decrees that by having black blood one cannot lay claim to any identification with humanity.

Because he can never unravel the significance of his "nigger" identity and his early childhood encounters with sex which become tied to the "nigger" identity, Joe is doomed. Unlike Gail Hightower in the novel who is also the victim of a complicated past, Joe is unable to take the journey back into his past to discern the reason for his outcome. Unlike Hightower, he has no understanding of the roots and beginnings of his frustrated destiny. Hightower finds a clue to the significance of his periodic need to take his grandfather's patched Civil War uniform from the old trunk. He errs at first by believing he does not have the choice to remove himself from the past, consequently holding himself in bondage to the past. But eventually he is able, at least, to realize the extent to which he has determined his own fate through choice. Joe, on the other hand, is never able to reach back to an understanding of the psychology that determined his being.

Joe Christmas' story is an allegory of the myth making process and of man's enslavement to the myths he creates. Like the community for which he becomes the scapegoat, Joe is an example of how human beings can become pathetically attached to memories of the past. Even when memories become destructive, humans are often reluctant to relinquish them owing to the tragic human dilemma that identity is bound up with memories: to relinquish memories is to relinquish identity, to relinquish identity is to plunge into a void. But Faulkner sees a need to experience this void if one is to find deliverance from the anguish of the past.

Joe and the community stand face to face in a violent glare like two mirrors opposing each other in competition to reflect the image of the virtual nothingness which keeps them apart. Joe is like the tortured child who has only one parent and that one cruel. He is afraid to relinquish that parent and to trust his own minimal sense of free will. Thus, he does not take advantage of his opportunity to marry Joanna Burden. In his own words: "If I give in now, I will deny all the thirty years that I have lived to make me what I chose to be."[21] He uses the same rationale for his recalcitrance as the Jefferson community. In holding on to old grief, they perpetuate grief. In so doing, both lose sight of the freedom they do possess.

But when one looks at the beginnings of Joe's life, it is difficult to hold him responsible for its tragic outcome. Alienated, with no real sense of identity, from early childhood, between the vulnerable ages of five and eight, he is accused of having imbibed some of the most characteristically weighty human burdens: pride, vanity, lechery, and despair. Confused and anguished by his surroundings, he feels at the age of eight that he has to establish himself as a man among his adoptive parents, the McEacherns, if he is to survive. Tragically for him, he begins to define manhood as obstinance and defiance. He sees life as something to be won and paid for in hard terms.

Womanhood is antithetical to manhood; thus, women become anathema to Joe Christmas. He sees all women, including Mrs.

McEachern who tries hard to become his mother, as conspiring to compromise his manly posture and attempting to rob him of the hard price he has paid to attain it. She is unconscious that she disturbs him, yet he is certain she foreshadows his doom. As a woman, Mrs. McEachern simply reflects on a primal level the frustrations Joe became plagued by when the nurse at the orphanage mistakenly thought he had invaded her sexual privacy. Since he is never able to understand this significant event at the orphanage, Joe interprets the nurse's secrecy as ominous and learns through this association to fear both secrecy and women. By the age of eight he is so frought with emotional complications he declares that he has no human ties. He dares anyone to approach him with softness and spurns Mrs. McEachern's attempts to compensate for her husband's callousness as ineffectual in the face of himself as a man. The boy knows punishment and injustice before he really knows people, but he cannot understand why. He does not even know whether he is supposed to understand why. All of this is the root of his utter sense of alienation and of his restlessness.

The traumas of childhood undergone by St. Velery and Christmas are characteristic of those portrayed in other works by writers exploring mulatto crises. Christmas' story, however, is probably the most paradoxical and complicated of all. Similar to Joe is the boy Maurai in Langston Hughes' story "African Morning." Maurai, the son of an English colonial and a deceased African woman, attempts suicide. Living under the auspices of his father, but more like a servant than a son, the youth does not comprehend the reasons for his being an outcast in the general community. Consequently, he lives in isolation and despair.

Joe is even more like Olivia Blanchard Cary, in Jessie Fauset's *Comedy, American Style* (1933), who suffers the pain of rejection, alienation, and restriction foisted upon her as a child because her complexion is a little brown. Her early frustrations thwart the development of her later social relationships and eventually fill her adult life with suffering. As a child she falls into chronic depression and does not come out of it until she is later mistaken to be Italian. Thus, unlike Joe, Olivia, feeling white and less alienated from the mainstream of society, feels that she has greater access to her birthright—that she is not so far as she had been from being a full person.

Joe's circumstances have led him to believe that he is connected with absolutely no one. He sees himself as an eagle, "hard, sufficient, potent, remorseless, strong."[22] This defensiveness shuts him off from true knowledge of himself. He thinks that hardness fortifies him; yet his mind and flesh are only in bondage. Thus his adolescent sexual experience with the black girl in the barn is unwittingly shaped by the nausea experienced when he was caught playing with the toothpaste in the closet among the orphanage nurse's undergarments. After the recurrence of nausea when he and the other boys are with the black girl, sex becomes even more complicated for Joe because sex becomes intertwined with race. Notions of sex and race are molded into greatly perverted forms which return to torment him throughout his adult life.

What is more lethal is that the young Joe begins to contemplate his vengeance upon the world through self-abuse. At times he hurls himself into the dangerous predicament of "nigger," playing with his wretched identity as if he were waving a banner. This is his masochistic way of attaining gratification and exacting retribution in his attempts to wage war against what he has come to experience as the "ruthless justice of men."[23]

It is no mystery then why someone in Joe's situation spends so much of his life wandering through a world of lost boundaries. His pain is like that of many of his fictional mulatto counterparts, the major difference being that Joe does not have as wide a realm of choice. He has been so terribly shortchanged of the minimal provisions necessary for clear mental space. Consequently, manhood at eight or twenty-eight is the "rigid abnegation of all compromise."[24]

Lillian Carmier in Ernest Gaines' *Catherine Carmier* (1964) is found in a similar situation. Having been taught to hate blackness from her childhood, she as a mulatta necessarily hates a part of herself. Not only can she not go home to her mulatto family, she has no true sense of home or parentage because neither her partents nor the relatives who raised her give her any social identity. Like Joe, Lillian is headed for a life of continual frustration and trauma. However, at least she and her family exercise a range of free choice that Joe never has. Joe yearns to know who he is whereas Lillian desires to deny her identity. She is consequently caught up in a perpetual confusion of reflexes: hating that she is black, but also hating those whites she desires to be like.

The dilemmas of mulatta heroines Mimi Daquin in Walter White's *Flight* (1926) and of Clare Kendry in Nella Larsen's *Passing* (1929) also revolve around issues concerning black humanity's alienation in American society. But with Clare Kendry we see that she is one who has always put her own needs above all else and, therefore, in leaving the black community where she does have a social base, it is not so much that she is leaving, but that she chooses to leave. Similarly, Mimi Daquin's flight from place to place seems to be motivated by a general pursuit of personal freedom, but unlike Joe and St. Velery, she is working with a greater degree of choice. She is not tormented by her social identity or alienation. She simply wishes to be free of social intolerance. As Irving How has so aptly said of Joe Christmas: "His was always the adult condition."[25] Joe could never even choose to be a child.

The narrative line in *Light In August* is certainly difficult to follow. However, Faulkner makes use of complex narration to shape and reveal Joe Christmas' character. In effect, the reader is being asked to perceive Joe as a metaphor for aspects of human existence that are not easily unravelled. As such, Joe is the exemplar of mankind and the crisis humans often undergo in attempting to understand and assimilate history. The nature of Joe's existence and fate signifies that the problem of human redemption in Yoknapatawpha is really a matter of the community's coming to a clear sense of needing to save itself from its own distortions.

Faulkner suggests through Lucas Beauchamp, the mixedblood descendant of the revered McCaslin line, that there is a panacea for the mulatto trauma. From the narrator of "The Fire and the Hearth" we hear that

> it was not that Lucas made capital of his white or even his McCaslin blood, but the contrary. It was as if he were not only impervious to that blood, he was indifferent to it. He didn't even need to strive with it. He didn't even have to bother to defy it. He resisted it simply by being the composite of the two races which made him, simply by possessing it. Instead of being at once the battleground and victim of the two strains, he was a vessel, durable, ancestryless, nonconducive, in which the toxin and its anti stalemated one another, seethless, un-

rumored in the outside air.[26]

But in his portrayal of Clytie Sutpen, Faulkner suggests that Clytie is one who endures the stigma of mixedblood status with unrelenting will. She is first mentioned in *Absalom, Absalom!* as the "negro girl" accompanying Judith stealing out to witness her father's brutal wrestling match with his slaves. That Clytie's identity as Judith's half sister is not mentioned early on adds to the dramatic intensity when this relationship is later revealed. When she is first referred to by name the narrator attempts to characterize her in terms of her origin. She was begotten by the callous Sutpen on his "wild nigger," whom Miss Rosa Coldfield and Mr. Compson speak of with vehemence that implies a biological separation from humanity. The various storytellers in the novel are compulsive in their efforts to account for Clytie's disposition. On the basis of her name, strong disposition, and inclination to anticipate events of doom, Mr. Compson assumes that Sutpen, in ignorance, misnamed Clytie Clytemnestra when he really intended to call her Cassandra. But Clytie is more willful, like Aeschylus' Clytemnestra, than she is prophetic like the more timorous seer Cassandra. Mr. Compson is amiss in his reading of the classics as well as in his perceptions of Clytie.

Clytie's character dominates most situations. Her presence affects more than it is affected. Even during the war there is the sense that the wasted, desolate farmland is favorably affected by her disposition. Her character dominates even in those tasks which were automatically expected of her as a slave: chopping wood, keeping a kitchen garden, harnessing the mule, plowing. Therefore, we are incredulous upon hearing of Mr. Compson's speculation that Judith could not have thought seriously of committing suicide to join her dead lover because nobody would have been left to take care of Clytie. Although Clytie is a slave, she is still very independent of mind. Mr. Compson's speculation about her dependency reveals more about his own character than about Clytie's. Also, he is characterizing her according to the slavocracy's general notion that a bondwoman or man is dependent by nature.

Miss Rosa Coldfield is so astonished by Clytie's disposition that she speculates that Clytie is of another species. Both women have uncompromising personalities and are obliged only by harsh conditions to adjust to each other. One thinks of Clytie the individual rather than Clytie the slave when she learns to plow and cut wood as well or better than the man tenant farmer, Wash Jones. Even Miss Rosa, who never forgets that Clytie was slave property, finds it necessary to explain that, with the hardships the three women endured during the war, tasks were not done on the basis of age or color but according to a standard of greatest good and least expense. Miss Rosa simply cannot ignore Clytie's individuality. Furthermore, Miss Rosa is particularly careful to indicate that Clytie defies all the prejudices which the culture attributes to black being. Clytie's presence is so powerful that Miss Rosa stresses at the beginning of both her major descriptions of Clytie that the bondwoman is not witless. Yet Miss Rosa still does not see blacks as human beings. She cannot conceive of blacks as possessing a mentality from which there would emanate the will to participate in the ordering of their own lives.

That Clytie never considered herself a slave demonstrates a sense of freedom that derives from her innate disposition, not from the fact that she lived under the roof of her owner-father. The young mulatta knows for sure who she is in the eyes of her father, that strange man who, upon his return from the war, rides up to the women in the field, leans from his horse and touches only his beard to Judith's forehead as a kiss and addresses her, "Well daughter," then turns to his slave daughter with only the acknowledgement that he knows her, saying, "Ah, Clytie." Upon returning to the war, Sutpen speaks to Clytie in the language of the master to his slave, "Well, Clytie," he says, "take care of Miss Judith."[27]

In Miss Rosa's limited and unsympathetic historical perspective, Clytie represents a disquieting relic from the racial, historical past in contrast to herself and Judith who are, in her estimate, victimized Yoknapatawpha citizens. Judith supposedly has ultimate control over her half sister, not because she has more force of character, but because she possesses the power of her social status as a white woman, granted and protected by Yoknapatawpha culture. Symbolizing a less privileged status, Clytie is the only character without a last name. Indomitable though she is, she is denied the legitimate label of her lineage.

Clytie is as integral to the atmosphere of the Sutpen household and legend as Dilsey is to the world of *The Sound and the Fury*. Her chroniclers speculate that she felt the tie to the Sutpen blood more strongly than she felt the master-slave relationship. We are meant to understand that she was acting as protectress of blood rights when, and if, she destroyed Bon's letters to Judith. Indeed she proclaims this blood bond even to Miss Rosa's face. She feels that she has participated with Judith and Henry in absolving the family of its sins. "Whatever he done," she cries out to Miss Rosa as the old spinster pushes her to the floor to enter the house, "me and Judith and him have paid it out."[28]

Clytie's refusal to let Wash Jones pass through the kitchen door while Sutpen is away serves structurally in the novel as a recapitulation of the initial impetus which set Sutpen on his ambitious road to "success" when the black servant denied him the right to enter the front door on the Pettibone Virginia plantation. Clytie is a vital participant who attends most of the novel's significant actions that occur during her life time. She not only assists in the physical management of the estate when Sutpen is away, but is also emotionally involved with Judith in maintaining Sutpen's room and waiting for his return. It is Clytie who probably hears with Judith the fratricidal gunshot at the gate when Henry kills their half brother, and she helps to carry Bon's coffin down the stairs to the grave. She witnesses Sutpen's crude and imperious betrothal to Miss Rosa, makes the trip to New Orleans to find Bon's orphaned child, attends to Judith's burial, and makes the final and ultimately adamant gesture of the Sutpen line when she sets the house afire to protect family rights, thus destroying herself, Henry and all of the past within reach of the flames.

Referring to the issue of miscegenation, Faulkner explicitly acknowledges that "the American is too fired always by the emotional situation."[29] It is definitely for emotional reason that in "Delta Autumn" the septuagenarian Uncle Ike McCaslin, the last of the Yoknapatawpha patriarchs, nearly goes into shock when he realizes that a mulatta kinswoman desires to marry his nephew Roth Edmonds, for whom she has borne a son. The old man has already been overwhelmed by the encroachment of civilization upon the outer wilderness of the Yoknapatawpha world which he equates with his youth, nobility, and innocence. A sudden racial intrusion into his inner family world would be intolerable. He does finally control his emotions enough to acknowledge and offer a gift to the child who is his descendant by two blood lines, that of the McCaslin masters and that of the McCaslin slaves. Yet the notion of a white person becoming intimate with black being through the sacred Christian ceremony is too much for Isaac to endure. His racial sensibility is like that of Miss Rosa who shirks at Clytie's touch. Caught in the grips of an ultimate horror, the old man's admonition is: *"Maybe in a thousand or two thousand years in America. . . . But not now! Not now!"*[30] It is precisely this terror in the white Yoknapatawpha mind which is responsible for generations of mulattoes caught in crises.

ENDNOTES

1. Lillian Smith, *Killers of the Dream* (N.Y.: Doubleday, Anchor Books Edition, 1963), p. 218.
2. Flannery O'Connor, "Everything That Rises Must Converge" in *The Complete Stories* (N.Y.: Farrar, Straus and Giroux, 1971), p. 414.
3. Quoted in Daniel J. Leab, *From Sambo to Superspade: The Black Experience in Motion Pictures* (Boston: Houghton Mifflin Co., 1976), p. 17.
4. Ibid., pp. 10-11.
5. Donald Bogle, *Toms, Coons Mulattoes, Mammies, and Bucks: An Interpretive History of Blacks in Films* (N.Y.: The Viking Press, 1973), p. 150.
6. Sterling Brown, *The Negro in American Fiction* (Port Washington: Kennikat Press, Inc., 1968; originally published in 1937 by Associates in Negro Folk Education), pp. 144-145.
7. Ibid.
8. Melvin Seiden,"Faulkner's Ambiguous Negro." *Massachusetts Review*, vol. 4 (Summer, 1963), pp. 675, 678.
9. Ibid.
10. M. E. Bradford, "Brother, Son and Heir: The Structural Focus of Faulkner's *Absalom, Absalom!*," *Sewanee Review*, vol. 78 (Winter, 1970), p. 77.
11. William Faulkner, *Absalom, Absalom!* (N.Y.: Vintage Books, 1972), p. 139. Originally published by Random House in 1936.
12. William Faulkner, 'Elly" in *The Collected Stories* (N.Y.: Random House, 1950), p. 211.
13. Ibid., p. 217.
14. *Absalom, Absalom!*, p. 74.
15. Ibid. pp. 98-99.
16. Ibid., p. 195.
17. Ibid., p. 205.
18. Ibid., p. 203.
19. Ibid., p. 208.
20. T. H. Adamowsky, "Joe Christmas: The Tyranny of Childhood: *Novel*, vol. 4 (Spring, 1971), pp. 240-251; Robert Slabey, "Joe Christmas: Faulkner's Marginal Man," *Phylon*, vol. 21 (Fall, 1960), pp. 266-277; William J. Sowder, "Christmas as Existential Hero," *University of Kansas City Review*, vol. 30 (June, 1964), pp. 279-284; Cleanth Brooks "The Community and the Pariah," *Virginia Quarterly Review*, vol. 39 (Spring, 1963), pp. 236-253.

21. William Faulkner, *Light in August* (N.Y.: Modern Library, 1967), p. 232.
22. Ibid., p. 140.
23. Ibid., p. 147.
24. Ibid., p. 130.
25. Irving Howe, "William Faulkner and the Negroes" *Commentary*, vol. 12 (October, 1951), p. 360.
26. William Faulkner "The Fire and the Hearth" in *Go Down, Moses* (N.Y.: Modern Library, 1955), p. 104.
27. *Absalom, Absalom!*, p. 276.
28. Ibid., p. 370.
29 William Faulkner, *Faulkner in the University: Class Conferences at the University of Virginia 1957-58*, ed. Frederick L. Gwynn and Joseph L. Blotner. (Charlottesville: University of Virginia Press, 1959), p. 157.
30 William Faulkner, "Delta Autumn" in *Go Down, Moses* (N.Y.: Modern Library, 1955), p. 361.

VI.

Dilsey Gibson: Her Touch With Time

Perhaps it is fundamental to human nature to load everything on the back of anyone prepared, whether from real humility or from weakness or indifference, to endure it.
–Balzac, PERE GORIOT[1]

Like many modernists, Faulkner viewed twentieth century Western man as often being trapped on a course of destruction by his obsession with time. Too often men like Jason Compson wanted to make time mechanical and thereby manipulate it. Likewise there were those like Quentin Compson who could not bear the forward progression of time and wanted time to stand still. There were others who were simply obsessed with living in a time long past. And there were others like Joe Christmas who were simply unable to unravel the meaning of time in their lives. Standing in contradistinction to all of these is Dilsey Gibson of *The Sound and the Fury* who, because she is relatively more free of ego and highly personal preoccupations, is also free of the tyrannizing aspects of time in time past, present, or future. She may be a victim of the historical past and present; however, she is not tyrannized by them. Her life is grounded in a sense of deep regard for humanity, rather than self, thus enabling her to move out of the past and to live beyond the present. For this reason Faulkner celebrated her above all his characters as a special embodiment of humanity. Dilsey possesses what Faulkner considered would untimately be the most beneficial sense of time.

Because Dilsey is in touch with Faulkner's esteemed verities of love, honor, pity, compassion and courage, Faulkner never intends for us to take her for granted. But in order to appreciate and apprehend the essence of Dilsey in contrast to most other major characters in *The Sound and the Fury*, one has to be able to envision great moral possibilities for humanity. One also has to be able to believe that even in the modern world, individuals are capable of acting in accordance with high moral vision.

Dilsey responds to the Compson misfortune but not to the Compson sense of time. From her point of view, the Compson family is in a season of misfortune and disjunction. A household is falling but it is not the end of things. The whole of life is in no way to be reduced to the Compsons, for they are, in the end, no more than their vain indulgences. From Dilsey's worldview, time has its own principal flow, measured out in its own durations. We see Dilsey actively and creatively trying to live out the moments of her own appointment in that duration. While individuals can try to rush time, as Quentin and Jason do, they are vain and foolish to think that they have any impact upon time itself.

Individuals relate to time out of a sense of their desires, needs, and potential. Seeing life through Dilsey's worldview, however, one may not realize harmonious existence within the sphere of principal time unless he acknowledges its virtual incomprehensibility. Perhaps time is not tyrannical for Dilsey because she rises above self-gratification, thereby granting more space for human revitalization. Though mankind may falter, for Dilsey it is not necessary that a man should lose himself completely to the whims of the temporal and the immediate. Man needlessly punctuates his brief moments in time's durations with presumptions and arrogance. For Dilsey, past (memory), present (the moment of and for deeds), and future (faith) form an eternal drama whose progress, while not of absolutely vertical ascent, still does lead toward human growth.

Dilsey is reluctant to have life defined by the negative activity thriving around her. Miss Caroline is a trial and Jason is an ordeal, but Dilsey refuses to let their particularly provoking characteristics usurp the crucial role of goodwill in her life. She knows that it is through human minds that existence is perceived, and that while human perception acts upon creation, it is certainly not all of creation. Dilsey's Christian vision is not simply about human perception, it is about seeing beyond human limitations. Her vision is revelation, which is something more cosmic and encompassing than what ordinarily moves before the eyes. Human sympathy is one's expression of the connection one has with the more encompassing eyes of the cosmos.

As Sally Page has stated, when Candace Compson is destroyed, the burden of motherhood in the Compson household falls upon Dilsey.[2] The actual mother, Miss Caroline, around whom so much of the Compson lifestyle revolves, has placed herself in the parasitic position of grafting onto other people's time. All members of the family, black and white, are forced to relate to Miss Caroline in some way. Faulkner has made Miss Caroline the antithesis of Dilsey. In characterizing Dilsey, Faulkner dramatizes Miss Caroline's self-pity as self-indictment. While Dilsey sympathizes with the ever deepening household misfortune, Miss Caroline demands more from it. Nevertheless, Dilsey manages to take advantage of her limited space and hold her own. Surprisingly, too, she manages to retain a sense of humor.

As Miss Caroline becomes more homebound, Dilsey is taken for granted as the natural and logical extension of the world outside Miss Caroline's upstairs chamber. Unlike Dilsey, Miss Caroline is so intent on bringing others under the dominion of her personal whims that even her most sympathetic biddings come to be discredited by those around her. As a result, Dilsey, who is the opposite, grows in stature in the household.

Through much tedious experience, Dilsey has learned that she has to handle Miss Caroline's whims decisively. Her tone toward Miss Caroline suggests that she is constantly struggling to maintain a distinction between what it means to be in service rather than in servitude to someone. Miss Caroline projects her convalescence so incessantly that Dilsey cannot have a diplomatically mature, adult relationship with her. Miss Caroline simply has to be handled and told what to do if Dilsey is to get any work done, or even simply *be*. The pressured tone in Dilsey's voice is generated also by the fact that her socio-historical space is the pivotal point of two worlds. She is hemmed in by the frustrations of two extremes, the world of her family cabin and the world of the whites in the big house.

Arch-antagonist that she is, Miss Caroline even dares to be petulant about Dilsey's own deserved signs of physical weakening and pain. With all of her readiness, however, Dilsey cannot really check the aptness of Miss Caroline for creating incessant annoyances that require of the maid a boundless disposition for humility and an enormously diplomatic will. Miss Caroline is highly accomplished at feigning discomfort, which she seems to believe is representative of the true Southern lady. She is also accomplished at throwing the strain upon the "back of anyone prepared, whether from real humility or from weakness or indifference, to endure it," as Balzac once wrote. Only someone bathed in Christian succor as Dilsey is, for instance, could endure the classic and magnificently orchestrated scene of humiliation in which Miss Caroline, having already caused the ailing figure to climb the steps that morning to make her hot water bottle, calls her again from the breakfast being prepared for her own comfort only to exercise her unchallenged dominion. The arbitrary summons is also an interruption of Dilsey's mournful singing, the manner by which she establishes and maintains communion with eternity amidst the hellish world in which she lives. As she toils heavily to mount the stairs, she is very much like the man Simon of Cyrene who was called from the roadside to carry the burdensome cross of Christ's crucifixion.

Later, when Faulkner portrays the weary Dilsey moving out into the desolate landscape in search of her tardy grandson Luster, we experience an instance of Faulkner's description at its most naturalistic, reminiscent of the sharp and barren scenes of Jack London's *The Call of the Wild* and Edith Wharton's *Ethan Frome*. We seem to be also in the world of T. S. Eliot's "Preludes," which closes with the image of "ancient women / Gathering fuel in the vacant lots."[3]

Dilsey's domain, the kitchen, is used by Miss Caroline as the place to banish retarded Benjy. Yet because of Dilsey's humane warmth, the kitchen which is naturally associated with warmth and nurturing remains so despite the belittling tendencies of the hypochondriac mother who is the very opposite of the worthy lady she supposes herself to be. Dilsey's kitchen is the back cell of the house proper, and because Miss Caroline perceives the service of the blacks as obligatory, both Dilsey and the kitchen exist to cater to her desires. Miss Caroline assumes the title of mother, but the duties of the office are actually relegated to Dilsey. "I'm going to tell Dilsey,"[4] the Compson children often say.

Like their mother, Quentin and Jason generally look upon black being through the lenses of condescension and contempt. They have a distorted, romantic, and paternalistic notion that slavery and its legacy have freed black being from the responsibilities of white men. Their concern is that they, as white Southern gentry, are the victims of Southern history. They believe in the "white man's burden."

Quentin perceives blacks as naive and paradoxical. Their behavior is conditioned by the white people they live among, not by qualities arising from their own sense of being. Thus, they are merely shadows of the true, white being. Dilsey would say, however, that Quentin wanders in the realm of his father's self-defeating assessment of life. He is bemused by his own sentiments and he never gets a perspective on the world outside of his own self-absorption. Thus, regarding himself as a victim of history, he has no will to act.

For Quentin only the world of self exists, but not so with Dilsey. For Dilsey, man has a living context which, if put into perspective of the totality of his experience in time, leads, if not to victory over the odds, at least to regenerative existence. Quentin's over-concern with time is the matrix of his anxiety. He relates to time subjectively, wishing to control it, to harness it according to his own desired ends. Not long before his suicide, he comments to a little Italian girl and thinks to himself when water is splashed on them by boys playing in the Charles River, "Hear them in swimming, sister? I wouldn't mind doing that myself. . . ." "If I had time. When I have time."[5] Quentin's use of the verb "to have" implies that he would, if possible, actually possess time. Dilsey on the other hand would speak rather of possessing opportunity in relation to time. She believes that one creates time, but does not control it. To the extent that time is perceived as an emanation of the dynamics of human consciousness, it is also a limitation. As a manifestation of God's mutability and duration time is something which one lives through by expedience or sensible compromise, or through great humility if he lacks the knowledge for making his way to compromise. To converse with, not about, the unknown or God, is to open the way to its reality. Dilsey communes with the unknown, God, and time through her work and her singing. In some moments it would even appear that she is actually speaking with God.

Dilsey and her family are not oblivious to the perception of black being held by the two Compson sons. While Quentin may be indirect in communicating his feelings, Jason is not. He thinks of the black person's labor as the white man's privilege, at least in an ideal state of peonage. But he does not have the resources to continue to exploit blacks; thus he perceives that they are exploiting him. Since blacks are not working to effect his plan, he would use his self-centered brain to try to reason black being out of existence. Historical time has no existence for Jason except when it serves his purpose. Thus he attempts to transform historical time into slick phrases used to flaunt his own ego and compensate for his family's notable decline.

Jason looks upon Dilsey, not unexpectedly, as "an old half dead nigger."[6] To Dilsey on the other hand, Jason is astonishing because of the ruthless limits to which he will proceed. It is out of this sense that Dilsey says, "You's a cold man, Jason, if man you is."[7] The general manner by which Jason imposes limits upon the creative possibilities of human existence is constantly exemplified in the hard-fisted, shallow, cold positivism of his language. Uncompromising and inordinately cruel, with a wit that communicates pale, bloodless humor, Jason sallies forth in life, girding about himself his particular, narrow identity.

The aging Dilsey knows that time will not bring about Jason's end as much as Jason will bring about his own end in time. Since Jason does not have the integrity to face circumstances with full acknowledgement of Dilsey's person, her racial humanity and her individual being, she knows that she will not be able to seek a sincere approach to living in the future with him. Dilsey can overcome what Jason feels about feeding "niggers"; however, Jason will not allow himself to see that what he considers "nigger" is really a projection of his own being as a white man. For Dilsey, God created mankind, but history has been mankind's creation. Dilsey knows that to ask God to answer to history would be asking God to bow before the likes of Jason, who neither has the humility to accept eternity, nor to participate in its fulfillment. In Dilsey's way of seeing, a life may be individual, it may even be unique, but it is not so individual oriented or as single as Jason would have it. Jason gives orders but Dilsey is the manifestation of Order.

Above all else, Dilsey is the comforter of helpless Benjy. She always appears to Benjy as a figure of influence and authority. Only she and his sister Caddy have shown him real affection. In contrast, Benjy's first impression of his mother reveals her as more prone to chastise than to comfort. It is Dilsey and Benjy who have established the strong emotional pact in the household. When Dilsey cries or raises a mournful song, Benjy mourns too. In anticipation of her husband Roskus' death, for example, Dilsey senses that through their timeless emotional bond, Benjy is capable of giving her as much or more solace than anyone else on the Compson place. As Olga Vickery has pointed out, after Caddy has left, Dilsey is the only one who truly remembers that Benjy is a human being.[8] Especially through Dilsey's realtionship with Benjy we see that the caring spirit is the only indomitable spirit. It is out of love that creation comes, which contrasts with the destruction that ultimately prevails when things are left in Jason's hands.

Dilsey has faith that, in time, meaning comes through revelation. God reveals things according to his own timing, she is often heard to say. She attributes cause and effect to the plans of Providence, the knowledge of which may be revealed if one is humble, patient, and attentive. She wants to eliminate Roskus' "no luck" attitude from her worldview, irritated by his superstitious inclinations and shortsightedness. He and their son T. P. delude themselves by thinking that they are somehow exempt from the hand of fate. What they think they see as ill fortune intended for others, Dilsey sees as pertaining to and affecting all. For Dilsey, luck is something which results as much from personal choice as from some abstract formulation about the hand of fortune. She does not have to look far to illustrate her point, reminding Roskus of his own encroaching physical disability.

Roskus believes in righteous retribution. Each Compson death signifies for him a gradual working out of the curse which he believes the Compsons have brought upon their house by renaming Benjy and not permitting their daughter Candace's name to be spoken there. He fears that their curse threatens him, too, because he lives on their land. Dilsey thinks that Roskus' notions of bad luck are as unlucky as bad luck itself. She thinks, for example, that it was Roskus' talking of bad luck that prompted their son Versh to go off to the loose living city of Memphis. When Dilsey says, *"Folks don't have no luck, changing names,"*[9] she obviously means it in the moral context that ill luck is actually rooted in such ignoble affectations as the social pride of Mrs. Compson. For Dilsey, superstitious thinking, too, is lacking in sympathy and understanding. It does not bring one to revelation and understanding which come only through reverence and humility. For Dilsey, action proceeds first from understanding; consequently much of her activity in the novel is impelled by tremendous moral urgency.

In response to critics who assert otherwise, it would be very unrealistic to expect Dilsey to be able to come down off the cross, as we might phrase it, and bring salvation to this pressing situation. For the most part, the Compson predicament is not a situation which can be saved by the sympathy of others. The heedless seem already to have done themselves in, and what they would need in respect to salvation from Dilsey, she cannot provide. There is no way possible from our worldview for the novel to end in absolute triumph over evil nor in a total affirmation of belief in the supplanting of evil by the good. As much as the good people can actually do is point out another direction to those inclined toward evil. Consequently, Dilsey's heroism lies in the fact that she demonstrates that pride and self-indulgence need not conquer the whole of life, that selflessness and compassion are higher realizations of the self. As an exemplar of goodness, she is as the blood of the New Testament which is offered for the remission of sins, leaving mankind with the responsibility of personal choice. While not suffering crucifixion, Dilsey suffers tremendous pain and mortification at the hands of Miss Caroline and her favorite son, Jason. Moreover, it is her mortification that leads most directly into the Easter Sunday imagery where she becomes the analogue for the "serene, tortured crucifix."[10] But even though she is not a victim of self-indulgence, all of her world too becomes a part of the novel's tragic essence.

The sense of time which unfolds around Dilsey in the final chapter is the most drawn out and punctuated of the entire novel. It is as if the cosmic weight of time has descended upon the particular morning, deliberately pacing, almost suspending the movement toward the finale. This weighty sense of time reflects the fact that before this morning is over almost all the Compson existence must pass before our eyes. This last chapter opens, ironically, focusing upon Dilsey with a frigid and uncanny tone, unlike the aura of warmth which has usually surrounded her. One has the sense of being led into something formidable. Even the natural atmosphere of the morning seems to have been wrought against Dilsey. She emerges from her cabin only to be met by stolid and chilling northwestern light which drops like fallout over the landscape and assails her. We watch this body of hers, worn down in size by time and which, with its "indomitable skeleton" and "impervious guts,"[11] appears to be what Dilsey herself is to Compson history, the remains. Both have witnessed the beginning and the end.

Neither the tone nor the imagery will let us forget that the heroic design here is reminiscent of the crucifixion of Christ. As we follow the movements of Dilsey this day, images are conjured up of the Passion and the road to Golgotha. Even the description of Dilsey's cabin area lends itself to this image. There is a trinity of mulberry trees in whose limbs jaybirds alight squawking ominously. According to Luster who serves as a mouthpiece for the local lore, these jaybirds spend their weekends in hell.[12] But we soon learn, as the last pillars have been pulled from the Compson wreckage by the girl Quentin's elopment with the money that Jason has been pilfering from her through the years, that the bluejays certainly do know where hell is. If Dilsey is to bear the cross of Christian redemption, she not only has to pass through but also endure this hell.

Faulkner has structured the scenes so that the first voice to complement that of the screeching bluejays that bleak morning is none other than that of Mrs. Compson. Being the antithesis of Dilsey, there is no one more capable than she to construct Dilsey's cross. The intrusion of her voice breaks the noble silence through which Dilsey has been holding her discourse with the early morning. Dilsey's humble desire for a special sort of peace on Easter Sunday is usurped by her mistress' petty, implaccable desire for attention and personal comfort. Yet Dilsey moves without dissent despite Mrs. Compson's cockcrow of incivility and her own increasingly painful physical afflictions. As the faithful servant of Christ she is braced, as she must always be, for the abusiveness of Jason or Miss Caroline.

In half a morning it seems that most of Compson history has repeated itself before our eyes. Miss Caroline as always, has demonstrated despicable theatrics. Dilsey has fetched Luster from the tree in which we first saw Caddy's muddy drawers. Jason has started out on his final highstrung course of action. Benjy has passed again through his constant and hopeless wailing. Somewhat akin to the words of Christ in the garden of Gethsemane saying, "Take this cup from me," Dilsey declares "I have stood all I kin."[13] Yet she manages to prepare for church to hear the Easter sermon, where she can stand at the foot of the cross of her true Master and not be humiliated, but regenerated.

Distressed though she is, Dilsey has not been so pressured by the events of the morning that she forgets that certain actions ought to be governed by general common sense. Seeing that her daughter Frony and Luster, out of plain vanity, risk ruining their new garments in the unpredictable weather, she finds no reason to delay in giving them a prompt lesson about their own lack of judgement. Reproaching them from her simple acknowledgement of their indigent exitence, she recognizes in her own family, too, the foibles of human nature, and recognizes as well that these foibles may persist quite nonsensically under what would be ordinarily deemed very adverse circumstances.

As Michael Millgate has pointed out, it is not only mischief but also pride that prompts Luster in that final scene of the book to show off before the town and drive to the left of the confederate monument, thus disorienting Benjy and starting another round of tumult and confusion with Jason.[14] It is out of pride, too, Dilsey feels, that Frony feels compelled to tell her that carrying Benjy to church so regularly has started the black folk and the white folk to talking. But Dilsey reflects that this talk could come only from a particular kind of folk she thinks of as "trash white folks" and "niggers" who need the fear of God put into them. Disregarding the uneasiness of the blacks and the complaints of the whites, Dilsey takes her love for Benjy as a natural part of human responsibility for human sorrow. What she sees in the others' ridiculing of human suffering is simply the cultivation of egoism.

While most of the church congregation are amazed and somewhat disgruntled by the visiting Reverend Shegog's undistinguished appearance, Dilsey waits for the man to deliver himself, not through his physical aspect, but through his spiritual intelligence. Described by the narrator as "a meager figure, hunched over upon itself like that of one long immured in striving with the implaccable earth,"[15] he is, in some ways, the reflection of Dilsey's own existence. Thus it is that

Dilsey and the minister seem to communicate on a higher level than the rest of the congregation. Reverend Shegog's essential message addresses pride and vain pursuit, through which Dilsey is reminded again of the suicide of Quentin some eighteen years earlier, the disinheritance of Candace, the prideful neglect of Benjy, the icy coming-of-age of Jason, the decay of Miss Caroline through self-pity, the death of Mr. Compson from alcoholism, the surmounting pressures of her household, and, now the trouble about the young girl Quentin. In her own words, Dilsey has seen "the beginning, en . . . de endin."[16]

The admonition is the same for all, and Dilsey and the congregation hear it in Reverned Shegog's words: "Wus a rich man: whar he now, O bredden? Wus a po man: whar he now, O sistuhn? Oh I tells you, ef you aint got de milk en de dew of de old salvation when de long, cold years rolls away!"[17] The meaning for both the minister and Dilsey merge in the crucified Christ whose visage is serene and tortured. Dilsey has endured time through her intimacy with Christ as the Lamb. To her, Reverend Shegog is revelation and light upon the darkness of the generations which she has seen. She comprehends sorrow and suffereing as perpetual attendants of man's earthly existence, but is overwhelmed by the tremendous presence of evil. Just that morning she reminded her grandson Luster about the unity of human beings in their inclination toward evil. "Dese is funny folks. Glad I aint non of em," Luster had said. To which Dilsey made the prompt retort, "Aint none of who? . . . Lemme tell you somethin, nigger boy, you got jest es much Compson devilment in you es any of em."[18]

Dilsey offers no testimony beyond her terse summation of life, experience, and time – that she has seen the beginning and the ending. For her to elaborate on the meaning of her words would probably be vain and self-indulgent, at which point the mystery of the meaning might vanish. She has experienced a sacred revelation, not only about the Compsons, but about life. She has seen the beginning and end of evil. Moreover, she has seen the outcome of good and evil.

When Reverend Shegog speaks of seeing "de resurrection en de light" and "de darkness en de death everlastin,"[19] Dilsey complements it with her own eschatological reckoning of having "seed de first en de last."[20] Believing that eternity lies in faith and vision, she goes home to the house with the rotting porticoes, unabashed by her engraving tears prompted by her own intimate knowledge of the blood of the Lamb. The spiritual freedom that comes from belief in the resurrection is there for those who can grasp its meaning. But it cannot be apprehended by those too caught up with the personal indulgences of human drama. As Walton Litz has stated, "Quentin and his father cannot see Jesus immediately. Instead, his figure comes to them filtering 'down the long and lonely light rays.' "[21]

So Dilsey has had her moment of ecstasy. Her faith has endured, although with difficulty in this world, given her proximity to Jason and to Miss Caroline, who also believes that she is a Christian and that she has directed her family according to Christain ways. Dilsey's trying morning might have been brought to a spiritual climax with Reverend Shegog's sermon, but she will still need to draw from it if she is to make it honorably through the rest of a long afternoon. For the Compson world in which she is intertwined has yet to reach its climax. Returning almost directly from the sacred service, Dilsey is confronted with Miss Caroline who has knocked the Bible off the bed onto the floor and, in all her hauteur, has waited steadfastly for the maid to return to pick it up. This gesture is the ultimate statement of Mrs. Compson's distance from Christian virtues, a precise exemplification of her doomed majesty, and a profound abjuration of any ties with individual conscience or spiritual authority. This is doubtless the lowest of low points on that Easter Sunday. Dilsey can find no words to match the occasion. Perhaps her only counter would be in words she once expressed to the callous Jason: "I thank de Lawd I got mo heart dan dat, even ef hit is black."[22]

Deeds have impact, especially if they have been performed in the presence of others. The Bible is Dilsey's sacred guide for conducting one's life. It is what holds her and what she holds on to. She feels the reciprocal responsibility of guardianship to ensure the endurance of the message and its messengers. For her this is a regenerative responsibility. In a sense, she has inherited the text which has become dispossessed through attempts to corrupt its virtues or to recast them upon the blacks by the whites. Miss Caroline's cultural legacy accentuates this. No humane perspective could come to her unless she had sincere involvement with her individual conscience. This would lead, however, to serious self-scrutiny in which she would never engage.

Dilsey realizes that the household has reached its lowest point.

After the episode with the Bible she compassionately says to Benjy, as she strokes his head in the yard and as he and Luster are preparing to take that final ride to the cemetery: "We's down to worse'n dis, ef folks jes knowed. . . . You's de Lawd's chile, anyway. En I be His'n, too, fo long, praise Jesus."[23] She has done the best that she could. She has endured "dis long time"[24] withstanding the temptation, in the midst of chaos, to descend into coldness. Withstanding such temptation is, according to St. Matthew, the only way human salvation will be accomplished, and Dilsey certainly seems to be on her way to accomplishing that.

Since human beings commune with themselves, their fellow beings, and God through their deeds and their acts of free will, Dilsey knows that in moments of freedom, to choose, human beings must blatantly reveal their inner being. These moments, then, are what make past, present and future. Some human suffering is explained simply by the fact that humans have limitations. But for human beings to generate suffering is, for Dilsey, tantamount to reducing the human estate to something bestial.

Dilsey also understands that man is often an unconscious instrument of nature. "Whut you do any of you devilment fur?"[25] she asks her grandson Luster. But man, because he does have consciousness, is responsible for some aspects of life. Dilsey knows that only God is all fullness, nature is part of the working of God, and man is part of God and part of nature. Thus, on Easter morning when she steps from her kitchen door into the yard to fetch the wood which the tardy Luster has not brought, she knows that she is up against the awful nature of mankind as well as the force of nature itself in history. She accepts the challenge, however, as part of that imperfection over which God Himself will eventually triumph.

As it has been pointed out in numerous studies, time-consciousness plays a crucial role in our understanding of the personalities of the main characters in *The Sound and the Fury*.[26] And although Dilsey's sense of time is not as extraordinary as that of Benjy and Quentin, Faulkner was no less concerned with it when he created her. Moreover, Dilsey's sense of time is highly significant; for Dilsey represents a culminating point through which Faulkner felt he had made his true contact with the transcendent. Consequently, Faulkner would speak continuously of Dilsey over the years, relative to all his other creations, with unrivalled pride.

Faulkner spoke often in his early writings of a basic need and urge within himself to create a semblance of the eternal which could withstand the chaotic flow of time. Dilsey Gibson is unchallenged in this instance. However, she is in no way meant to suggest that immemorial mammy whose reason for being is to supply the perpetual and edenic bosom for the master's offspring, distraught with the frustrations and sufferings of the world.[27] The objective relationship she establishes with Quentin and any others who harbor infantile or immature yearnings is proof of that. What Dilsey advocates makes for man's salvation and provides a basis for the rhythm of his eternity.

The figures on Byzantine friezes and on Keats' Grecian urn became Faulkner's favorite prototypes for the creation of his images of the eternal. In his early verse, fiction, and review essays, he created a cluster of images which later culminated in the singular figure of Dilsey. In a 1922 review essay of John Hergesheimer's *Linda Condon*, Faulkner wrote of the novel that "it is more like a lovely Byzantine frieze: a few unforgettable figures in arrested motion, forever beyond the reach of time and troubling the heart like music."[28] Then writing about A. E. Houseman's *The Shropshire Lad* in 1925 he wrote that "here was reason for being born into a fantastic world: discovering the splendor of fortitude, the beauty of being of the soil like a tree about which fools might howl and which winds of disillusion and death and despair might strip, leaving it bleak, without bitterness; beautiful in sadness."[29] In the same year, or shortly thereafter, he quite similarly described the phenomenon of light as "hollowed murmurous out of chaos and the long dark fury of time. It seemed strange that the candle flame should stand so steady above the wick."[30] In *Flags in the Dust*, just a few years later, the narrator says likewise with reference to Horace Benbow and the artistic sensibility in general:

> The meaning of peace; one of those instants in a man's life, a neap tide in his affairs, when as though with a premonition of disaster, the moment takes on a sort of fixed clarity in which his actions and desires stand boldly forth unshadowed and rhythmic one with another like two steeds drawing a single chariot along a smooth empty road, and during which the I in him stands like a tranquil deciduated tree above the sere and ludi-

crous disasters of his days.[31]

Finally we have Dilsey in *The Sound and the Fury* as she emerges from her cabin on the trying Easter Sunday morning under the shadow of the forces of death, human vanity, and greed, among which she is the major force of annealment and resurrection:

> She had been a big woman once but now her skeleton rose, draped loosely in unpadded skin that tightened again upon a paunch almost dropsical, as though muscle and tissue had been courage and fortitude which the days or the years had consumed until only the indomitable skeleton was left rising like a ruin or a landmark above the somnolent and impervious guts. . . .[32]

At the end of the essay, "Verse Old and Nascent: A Pilgrimage," published in the April 1925 issue of *The Double Dealer*, where he recounts his early encounters with the world of poetry, Faulkner had made an incantation-like appeal: "Is there not among us, someone who can write something beautiful and passionate and sad instead of saddening?"[33] The tone of his query is reminiscent of the moment of elation and affirmation in Joyce's *A Portrait of the Artist as a Young Man* when the maturing Stephen Daedalus reveals: "Yes! Yes! Yes! He would create proudly out of the freedom and power of his soul, as the great artificer whose name he bore, a living thing, new and soaring and beautiful, impalpable, imperishable."[34] The young Faulkner's efforts to bring a Dilsey-like figure into being are of this spirit; for it is Dilsey who makes his creation sad while not saddening. She is the "tranquil deciduated tree" as well as the candle flame above the wick.

On the more whimsical side, in *The Sound and the Fury*, Faulkner enshrined his accomplishment in creating Dilsey by using a magnificently dramatized conceit prompted by the saucy young Caddy. As Caddy and Dilsey discuss the Compsons' changing of the name of their idiot born son from Maury, after Mrs. Compson's brother, to Benjy, the young girl is incredulous that Dilsey contends that her own name will outlive her physical existence in time:

> *'Huh,' Dilsey said. 'Name aint going to help him. Hurt him,*

neither. Folks dont have no luck, changing names. My name been Dilsey since fore I could remember and it be Dilsey when they's long forgot me.'

'How will they know it's Dilsey, when it's long forgot, Dilsey,' Caddy said.

'It'll be in the Book, honey,' Dilsey said. 'Writ out.'

'Can you read it,' Caddy said.

'Wont have to,' Dilsey said. 'They'll read it for me. All I got to do is say Ise here.'[35]

Of course, we know that the "Book" Dilsey refers to is the Bible with its traditional entry of family names as well as the Bible as the great roll prophesying the names of all who are to enter the heavenly gates. But there is another line of logic about this wonderfully constructed passage which is the result of the artist Faulkner's immortal accomplishment. This logic suggests that the "Book" is also *The Sound and the Fury*, the work to which Faulkner would constantly refer in his later years as the "splendid failure." It was the book he said that caused him the most grief.[36] Yet in *The Sound and the Fury* he was to create his most triumphant symbol of the human being's strength to survive human folly and misery. Several years later he wrote to the novel's French translater what he later reiterated many times in tribute to Dilsey: "There was Dilsey to be the future, to stand above the fallen ruins of the family like a ruined chimney, gaunt, patient and indomitable."[37] And as if this were not explicit enough he said again in 1956: "Dilsey is one of my own favorite characters, because she is brave, courageous, generous, gentle, and honest. She's much more brave and honest and generous than me."[38]

To speak too simply of Faulkner's concept of time, particularly that sense of time used by artists to exemplify the modern fractured consciousness, would be to misread or oversimplify a much more complex matter. The fractured view of time is only one dimension of Faulkner's world. While he finds the modernistic experience of time and reality fascinating and crucial to communicating his insight into existence in the Yoknapatawpha world, he does not intend for us to overlook those less sensational type characters like Dilsey who may bear the greatest clues for human survival. Faulkner finds something very worthwhile in illuminating the stature of a Dilsey who manages to endure chaos while standing in its midst, or a Lena Grove who can go on generating human kind in sheer ignorance of the chaotic, or of the anonymous man plowing the field in *Intruder in the Dust*, continuing his work at close distance to not only the chaos around him but also the danger. Faulkner treats the chaotic mind with profound sympathy and, of course, with profound depth. But he is as baffled by it as he is fascinated. In Faulkner's works the chaotic mind is a hallmark of what we have come to refer to as the human condition, and points to the fact that if man cannot survive his mind, then he *is* doomed.

The critic who is more preoccupied with modernistic complexity, as Jean-Paul Sartre is in his analysis of *Light in August*, will tend to speak in a very limited way about Faulkner's dealings with time. This type of critic often also speaks too absolutely of Faulkner's concept of time.[39] One cannot help but wonder why a character with the stature of Dilsey is completely ignored in the course of many of the discussions of time in Faulkner's works. Perhaps it would be argued that Dilsey's spiritual traits are negligible, that her courage and compassion are already familiar to us. Maybe the same is thought about Lena Grove in *Light in August* as she follows her simpler instincts of time to find the father of her child, journeying through three states. But without giving consideration to the contrasting senses of time, especially where major characters are involved, it is difficult to see how one could make a reliable judgement of what Faulkner's concept of time actually is. Faulkner looks upon Dilsey and Lena as mainstays in time, and as far as the fragmented sense of time is concerned, he seems to believe that in time it will bring about its own destruction. Indeed, Faulkner sees the conflicts in the South as well as within himself as having to do with the fragmented sense of time by which the region has come to look upon life.

Some men confuse time "with its mathematical progression," the narrator of "A Rose for Emily" declares.[40] "You were born with the habit of consuming time. Be satisfied with that. Tom-o-Bedlam had the only genius for consuming time: that is, to be utterly unaware of it," comments a character in *Mosquitoes.*[41] In this way Benjy consumes time as he hears the ticking of the clock and has no response. But Dilsey never forgets that the clock itself is the creation of mankind. Subsequently, the clock demonstrates man's imperfections as we see with the old one-handed clock over the cupboard in the Compson kitchen which Dilsey is always correcting. In her understanding, the clock is several imperfect removals from the true time keeper, God. For Dilsey, time dissolves, and, thus, maintains a whole relationship between the sum of its dimensions: past, present and future. When Dilsey calls out the correct hour relative to the number of strikes given by the old clock, she sounds sympathetic for the old machine's condition, probably because she knows that the clock strikes only to call attention to the time and condition of man. The clock is only a microcosm of duration. Human existence will be forever subject to beginnings and endings. And as the hour approaches one o'clock on that turbulent Easter Sunday and she decides that Jason is not coming home to eat, Dilsey knows that she has been in touch with just one microcosm in time's eternal duration.

Indeed the clock is the *reductio ad absurdum* of human existence because by it men attempt to relegate time to units which are defined, precise, and calculable. The clock cannot measure the more abstract multidimensional continuum which makes time far more than a mechanical influence. As Dilsey perceives it, any influence which may seem the result of the clock itself is more a projection and extension of the impetuousness of human beings who calculate by it than it is an influence which exists in and of itself. Quentin's grandfather's term "mausoleum" is an apt image of the clock for those who think of time as finite units. When Quentin pulls the hands off the watch given to him by his grandfather, one feels that time has been freed to return to its own realm outside human manipulation.

Faulkner never intended that Dilsey be taken as a symbol that the forces of chaos would be defeated.[42] He intended that she provide a perspective from which we might view chaos, from which we ourselves might emerge from it. By transcending her painful existence, Dilsey reaffirms the possibility of transcendence itself.

ENDNOTES

1, Honre de Balzac, *Pere Goriot* (N.Y.: Signet Classics, 1962), p. 21. Originally published in 1834.

2. Sally R. Page, *Faulkner's Women: Characterization and Meaning* (Deland, Fla.: Everett/Edwards, Inc., 1972), p. 21.

3. T. S. Eliot, *The Complete Poems and Plays, 1909-1950* (N.Y.: Harcourt, Brace and World, Inc., 1952), p. 12.

4. William Faulkner, *The Sound and the Fury* (N.Y.: Vintage Books, 1963), pp. 58, 59.
5. Ibid., p. 170.
6. Ibid., p. 230.
7. Ibid., p. 258.
8. Olga Vickery, *The Novels of William Faulkner* (Baton Rouge: Louisiana State University Press, 1964), p. 47.
9. *The Sound and the Fury*, p. 71.
10. Ibid., p. 368.
11. Ibid., p. 331.
12. For further significant information, though not much interpretation, on the use of folklore in this novel, see Charles D. Peavy, "Faulkner's Use of Folklore in *The Sound and the Fury*," in *Journal of American Folklore*, vol. 79, no. 313, July-Sept., 1966.
13. *The Sound and the Fury*, p. 357.
14. Michael Millgate, *The Achievement of William Faulkner* (New York: Vintage Books, 1966), p. 103.
15. T. S. Eliot, p. 367.
16. *The Sound and the Fury*, p. 357.
17. Ibid., pp. 368-9.
18. Ibid., p. 344.
19. Ibid., p. 370.
20. Ibid., p. 371.
21. Walton Litz, "William Faulkner's Moral Vision," *Southwest Review*, Summer 1952, p. 208.
22. *The Sound and the Fury*, p. 258.
23. Ibid., p. 396.
24. Ibid.
25. Ibid., p. 344.
26. Jean-Paul Sartre is probably the most noted figure who stands at the beginning of this trend with the publication of his 1939 essay, "Time in Faulkner: *The Sound and the Fury*" ("A Propos de Le Bruit et la Fureur," *La Nouvelle Revue Francaise*, 52, 1939). The problem is not with all of what Sartre says, but with his generalization of all of Faulkner. Cleanth Brooks in *William Faulkner: The Yoknapatawpha Country*, among other critics, has written on the misleading aspects of this trend; also Henry J. Underwood, Jr., "Sartre on *The Sound and the Fury:* Some Errors," *Modern Fiction Studies*, vol. XII, no. 4, Winter 1966-67.
27. George Kent, "The Black Woman in Faulkner's Works, with the Exclusion of Dilsey, Part II," *Phylon Quarterly*, vol. 36, no. 1, Spring 1975, pp. 55-62.
28. William Faulkner, Review essay of John Hergesheimer's *Linda Condon* in *Early Prose and Poetry*, ed. Carvel Collins (Boston: Little, Brown, 1962), p. 101. Originally published in 1922.
29. William Faulkner, "Verse Old and Nascent: A Pilgrimage," in *Early Prose and Poetry*, p. 117. Originally published in 1925.
30. William Faulkner, "Mistral," in *Collected Stories* (N.Y.: Random House, 1950), p. 862.
31. William Faulkner, *Flags in the Dust* (N.Y.: Vintage Books, 1974), p. 195.
32. William Faulkner, *The Sound and the Fury* (N.Y.: Vintage Books, 1963), p. 331.
33. William Faulkner, "Verse Old and Nascent," in *Early Prose and Poetry*, p. 118. Originally published in *The Double Dealer*, April 1925.
34. James Joyce, *A Portrait of the Artist as a Young Man* (N.Y.: The Viking Press, Inc., 1964), p. 170. Originally published in 1914.

35. *The Sound and the Fury*, p. 71.
36. *Faulkner in the University*, p. 77.
37. Joseph L. Blotner, *Faulkner: A Biography* (N.Y.: Random House, 1974), vol. I, p. 571. Originally quoted in Maurice Coindreau's introduction to his translation of *The Sound and the Fury* (*Le Bruit et le Fureur*, Paris, 1938).
38. Interview with Jean Stein (1956) in *Writers at Work: The Paris Review Interviews*, ed. Malcolm Cowley (N.Y.: The Viking Press, 1959), p. 130. Originally published in the *Paris Review*, Spring 1956).
39. Sartre, op. cit.
40. William Faulkner, "A Rose for Emily," in *Collected Stories*, p. 129.
41. William Faulkner, *Mosquitoes* (N.Y.: Boni and Liveright, 1927), p. 319.
42. Two fine articles on the final section are: Beverly Gross' "Form and Fulfillment in *The Sound and the Fury*" (*Modern Language Quarterly*, vol. XXIX, no. 4, December 1968); Margaret Blanchard's "The Rhetoric of Communion: Voice in *The Sound and the Fury*" (*American Literature*, January 1970). The first article discusses the last book of the novel as a "poetic rather than a dramatic resolution of forces." The second is an apt analysis of the dimensions of the narrator of the last book. The article which attempts hardest to challenge what was often designated as Dilsey's moral ordering of the novel is probably John V. Hagopian's "Nihilism in Faulkner's *The Sound and the Fury*," in the Merrill Studies in *The Sound and the Fury* compiled by James Meriwether. The intent of the article as stated by its author is "to demonstrate that a structural analysis of the closing chapter of *The Sound and the Fury* does, in fact, reveal nihilism as the meaning of the whole." This essay proceeds too often with a one-dimensional misreading as is shown by its interpretation of Dilsey's "mangy and anonymous fur" in only negative terms. The author tends to make the meaning of his "closures" into absolutes, thus minimizing the power of the metaphorical context. He also seems to be undergirded by an effort to discount critical interpretations instead of accounting for and interpreting the text. Furthermore, his argument that the final closure of the novel is cast in nihilistic terms does not seem to acknowledge that the ultimate goal of the existentialist is transcendence of the nihil, not simply nihilistic reductionism. For, one could very well undertake a structural study of the novel and find in its form a symbol of transcendence, the mandala, as an image of individuation on the part of its creator.

VII.

Lucas and Nancy in the Heroic Design

Together with Joe Christmas in *Light in August* and Dilsey Gibson in *The Sound and the Fury*, it is Lucas Beauchamp in *Intruder in the Dust* and Nancy Mannigoe in *Requiem for a Nun* who have the most prominent roles of all the black characters in the Faulkner canon. Unlike Joe Christmas, a man alienated from society because he does not know his identity and because the world is afraid of what his identity might be, Dilsey, Lucas, and Nancy, while not free from the racial indignities imposed upon black being out of the white Yoknapatawphan's sense of racial superiority, have managed through perseverance and magnanimity of vision to find and exercise for themselves an exceptional degree of moral choice and freedom. In a sense, they chronicle Faulkner's personal growth and belief in the human being's higher potential. These black characters recognize that although evil is a part of human nature, one can nevertheless make choices. This perception is the primary force that frees Faulkner somewhat from his racial heritage, that is, he shows through these characters that the human being can choose and that one is not so bound to a fixed destiny as one's situation might imply.

Dilsey, Lucas, and Nancy, among others, function as initiators and agents of regeneration. They share a bond of fortitude and comprehend the necessity for sustaining good, not only because they are among those who try to maintain dignity and decency regardless to the condition in which they find themselves, but also because they understand that the need to aspire toward the good is essential to human survival.[1] It is ironic that they should be given this function, or as some might say, this burden, since they have all suffered so much and since the white Yoknapatawpha mind generally perceives the existence of black being as a symbol of misfortune and the unregenerative nature of man.

The perception is, of course, the dramatic and ironic tragedy of the white Yoknapatawphan himself who has chosen to mold his identity out of his own mythic view of reality and history. But if the roles these black characters play are to be considered burdensome, they are burdens which, because of their vision, they have chosen to assume from their own sense of human responsibility. A greater irony in this regard points more toward Faulkner, however. By having the black peon serve as an agent for the development of the white man's freedom and sense of responsibility, Faulkner contradicts much of his own public chauvinist talk made during the fifties about the duty of the white man to teach responsibility to the black.[2] In his fiction, it is often just the other way around.

Although these black characters appear as redemptive heroes, they are not self-consciously so. They are simply being themselves in relation to other human beings in a particular place and time. They are characterized by independent thinking, the nature of which is sometimes eccentric. Their existences having been proscribed by the Yoknapatawpha society, they gain much of their heroism by standing stoically in moral contrast to their surroundings. Because Faulkner understands that the Yoknapatawphans do not appreciate the moral worth of black being, he purposely creates the story of Charles Mallison's initiation into manhood in *Intruder in the Dust* with Lucas Beauchamp functioning as the major agent. Dilsey and Uncle Parsham Hood are perhaps the least self-conscious in their redemptive roles. As an exemplary character, Dilsey serves more as a force of resistance in the midst of the action than as a character who effects or generates action. Indeed, all of these characters act in some way as forces of resistance because they work to thwart catastrophe. But Nancy and Reverend Sutterfield, on the other hand, consciously set out to redeem. That is, disregarding their own historical or prevailing victimization they feel morally concerned about the welfare of other members of the community, and try to deliver them from moral destitution. It is only Nancy among all of them, though, who has the fervor of a martyr.

These black characters are astounded by the proportions that evil has taken and continues to take in their worlds. For them, there is no personal freedom unless there is freedom in relation to other human beings. Dilsey, Lucas, and Nancy are not prompted by self-sacrifice as much as by a sense of moral economy. They have a good intuitive estimation of what, in the end, is of lasting value in the world.

However, the heroic proportions in which these particular characters are cast serve to emphasize the discrepancies in the quality and dimensions of Faulkner's other black characters. By being cast in the extreme they highlight the absence of a middle or more normal range of blacks. Yoknapatawpha is a county in which, according to Faulkner's own demographic statistics, the blacks outnumber the whites two to one. The range of character development in the entire Faulkner canon is quite limited when, for instance, it is put beside Charles Chesnutt's *The Marrow of Tradition* (1901) and Jean Toomer's *Cane* (1923) in which a vast profile of the black being is presented.

Faulkner's characters of heroic proportion show no regret for the past. They are a little sentimental about tradition, but know that destruction of the past also means the dissolution of corruption. They know this corruption well because they have been its prime victims. Dilsey, Lucas, Nancy, and Reverend Sutterfield have the courage and compassion to assume responsibility for what they see. They are not like the Quentins who, Faulkner says, speak truth when they know they are about to die because they know they will not be around to have to defend it.[3] Neither do they simply moralize. They act out their beliefs with a greater sense of freedom than the white Yoknapatawphans who are deluded by thinking that their holding the reins of power makes them free.

In his *Faulkner and Dostoevsky*, Jean Weisgerber has done an informative job investigating the influence that Dostoevsky's philosophy of atonement played in Faulkner's effort to find that redemptive formula that would lift the curse Faulkner thought to be on the South, resulting from the white people's violation of the land, the native inhabitants, and the subjection of the blacks to slavery.[4] However, in the formula Faulkner eventually tries to work out in his fiction, atonement is not just the quieting of one's soul; it is a vigorous life-giving force. After all, the path to redemption according to Faulkner is not meant to cleanse the Yoknapatawphan of his sins in preparation for heaven. It is meant to prepare the Yoknapatawphan simply to live in Yoknapatawpha.

For Faulkner atonement is a matter of the individual conscience coming to terms with its existence and thereby learning to live more humanely. Out of his preoccupation with the subject, he arrived at the formula which he repeatedly referred to in his last decade as "The Trilogy of Man's Conscience," an ethical schema outlining man's moral states and choices. In this schema, one man says, "This is dreadful, terrible, and I won't face it even at the cost of my life;" the second says, "This is terrible but we can bear it;" the third says, "This is dreadful, I won't stand it, I'll do something about it."[5] Most characters in the Yoknapatawpha world do not even make their way into the first category, although characters like Isaac McCaslin, Gail Hightower, Gavin Stevens, Uncle Buck, and Uncle Buddy belong in the second. It is Dilsey, Lucas, Ratliff, Miss Habersham, Nancy, Charles Mallison, and Aleck Sander who demonstrate the ability to act within the third and only category that can lead to the renewal and restoration of life. Because there are not many good candidates, Faulkner even has the problem of generating for his audience and himself a sense of the potential for redemption in the damned society. The persistence of his attempts to mark out a trail for the spiritual redemption of Yoknapatawpha County is clearly manifest in the theme and structure of *Go Down, Moses*, as well as in his extra-fictional statements of the 1940s leading to the publication of *Intruder in the Dust* in 1948. Indeed, it is noteworthy to watch Faulkner's total characterization of Lucas during this period. Lucas' development is indicative of Faulkner's maturation in permitting blacks to live more nobly.

In "The Fire and the Hearth" we see Lucas as a man of pride who places special value on the fact that, although black and a product of slavery, he is, besides Isaac McCaslin, the oldest male descendant of the original McCaslin line. According to the bequest of the original owners, the land Lucas had been cultivating since before the birth of its present holder, Roth Edmonds, is his to live on for the rest of his life. But he also has his own special sense of affinity to the land derived naturally from the years given to farming and living on it. Through his relationship with the land and out of blood pride, Lucas demonstrates his willfulness in his relationship with Roth, whom he never forgets is a product of the female rather than the male side of the family. In Lucas' view, his white cousin-landlord's would-be voice of authority is childish. Lucas is disgruntled with Isaac McCaslin as the male heir for relinquishing the land to his kindred Edmondses to relieve himself of the responsibility of the curse incurred by the initial taking of the land and the enslavement of human beings to work it. For Lucas this is a cowardly act, especially for a McCaslin. He sees it as a basic weakness in the man, unable to shoulder the responsibilities of his heritage. Faulkner himself implies that repudiation is not enough when he places Isaac in the second category of his ethical schema.[6] Blood kin or not, Lucas sees the Edmondses as newcomers and intruders who have caught Isaac in his weakness and deceitfully deprived him of his patrimony.

As a curious and complex traditionalist Lucas is incensed by the introduction of electricity and automobiles. They, too, are intrusions, new and unnecessary comforts that the old people, who were better men, could do without. Proud to be a farmer he scorns anything, work or equipment, that is not first rate. At the age of sixty-seven, he is trying through farming and the making of bootleg whiskey to work to pay for his retirement so that he can tell Roth Edmonds to allot the farmland to someone else. Lucas anticipates that Roth will demand to know how he expects to support himself in retirement. But Lucas is prepared to remind the white man that nothing can be exacted of him, and certainly not by one Lucas considers to be of less worth than himself.

Lucas intends never to let Roth forget that his elder black cousin belongs to the old stock made up of courage, honor, and pride—the stuff that has made mankind endure—and that he is not asking for charity but is prepared to pay rent for the cabin in which he and his wife Molly live, when he decides to stop farming. Lucas Quintus Carothers McCaslin Beauchamp is a self-created man who changed the spelling of his name from that of his revered white patriarch Lucius Quintus McCaslin. He is proud of his heritage but is just as proud to be distinct from it. To the extent that Lucas can maintain control over the racial situation, he refuses to participate in the self-castigation that is expected of his caste. He will not live in a self-deprecating manner. This is the essential Lucas with whom we come into contact in *Intruder in the Dust*.

In a number of instances in "The Fire and the Hearth," however, Faulkner downplays the character of Lucas, appearing sometimes ambivalent about the kind of character Lucas is to be, whether to allow him singular integrity or to exploit him for comic effect. There are times when Lucas, like Simon in *Flags in the Dust*, approaches the stereotypic black buffoon. The manner in which Lucas is treated comically is not consistent with his more stoic and serious disposition which we encounter in *Intruder in the Dust.* One senses that Faulkner is still experiencing some difficulty with the serious articulation of the black male image. Without doubt, a man like Lucas, whose lifestyle is profoundly ordered by his own strong will, like any other human being, is sometimes genuinely funny. But an emphasis on comic extremes does not give a sense of fullness to his character as much as it makes him seem irresponsible. This man, who respects courage and responsibility would not, believably, jeopardize his marriage or sell his landlord's mule to set out on a highly impulsive search for gold the way Faulkner portrays him. One can understand Lucas' involvement with the bootleg whiskey enterprise, however, because he wishes to be autonomous. In order to ameliorate what at times becomes a ridiculous characterization of Lucas, Faulkner attempts to heighten Lucas' character by executing some of the scenes from a more cosmic rather than terrestial stance. The more typical Lucas respects skill and discretion. For this reason he refuses to let his daughter marry his prospective bootleg competitor because the man is indiscreet and takes little pride in the kind of whiskey he manufactures. Lucas does not want his secret operation which the revered McCaslin line has engaged in for so many years, and which he has managed to operate right under Roth's door without discovery, to be ruined.

It is apparent that Faulkner was conscious of the problems he was having in creating Lucas' character, but instead of recasting it, he attempted to account for some of Lucas' unscrupulous actions by having the narrator say that Lucas was "enveloping himself in an aura of timeless and stupid impassivity." In other words, Lucas was being transformed from "Negro" to "nigger."[7] Thus the character bears the burden of the artist's weaknesses. When we encounter Lucas again in *Intruder in the Dust*, it is to Faulkner's artistic and moral credit that he develops the greater Lucas, not only sustaining that greatness without compromise but also rendering him as an exemplary force essential to the fulfillment of Faulkner's more mature vision of the Yoknapatawpha reality and its deliverance.

While we have to concede that *Intruder in the Dust* is very much Charles Mallison's book, another one of those classic treatments about the education of a young man, Lucas, as warden and agent of the youth's initiation, is the dominating presence in the story. In his intrusion into the maturation process of the boy Charles, he becomes what Sam Fathers is to Quentin in "A Justice" and to Isaac McCaslin in "The Bear" and "The Old People." Faulkner seems to hope, however, that Charles might grow into a greater sense of responsibility and courage than either of his counterparts who in a sense reneged on the moral responsibilities with which they were faced. Lucas' moral stature is influenced from the beginning by his apprehension of a possible peril which could come to someone else—in this instance an adolescent boy—and from his assumption of the responsibility to prevent that peril. Eventually their relationship will be based upon a mutual assumption of this kind of responsibility.

From their first encounter when Charles has fallen into the cold creek, Lucas knows that this boy, like any other white boy in the Yoknapatawpha world, is preparing to take on the distorted assumption that being white makes him free, especially from the authority of any black person. Thus, the old man and the boy become engaged in a drawn out battle over integrity and authority in which the boy has to learn that the greatest authority derives from mutual respect and mutual obligation. It is a complex battle in which the psychological intensity, because of peculiar social strictures, cannot be overestimated. For, with the frustration arising out of its past defeat, the Yoknapatawpha world has locked itself into an attitude of recalcitrance which makes it dangerous for anyone, white or black, to attempt to reverse the sacred social ritual which provides for and protects white manhood.

Mark Twain once described *The Adventures of Huckleberry Finn* as "a book of mine in which a sound mind and a deformed conscience come into conflict and conscience loses."[8] The Yoknapatawpha world of *Intruder in the Dust* involves us in another version of the deformed conscience. Lucas knows that deformity of conscience, and the risks he takes in dealing with it make him that much more of a courageous and admirable character. Here, too, as in *Huckleberry Finn*, the deformed conscience loses or, as Faulkner puts it, the heart wins out over the mind. The distorted reality has to be challenged and deracinated or else there is no freedom.

According to Faulkner, this story of Charles Mallison's initiation into manhood actually began as a detective story for his children.[9] In the general way of a detective story it is a story about a crime, specifically a murder. But in its own very cogent way it is also an anti-investigative detective story, whose departure from the norm provides a natural vehicle for the moral impact of the story, superseding the expected moral ramification of the murders. It is anti-investigative in that the people shun carrying out a truthful investigation because it may lead to community indictment. It is anti-investigative because in its usual manner of relating to black being the Yoknapatawpha mind has already drawn the conclusion that Lucas Beauchamp, the black man holding the recently fired gun and standing over the body of a dead white man, is the one who has committed the murder. Such circumstances would almost inevitably pinpoint anyone, white or black, as a suspect but not as a murderer.

Faulkner impresses upon us that Lucas is viewed as more than a suspect; in the eyes of the Yoknapatawpha whites he is guilty. To enhance this fact further and maintain the anti-detective situation, Faulkner has not, in the beginning, shrouded the murder with suspense and mystery but has shown that the mystery has to do more with when the lynching will take place. The suspense of lynching dominates the story even when coupled with the probability that the murder was committed by someone else. Although the true murderer is eventually discovered despite the anti-investigative bias of the community who would have been outraged at the thought of opening a white man's grave to save the life of a "nigger," the mystique of the rite of lynching, the earmark of injustice against black being, still pervades the atmosphere.

It is out of their respective caste relationships to lynching in all of its emasculating forms that the steadfast old man and the young boy become inextricably bound from their first meeting, a relationship taking on sometimes allegorical and symbolic proportion in the crisis of Yoknapatawpha redemption. Besides detective story conventions, the action of this novel is also punctuated by many of the characteristic signs of traditional initiation rites: the hunt, the baptism, the sudden appearance of the warden and his spellbinding effect, his isolated and somewhat curious domicile, the bridge, the gate, the call, the task, the trial, the accomplishment, and the boon.

The first of this imagery of initiation, the hunt, sets an ironic tone for much of the other imagery to follow. There is, at the beginning of the boy Charles' and Lucas' first meeting, a hunt which leads to a crisis represented by a chilling baptism of the twelve-year-old Charles in an icy creek. What began merely as a rabbit hunt leads to something far greater than what the boy is capable of comprehending in those first years. Indeed, what he has taken from the hunt in the place of a harmless rabbit is a monumental burden of anxiety about his identity, although according to the dictates of his culture there is not much difference between a black man and a rabbit since both are equated with meekness. Lucas eventually alters the boy's general perceptions of the reality into which he is growing and the assumptions he considers basic to his manhood. Even more, Lucas' manner of handling the relationship from the start makes the boy's experience all the more frightening because what was at first so real to the boy later becomes highly ambiguous and illusory.

The complications in which Charles becomes entangled arise out of the fact that he perceives himself not as boy but as a white boy. He cannot understand or accept a black man's not coming immediately to his service when he was nearly drowning in a frozen creek. Even more, he is morally outraged that the black man would order the two black youths attempting to rescue him, to stand out of the way. In this initial incident Lucas deliberately disturbs the boy's self-image. What Lucas has in mind, however, is something more. He resists letting any white think of himself foremost as white, a special order to which black being is expected to surrender. He means, rather, to impress upon Charles that he is simply a boy and by disturbing his distorted self-concept Lucas offers him a new pathway to maturity. Since the Yoknapatawpha culture denies any responsible role of leadership to black being, the boy cannot help but become frustrated and refuse this initial challenge to his maturation.

To show the strength with which the myth of his whiteness has gripped the twelve-year-old Charles, Faulkner has set the force of the boy's mind in competition with a man who is not only of overwhelming physical stature, but also of intractable disposition. That Lucas is watching but not reacting while the boy scuffles to get out of the icy water with the aid of his attendants is not simply for the melodramatic effect, although this is achieved. The delay and sudden command to Joe and Aleck Sander to move the pole out of the way is perhaps the best dramatization of Lucas' character that Faulkner could have managed. When Lucas' presence is at last made known, it is set forth as a sharp and haunting intrusion. Delivering the command with his towering presence, he wants Charles to reclaim himself through his own independence.

The greatness of Lucas' stature is dramatized by a carefully detailed account of Charles' climbing out of the water and gradual awareness of the separate portions of the even more chilling man's body. His eyes move first along the booted feet, then upwards along the long legs, and slowly up to the face of the huge black man standing self-composed with an ax, an ancient symbol of the force of light, on his shoulder. Such an undaunted and appalling figure in black skin cannot be a real man in the Yoknapatawpha world, however. Drawing upon the cultural framework in which he has been raised, Charles classifies Lucas as an ogre. But even that classification is complicated by noticing that the black man is wearing a pelted hat similar to the one his revered grandfather had worn. Thus, he is not only outraged but also mystified. Lucas, who is certainly no Nigger Jim, is mandating that there is no territory for Charles to "light out for" other than that territory which is there within himself. This time it is the black not the white man who issues the dictates of freedom.

Lucas is assuming the rights and responsibilities of an adult regarding the welfare of a child, generally granted by society but not to its black peons. And in the manner of the adult with the authcrity and the entrancing power of the wizard, Lucas makes his commands with no expectation of refusal. He directs the three boys to come with him to his own house, while Charles is amazed that his wish to return to the house of Roth Edmonds is neither denied nor acknowledged. Lucas has brought him to the crossroads of conscience and manhood sooner than Charles has expected to arrive there. His desire to reenter his old world is in vain, although it will take him four years to learn that. Simply by the force of his commanding presence, Lucas leads Charles over a low bridge, past the forbidden gate leading to Roth Edmonds', with Charles thinking that he still has the will to turn and enter it. He assumes that his will is still greater than that of the black man, but under the power of this new presence he rationalizes its loss. It is as if Lucas, who significantly never looks back, is drawing Charles out of the realm of the more socially acceptible world and closer to the true heart of things. As the initiating wizard would, Lucas moves decisively as he directs the boys through the unmarked and untended ways.

It is natural for Charles to perceive the domain to which he is taken as strange and forboding since not only is he out of his native physical realm but also out of his native psychological realm. Charles is being carried away from the regular frame of reference onto Lucas' house on the hill, symbolic of another plane where he will enter the second phase of his initiation into a higher consciousness. Lucas disturbs Charles because his presence is powerful and unique, undermining the credibility which Charles has in his racial fathers who supposedly have taught him all he would need to know about black being. Defenseless in his posture of whiteness and, consequently, humiliated, the boy's anger is misdirected onto Lucas rather than his fathers.

Lucas' insistence that the boy strip off all of his clothes in his presence and wrap himself in one of their quilts only heightens Charles' feeling of abandonment and humiliation. Lucas will not take no for an answer, and by demonstrating his authority appears to be carrying the boy symbolically through another step of the initiation. Charles must lay himself bare before his warden; he must wrap himself in his warden's garments no matter how much he resents what he considers their "nigger" smell, and he must eat the food prepared by the warden's wife no matter how much he considers it the peculiar food of "niggers." If he was humiliated at the creek he is even more so now because he, as a white man, has gained a greater intimacy with what he perceives as despicable. Lucas might realize that it is not the boy's fault, at his age, for reacting in such a way to kindness, but probably does think it tragic that the boy is already unable to respond with simple gratitude to the care shown him by another in a moment of crisis.

If this is the way Charles has already been conditioned to view life, Lucas will take no responsibility for reinforcing it. Thus, Lucas only watches as the boy makes his final gesture, attempting to assert his authority and status as a white man. Charles believes he is ridding himself of an humiliating experience and also any indebtedness to a "nigger" by paying Lucas with money. He does not yet know that that which Lucas has to offer, more than warmth and food and dry clothing, is a new life, which cannot be paid for with money. Lucas spurns the money, and Charles, indignant and frustrated, drops it onto the floor. As the old man orders Joe and Aleck Sander to pick it up and give it back to their ward, Charles knows in a very furious and tragic way that the battle is on between himself and Lucas. He clings to the belief that he cannot live honorably as a white man unless he maintains his authority over black being. While in fact the victim of the white man's compulsions, yet thinking that he is victim of a black man, Charles starts what he does not know will be a four year gambit by throwing away part of the seventy cents which Lucas has scorned into the creek, as he and his companions go back to hunt in the woods.

Charles is no longer preoccupied with shooting rabbits in the woods, however. Indeed, he is so debilitated by his experience with Lucas that he fumbles every opportunity to shoot the rabbits which run before him. Like the white men in the area who have known and scorned Lucas for years, Charles has another rabbit on his mind now, not the meek and submissive hare, but its shrewd counterpart in the form of Lucas.

In this brief moment in the boy's life Faulkner has presented what might be called a microcosm of his work in psychological realism up to the period beginning with *Go Down, Moses*. For what Lucas has sparked in the boy is simply the fury and outrage which has been manifest in the Yoknapatawpha community in different forms as represented in *Flags in the Dust, Light in August,* and *Absalom, Absalom!*. In these earlier works we feel the reality of doom and Faulkner's groping for a technique to eradicate it. In *Light in August* he uncovers the highly concealed core of the intricate and mythic modes of the mind. And in *Absalom, Absalom!* he goes a little further by using narrative technique as a means of exorcising the myths, by using the cord of the narrative to pull us into the heart of the labyrinth, where often the minotaur of self is so utterly surrounded with the myths that it seems fatally doomed. Thus, in *Go Down Moses* Faulkner attempts to cure the historically depraved conscience through the use of repudiation in the case of Isaac McCaslin. Faulkner knows before he finishes the book, however, that repudiation of the historical sin and its objective manifestations will not be wholly effective. Consequently, he ends that book with another call for Moses, another call for deliverance.

The deliverance formula Faulkner subsequently supplies us with is that of *Intruder in the Dust*. Charles Mallison, in whom the overwhelming tension between the defeated past and the humiliating present begins to abate, is the first initiate of this formula, which as Faulkner prescribes it, is to look at the circumstances of one's existence and to be better in relation to them than one ordinarily might. One then confronts one's conscience and acknowledges that one can make choices which lead to freedom. The nature of this choice for the Yoknapatawpha male is best articulated by Charles' lawyer uncle, who grows, too, through the boy's experience. According to Stevens, "For every Southern boy fourteen years old, not once but whenever he wants it, there is the instant when it's still not yet two o'clock on that July afternoon in 1863. . . ."[10] Thus, there is the choice of being realistic about one's time and condition or of being foolhardy in the face of predictable doom by trying to hold on to the past.

But the matter of choice is not a simple affair. Charles does not want to choose not to be a man. Lucas knows that the boy does not even understand the choices being offered, for he has not been given a definition of manhood, but of white manhood. And while it is not without its comic elements, it is also tragic to watch this juvenile caught in a silent rage over the adult integrity projected by a true man. At every juncture during the four year period before Lucas confronts Charles with the final major task, the man counters every move the boy makes to identify with white manhood. Charles' obsession even leads him to attempt to free himself of indebtedness to Lucas by sending gifts to Lucas' wife Molly. But he is only more enraged when he finds that Lucas can still play the game better. In one instance Lucas not only sends the youth a jar of molasses in return for the gift given to him and Molly, but he sends it (most unsuitably for the boy's white consciousness which projects blacks as servants to white men and not the other way around) by a white boy on a mule.

R. W. B. Lewis has written that Faulkner came to his eminence among French intellectuals because his works provided a central context for the major issues with which these intellectuals were involved concerning "questions of existence and salvation, of the degree of rationality in the universe and the degree of man's dependence upon it."[11] This is very much the issue which holds us in suspense as we witness the atmosphere of lynching that grows around the arrest of Lucas Beauchamp for what most have come to believe was his killing of a white man. It is the opportunity for all in the community who have long resented his intractability as a black man to unleash some of the more irrational forces in their universe.

Intractable, ineffable, Lucas defies the stereotypes that the Yoknapatawphans wish to assign to black being. In maintaining his individuality he is not typical of any group, white or black. He does not come to town on Saturdays as most country people do. When he does come, it is on the weekdays and he wears a vested suit and a gold watch chain, and carries his gold toothpick in his mouth. His standard comment about his identity is that he belongs to the old McCaslin line. This establishes for him what he perceives as a more heroic heritage than can be claimed by any of the more recent whites in the area.

For Lucas, his gun, his watch chain, and the toothpick are symbols of his McCaslin lineage, although he is also always quick to assert his independence from that lineage by informing his curious public that none of it was given to him, that he bought it all himself from the old patriarch. Lucas sees himself as a natural aristocrat because he comprehends that nobility is not based on emblems of power but on the old verities of fortitude and compassion. In demonstrating his indomitable courage he exasperates the already defensive self-concept of many of the white males around him by highlighting their perversion. He pierces their veneer of manhood and they respond with frustration, feeling the weight of Lucas' being upon them, which reflects the limitations of their own power. They may be apprehensive that Lucas' attitude may be present in other blacks as well. They see in Lucas: "the Negro who said 'ma'am' to women just as any white man did and who said 'sir' and 'mister' to you if you were white but who you knew was thinking neither and he knew you knew it but who was not even waiting, daring you to make the next move, because he didn't even care."[12]

Many white Yoknapatawphans are so desperate about maintaining their self-image and are so intent upon using violence to defend it that they feel that any black person like Lucas who does not bow to their system, is a fool. When the lawyer Gavin Stevens interrogates Lucas about the trouble for which he has been arrested (and for which he might be lynched at any moment), he is awestruck that Lucas, who refuses to plead with him for mercy, will not alter his behavior even under these difficult circumstances. The boy Charles recalls hearing how Lucas, under the imminent threat of assault from a notoriously violent white man at a country store, was called a fool because he would not run. The man did not like Lucas' self-composure and Lucas did not mind acknowledging to the white man that his dislike really did not matter. Later, when the truth of Vinson Gowrie's murder is made clear, the community is even more appalled that as a black being, Lucas would be willing to risk divulging the corruption of some of the most callous of white men.

Black writers have often superbly captured the tensions involved in these type confrontations. For example, in his story, "Three Men," Ernest Gaines gives a dynamic illustration of what happens routinely when a black person finds himself confronted with a system like that of the Yoknapatawpha world. What Gaines manages to illuminate in his characterization of Proctor Lewis, who has turned himself in for a killing, is that whites expend a great deal of energy attempting systematically to humiliate the blacks. Whites do this by seeking to denigrate black being in the presence of black being itself. They also seek to hold blacks in a double bind through action and through language. The action and the language of the whites are not only heavily coded but are often rigged to explode. Gaines' character is wise in knowing that he has to weigh every word said to him in order to know exactly when and where not to answer and how the answer should be put. He is supposed to understand, above all, that once he is in a white man's presence he is at that white man's mercy. This results in very strong, residual tension between black and white being. However, for the blacks the tension is not supposed to be expressed. Even if choking to death from tension, under the old Southern behavior code the black person is not supposed to let it show.

Depicting black humanity as living with grace under pressure is a major theme for Ernest Gaines.[13] But for the white man this manner of black survival is perceived as subservience because nowhere in the white man's worldview is there any allowance for blacks to possess a quality such as grace. To say that a black man had grace would be to elevate him in stature, which would threaten the white man's sense of superiority. Consequently, the fact that the black person may perceive himself as graceful rather than obedient is dangerous.

Lucas refuses to dignify this perennial predicament which the white man would assign to black being. It is as if the black man, while pushing one heavy stone up hill, knows that there is a heavier stone already at the top waiting to crash down upon him. That which is held in the black person's mind, then, easily determines whether he lives or dies. He runs great risks for thinking too openly.

We are always conscious that the irrational runs high in the Yoknapatawpha world where race is concerned. Lucas is never thought of simply as an accused murderer caught at the scene of a crime, but as a black man who has killed a white man. In addition he is that "biggity stiff-necked stinking burrheaded Edmonds sonofabitch,"[14] who, in not feeling compelled to address white men as mister, may let death by a lynch rope become the crowning achievement of his life. Contrary to public opinion, Lucas is not so egotistical as to be blind to the nature of his crisis. Lucas knows that he has to involve himself in his own plight if he is to be acquitted. He knows he cannot rely upon Yoknapatawpha rationality, for the lynch mob has already gathered in front of the jailhouse. In fact, all of the blacks in Jefferson feel the terror in the air, and for that reason no black person is seen on the streets.

In understanding, too, that the county attorney, Gavin Stevens, is ready to convict him on the basis of his personality, Lucas has to work shrewdly to put the law on the defensive. While the Harvard and German educated attorney is critical of both "whitefolks" and "niggers," he is not so distinct from either as he would like to be. Stevens' thinking is simply more intellectualized than theirs, for he believes, too, that Lucas has killed Vinson Gowrie and assures Lucas that he does not defend "murderers who shoot people in the back."[15] Under the irrational sway of racism, Stevens also has contempt for the man who never acted the role of a "nigger" once in his life. Contempt is what he feels when he approaches the old man's cell. Stevens is indignant that in a severe crisis Lucas remains unbowed. The dignified Lucas has removed the mattress from the cell bed and spread clean newspapers over the springs to sleep on, not wanting to be contaminated by the traces of other folk. Characteristically, too, Lucas does not rise immediately upon opening his eyes and recognizing the approaching white people. Lucas has not made up his mind to die, but he has made up his mind to live with honor.

Stevens is appalled that Lucas charges him, as county attorney and citizen, with the responsibility for justice. Since, like his fellow citizens, Stevens has already convicted Lucas in his mind based on what he has heard, he is only waiting for the black man to plead for mercy, not just before the law, but also before the power of whiteness. But Lucas refuses to assume the role of victim, and refers only incidentally to the violence of his possible lynching as something to be dealt with. He knows that Stevens together with the rest of white Yoknapatawpha would be horrified to implicate the kin of a murdered white man in order to save a black man. Thus, in seeing Stevens as part of the Yoknapatawpha condition Lucas understands that he cannot even trust his own attorney with all the facts.

Charles is beginning to believe that the old wizard has forgotten him, and also believes that he is nearly free of the debt which for four years he has unsuccessfully tried to rid himself of when Lucas is arrested and brought into town by the sheriff. At this moment in the life of the community, Charles wants more than anything else to identify with the other white men who are overjoyed in seeing that the bold Lucas Beauchamp has fallen, and that they can now use him to illustrate once again that the white man reigns supreme. Thus, until he learns otherwise and is consequently embarrassed for having once more miscalculated the old black man, Charles is convinced that in the midst of his troubles with white power Lucas openly shows disdain for white men. Charles simply needs to believe that there is justification for the black man's certain and imminent punishment. The boy has inherited the racial evil of the culture, and the attempt of this evil to overtake his being is manifest in his growing struggle with his emotions.

That Lucas' hat falls to the ground as he emerges from the sheriff's car symbolizes for Charles the dethronement of the black man who seems to have always worn the hat to accentuate his pride. Lucas' loss of the hat is the complementary action to the boy's having been made to undress himself before the old man on their first meeting.

When Lucas eventually presents Charles with the ominous task by which he may gain his freedom, the central "questions of existence and salvation, of the degree of rationality in the universe and man's dependence upon it" become more overwhelming for the reader. For we do not know at this point whether this young boy, whose emotions are charged by humiliation and vengeance, is capable not only of carrying out the terrifying task of going into the night to open a grave, but whether he is first capable of transcending his racial emotions.

Because we have heard him anguish for four years over his failure to subdue Lucas, we are afraid that Charles may be too fatally imprisoned by the contempt emanating from the myth of race to make the daring choice. We know, too, that because he has been seeking to be free from Lucas, to be a white man, he feels Lucas' arrest and probable death now places that freedom within his grasp. Since his obsession with Lucas is the same as the community's: to make a "nigger" of him, the boy anticipates that what he had not been able to do alone will now be done by the mob. From his point of view, "They're going to make a nigger out of him once in his life anyway."[16] The great irony is, however, that Lucas' predicament will really help to make a man out of a boy. What greater physical or spiritual task could be required of the initiate to manhood other than to demonstrate his ability to raise the dead? Besides, Lucas' request is all the more challenging because not only does it mean violating a basic taboo about the rights of the dead; it means violating the grave of a white man; and ultimately it means violating the grave of a white man for a "nigger."

When confronted with this task all that Charles can do is respond to his instincts, listening to the conflict which has been shaped by the community and his heart. As he stands alone with Lucas in the jail he feels compassion for Lucas who is making him aware that a proud old man can honorably ask a young boy to help save his life. Even though he is not yet sure whether he can perform Lucas' task, Charles begins to understand that he as well as the old black man is locked behind bars. What he perceives is that they just happen to be on different sides. In perceiving the frightful affinity he also has with the white men forming the lynch mob, however, Charles becomes more inclined to take on Lucas' task. He knows that murder and the resulting shame are too great a price to pay for association with these white men, that he cannot have a secure emotional relationship with a lynch mob. Recognizing this, he wishes he could protect not only himself but the lynch mob too from entering upon a course of criminal deeds. Thus, because Lucas has had the strength to act like a true man, Charles' new recognitions will give him the strength to attempt the same.

In the end, Lucas, the eccentric old gentleman, is able to quip with the youth about their common experiences of falling into icy creeks, so to speak. The youth, by watching the proud old man make a candid acknowledgement of his nearly ill-fated predicament learns something about the virtue of humility. Through his experience with Lucas, Charles begins to distinguish and appreciate the difference between humility and submissiveness, and of how the latter reduces the stature of all involved. Lucas, the man of tradition, causes a rupture in traditional values. The tradition he represents, however, is that which cultivates human values in which the old nurture the young, where dignity is acknowledged in any man who lives by it, and where each shares responsibility for the other person's fate. Characteristically, Faulkner is not only seeking redemption for the captive but also for the captor. Lucas and Charles are both heroes in this novel because they do not succumb to the Yoknapatawpha terrors they face. Because they have courage, they not only make the necessary journey beyond the culturally defined boundaries but, like all great heroes and heroines, return bearing the boon for humanity.

* * *

* * *

The role Faulkner creates for Nancy Mannigoe in *Requiem For a Nun* is not only daring but difficult. It is hardly a role that one could justify in Christian or humanitarian terms. It is abstrusely philosophical and quite pagan. Yet it is the role of a redeemer who offers sacrifical love and faith in the outcome of her deed as the motive and justification for murder. Faulkner sympathizes with this struggle to create order in the corrupt world of Temple Drake. He makes Nancy the nun for whom the requiem is ultimately played, a role which is among the most compelling in Faulkner's total attempt at making a workable redemptive formula for a heroic design.

In *Intruder in the Dust* spiritual renewal is arrived at through secular means, and in the case of Dilsey in *The Sound and the Fury* the context is basically religious in the orthodox Christian sense. But in *Requiem For a Nun* Nancy takes us into an abstruse and paradoxical realm. Christian religion does provide doctrine to help elucidate its rituals and symbols, but Nancy has no system of articulation other than her ritualistic deed and her terse injunction that one must *believe*, which she reiterates after having been tried and convicted. That she has no clear means of articulation may well be due to the fact that she has stepped far beyond traditional boundaries.

In *Requiem For a Nun*, Faulkner acknowledges the social victimization of black being, but places most of the emphasis on the white woman Temple Drake Stevens as having a great moral problem. The plot of the novel in its most elemental form is concerned with what happens when Temple and her nurse maid confidante, Nancy Mannigoe stand at odds. Nancy is unable to convince Temple of the inevitable harm to be brought upon both of Temple's children if Temple runs off with her lover, taking her infant daughter by her husband but leaving the young son she has had by another man. Since her arguments with Temple go unheeded, Nancy intervenes by smothering the infant in her crib. Thus, Faulkner portrays Nancy as offering the child and herself as a sacrifice since the nurse-maid certainly knows the probable consequence of the murder will be her own death. By portraying Nancy as standing confident in her convictions,

Faulkner attempts to promote his theory and belief in the great value of individual acts of conscience. He seems to be using Nancy's sense of life to open up a vista for the salvation of mankind. But a risky opening it is.

Few would disagree that the act of infanticide is a very heavy burden to place upon any human being, especially one like Nancy who already bears the burden of having been a prostitute and dope addict. One might argue also that the image of black being has been portrayed gruesomely enough in American fiction without having to take on the additional weight of such a deed as Faulkner has Nancy commit. But it is owing to the burdensome social victimization that Nancy has suffered that Faulkner wants her as the murderer to be the focus of our sympathy. It was not out of sheer unconscionableness that he placed Nancy in such a situation. Perhaps he was trying to use her condition to accentuate his theme of sacrifice. Faulkner clarified his sense of Nancy when he described her as having led,

> that tragic life of a prostitute which she had had to follow simply because she was compelled by her environment, her circumstances, to be it. Not for profit and any pleasure, she was just doomed and damned by circumstances to that life. And despite that, she was capable within her poor dim lights and reasons of an act which whether it was right or wrong was of complete almost religious abnegation of the world for the sake of an innocent child. That was–it was paradoxical, the use of the word *Nun* for her, but I–but to me that added something to her tragedy.[17]

From Nancy's inscrutable face, one gets the impression that her reality is not universally comprehensible. There is the sense that she is absorbed by a pathos that goes far deeper than her particular identification as a black woman accused of infanticide. Her self-consciousness designates her as having witnessed a call for justice beyond that recognizable by general humanity. Thus, she does not even look at the people who surround her in the courtroom, gazing instead, unwittingly, beyond them. She has even confounded the attorney by pleading guilty when he has advised her to plead not guilty to invoke the mercy of the court.

After the murder, although she does not want pity, Nancy does speak with the expectation that her point of view will be considered. When she sits in the dark kitchen of the Stevens' house chanting her confession, she seems to think that she is making a covenant between her conscience and God, and that in so doing is making herself invincible. She goes to jail chanting her words of confession, moving into greater realization of the daring ramifications of her act. Nancy does not hope for a pardon to save her from the ultimate suffering she will have to undergo if the act is to remain purposeful for her. To wish for deliverance would imply that she has inflicted greater suffering upon the innocent child than she herself is willing to take on. For Nancy, one should not simply hope after having made a specific commitment to salvation; one should just believe. She continuously uses the word *believe*. Simply to hope is to fall short of greater spiritual possibilities. Sin can be worked out only through suffering and belief. Abstruse though it is, this is Nancy's formula for human redemption. Even the philosophical district attorney, Gavin Stevens, has to ask her for clarification of her point. What we have finally is other people standing at Nancy's feet seeking answers about human fate.

In Faulkner's search for a formula of redemption, *Requiem For a Nun* is one of his large, essential metaphors. The world of its language and deeds is so much larger than real life that we have to accept the book on its own terms if we are to have any appreciation for it. We might call the action of this novel an allegory of the experience of how one might go about working out redemption. There is the overwhelming question of spiritual authority, of whether one can justify the killing of an innocent child in seeking the salvation of another human being or even of mankind, which lingers, however.

Faulkner's difficulty in laying out a redemptive formula has a lot to do with the often obscure nature of the dialogue in the novel; consequently, critics have debated the expressiveness and non-expressiveness of the novel's characters. Michael Millgate speaks of the theatrical version of the book as "highly formal and almost ritualistic, proceeding as if in a series of merging tableaux. The writing, too, seems ponderous and heavily stylized, sadly lacking in dramatic life. . . ."[18] Yet, we might say that considering Faulkner's preoccupation with providing a ritual formula per se, the language of the novel fits as it is. For as Lawrance Thompson suggests, what we have is "the allegorical morality play: Temple is cast in the awkward role of Everyman; Gavin Stevens plays the role of Conscience; Nancy is an uncomfortable Christ; and the governor only clumsily symbolizes the ultimate Judge."[19] Still, though, the novel needs elucidation. And while Faulkner is often a genius at dramatizing the dynamics controlling a character's consciousness, the lack of this in *Requiem For a Nun* makes it difficult for one to assign credibility to the major action. We cannot help but wonder what Nancy's deliberations were as she made her decision to sacrifice the child.

Concerning the question of Nancy's motives, one must acknowledge James Baldwin's observation that there is a tension in this novel, which he reads as a "preposterous bore." The tension, he feels, is a result of Faulkner's suspicion that Nancy murdered the baby out of "pure exasperated hatred."[20] For Baldwin, it seems to be a question of what Nancy is purported to be versus what she is as defined by her social condition. He also feels that Nancy's sins make for more interesting drama than those of the dull mistress for whom she takes "such drastic means of saving."[21] Again, Baldwin's contentions appear to grow out of the fact that Nancy's inner consciousness is not dramatized. Furthermore, Baldwin asserts that "the key to the tale is to be found in who tells it,"[22] and that in his search for a redemptive formula Faulkner "may have needed to believe in a black forgiveness."[23] Baldwin sees the novel as too much like the bloody revenge of the Old Testament for anyone, even Faulkner, not to be forced to question Nancy's motives. What he calls the play's "turgidity," then, is caused primarily by Faulkner's indecisiveness, generated both by his effort to make Nancy's motive seem transcendent as well as his fear that it is not. What Baldwin is pointing to is what has been the problem of the drawing of black characters in much of American literature, specifically a disregard for the integrity and consciousness of black being.

What follows from Baldwin's argument is that Faulkner was really not clear about the true stimulus for his creation of *Requiem*. Faulkner once stated that his intention was to see what became of Temple Drake[24] and, in essence, to give Temple another chance after *Sanctuary*. Thus, to accept this as his true motivation, one has to believe in Nancy's spiritual capabilities as Faulkner himself proposes them. But Baldwin is right in saying that in "seeking to exorcise a history which is also a curse," Faulkner hopes that the old order will "redeem itself without further bloodshed . . . and without coercion."[25] And it is obvious that Faulkner, with his use of gothic effect to shock and awaken, hoped that the dramatization of a human sacrifice would halt the greater bloodshed, as Baldwin points out.

But if the Yoknapatawphans were not prepared to open a white man's grave to save a black man, it is not surprising that they would also not be able to comprehend the philosophical objectives surrounding Nancy's deed. What else but death by hanging could they hand down as a sentence since they hardly realized that Nancy consciously made a sacrifice of her own life when she took the life of the infant?

Faulkner's use of infanticide in *Requiem* certainly reminds one of his exchange with the readers of the Memphis *Commercial Appeal* about white men who murdered black children in a Mississippi home during the Christmas season of 1949 being given two life sentences and one ten year sentence. Faulkner thought he could shock the public into seeing that the men should have gotten the death penalty and into comprehending the value of all human life when he commented that when these men were paroled he hoped that if they murdered again their victim would at least be white.[26] He thought that if one used the life of a child as a sacrifical victim, then one had certainly reached the moral end. Later, too, in commenting on the murder of the adolescent black boy Emmett Till by white men in the summer of 1955 in Mississippi, Faulkner linked the value placed upon children with the conditions of human survival. Societies which murder children, for whatever reason, probably would not survive and did not deserve to.[27] Perhaps Faulkner thought that by his sacrificing a child in *Requiem* he could make the world more aware of its insensitivity.

It would be a simplification as well as an underestimation of Faulkner's art to say that the whole matter of Nancy's daring act merely relates a situation in which one expects good to come out of evil. For Nancy is not convinced, and neither is Faulkner, that either is living in a civilized world where one can always make effective appeal to the human intellect. It is for that reason redemptive covenants must be recast. Thus, in Faulkner's subsequent and even more abstruse work, *A Fable*, we see him still pursuing a redemptive formula, for an even larger reason—the eradication of war. We hear from the corps commander:

> 'It is man who is our enemy: the vast seething moiling spiritless mass of him. Once to each period of his inglorious history, one of us appears with the stature of a giant, suddenly and without warning in the middle of a nation as a dairymaid enters a buttery, and with his sword for paddle he heaps and pounds and stiffens the malleable mass and even holds it cohered and purposeful for a time. But never for always, nor even for very long: sometimes before he can even turn his back, it has relinquished, dis-cohered. . . .'[28]

In his discussion of Faulkner and Dostoevsky, Jean Weisgerber shows how Nancy follows the example of Dmitri Karamazov, performing the sacrifice "for all the 'babes,'" as Dmitri takes on suffering for all mankind.[29] Nancy feels that she shares the experience of Temple's guilt because Temple has not only to be awakened to the nature of evil, but also to the nature of good as she comes to comprehend Nancy's sacrificial act. Yet the act is indeed all a terror, and perhaps Faulkner would agree with Flannery O'Connor in saying that we look for redemption but we have forgotten the cost of it.[30]

If this world is unable to accept Nancy's humanity as a fact of existence, it could hardly empathize with the basic drama of *Requiem*. The Yoknapatawphans are preoccupied with delivering Nancy's sentence and are therefore obstructing their own experience of regeneration. If the Yoknapatawpha world would come to see that it has the opportunity to exercise moral choice and, in turn, remove itself from perennial frustration and death, Faulkner feels their lives would be more constructive and genuine. The experience would, in effect, exorcise the curse of history reflected still in the peon status of the blacks. In order for this to happen, though, someone other than black being would have to make some major sacrifices. From what Faulkner has actually shown us, consciously or not, the blacks, though pushed toward the gutter, are waiting for white being to catch up with the black being's humanity.

Weisgerber argues that Faulkner, like Dostoevsky, wants political and moral freedom to be inextricably linked. That is, Faulkner wants political freedom to be recognized as the fruit of moral freedom, and for that reason he wants the South to handle its own racial issues. To continue to divide political and moral freedom would further shatter the wholeness which man should want to achieve. If political and moral freedom were to be inextricably linked, however, the Yoknapatapha world would have to carry itself through a major catharsis, which is what Faulkner seems to have been trying to do through *Requiem*.

What separates Faulkner's treatment of black existence from most of his white Southern predecessors is that whether he is capable of successfully representing the black consciousness or not, he does acknowledge through Dilsey, Lucas, Nancy, and others the possibility of presence of mind in black being. On its most profound level the relationship between black and white being is an ontological and phenomenological problem. It is a problem of the dual relationship between the self and the other or the subject and its object. And black being in the Yoknapatawpha mind generally has the quality of otherness, of being something other than true humanity. As high priestesses and priests in Faulkner's rituals of redemption, the blacks, in a sense, have to wrest for themselves their places of responsibility since no right of authority is accorded to them by society.

Given their position of otherness in the culture, the redemptive roles assumed by the blacks are to some extent unavoidably ironic. We feel the thrust of that irony in Isaac McCaslin's acknowledgement that Sam Fathers set him free. Nancy, Sam Fathers, and Lucas are all used to instruct white initiates in self-realization and self-discovery. There is irony here because the acts of heroism carried out by these black characters do not stem so much from their being free in the society as much as from the fact that, given all circumstances, they would insist upon the freedom to assume their degree of responsibility. Of course, the greater question with respect to such heroism is whether the world itself will respond positively enough to their heroic acts, in order to keep the flame of freedom not only from smothering but to keep it growing as well. For while these heroic acts are individual, we cannot forget that for Faulkner they are formulaic, and something greater than the individual act is expected to come out of each of them. When Faulkner says that these individuals act without thought of reward, he does not precisely communicate all of what he intends. They act without expectation of immediate self-gratification, but they do hope that there will be a reward for all of mankind. By performing good themselves, all men might act better toward each other without selfish motives. Faulkner's heroic black characters act for the cause of good and for man's immortality, and they do it at the price of personal suffering.

ENDNOTES

1. William Faulkner, *Faulkner in the University: Class Conferences at the University of Virginia 1957-1958*, ed. Frederick L. Gwynn and Joseph Blotner (Charlottesville: University of Virginia Press, 1959), p. 54.
2. Ibid., p. 210.
3. Ibid., p. 18.
4. Jean Weisgerber, *Faulkner and Dostoevsky: Influence and Confluence*, trans. Dean McWilliams (Athens: Ohio State University Press, 1974).
5. *Faulkner in the University*, p. 62.
6. Ibid., p. 246.
7. William Faulkner, "The Fire and the Hearth," in *Go Down, Moses*, p. 60.
8. Cited in F. Anthony de Jovine, *The Young Hero in American Fiction* (New York: Appleton-Century Crofts, 1971), p. 19.
9. *Faulkner in the University*, pp. 141-142.
10. William Faulkner, *Intruder in the Dust* (New York: Modern Library, 1967), p. 194.
11. R. W. B. Lewis, "William Faulkner: The Hero in the New World," in *The Picaresque Saint* (New York: J. B. Lippincott, 1956), pp. 180, 187-209.
12. *Intruder in the Dust*, p. 18.
13. Interview with Charles Rowell in *Callaloo*, vol. I, no. 3, May, 1978, p. 44.
14. *Intruder in the Dust*, p. 19.
15. Ibid., p. 60.
16. Ibid., p. 32.
17. *Faulkner in the University*, p. 196.
18. Michael Millgate, *The Achievement of William Faulkner* (New York: Vintage Books, 1971), p. 223.
19. Lawrance R. Thompson, *William Faulkner: An Introduction and Interpretation* (N.Y.: Barnes and Noble, 1963), p. 132.
20. James Baldwin, *No Name in the Street* (N.Y.: Dell Publishing Co., Inc., 1973), p. 45.
21. Ibid.
22. Ibid.
23. Ibid.
24. *Faulkner in the University*, p. 96.
25. *No Name in the Street*, p. 46.
26. William Faulkner, "To the Editor of the Memphis *Commercial Appeal*," in *Essays, Speeches, and Public Letters*, p. 204. Originally published in the Memphis *Commercial Appeal*, March 16, 1950.
27. *Essays, Speeches, and Public Letters*, pp. 222-23. Originally published in the New York *Herald Tribune*, 9 September 1955.
28. William Faulkner, *A Fable* (N.Y.: New American Library, 1966), p. 47.
29. *Faulkner and Dostoevsky*, p. 290.
30. Flannery O'Connor, *Mystery and Manners*, ed. Sally and Robert Fitzgerald (N.Y.: Farrar, Strauss, and Giroux, 1961), p. 48.

VIII.

The Comic End

Comedy can be a means of mastering our disillusions when we are caught in a dishonest or stupid society.

–Wylie Sypher[1]

All that is serious in life comes from freedom.

–Henri Bergson[2]

There are several black characters who play rather genuinely comic roles in Faulkner's Yoknapatawpha world. They transcend the more stereotypic role into which many of Faulkner's black characters were cast when he yielded to the dictates of Southern tradition. This group of more artistically and humanely developed characters are not so much the object of comedy as they are the manipulators of it. They are made to function more as enhancers of Faulkner's developing vision, and not as enhancers of the old Southern way of life.

What is apparent in these particular characters, moreover, is that Faulkner grants them a high sense of awareness of their relationship to the culture which they know is juggling them. They are not as submissive in their roles as some critics have held.[3] One might say that while they are biding their time and eking out the best existence that they can for the moment, they are also maneuvering whenever possible to gain control over their immediate situations. There are three blacks who demonstrate these characteristics especially well. They are Old Job in *The Sound and the Fury*, Old Het in *The Town* and Ned McCaslin in Faulkner's last novel *The Reivers*. Almost all of Faulkner's other humorous black characters excepting a few like Tom-Tom Beauchamp, Turl, Minnie and Deacon fall, however, into the unfortunate use as objects of the white man's racial humor.

As Harry Campbell and Ruel Foster point out in their early study of Faulkner, Faulkner's multifaceted humor often functions "in a structural sense–that is, it may contribute an additional conflict to the plot and it may serve to balance other conflicts in the plot. . . ."[4] Old Job, Old Het, and Ned bring varying degrees of complication and meaning to the plots. They are not simply inserted within the stories to provide comic relief. Consequently, Faulkner has to provide them with a minimal level of sophistication.

Old job, of *The Sound and the Fury*, is not really a comic although he provides us with some comic intrigue by placing the intrepid Jason Compson in a comic situation. Old Job manages for an instant to halt Jason's momentum and in doing so gives us faith that Jason may not move forever so callously against the innocents.

Jason feels about Uncle Job as he feels about all the other "niggers." Job is just another "trifling nigger" sucking the blood out of the ambitious efforts of deserving white men like himself. What particularly irritates Jason about Old Job is that Job does not acquiesce to intimidation. Jason presumes, though, that he can make his derisive pronouncements about Job and the other black folk and have them received with silence or some other form of acquiescence. When he finds that Job is not afraid to match wits with him, his only recourse is to overthrow the rules with which he has initiated the exchange himself and to descend to the use of epithets.

Old Job intends to convey, through his salty and risky replies, that Jason deserves not more respect under any circumstances than such a man as Jason is capable of giving. Job exposes Jason to himself and to the reader as the man "whut so smart he cant even keep up wid hisself."[5] It is only on the day after their exchange that we learn the fullest implications of Job's characterizations when Jason is outraged that his niece has eloped with all the money he has stolen from her. We also know from Old Job's response exactly what Jason's standing is in the business in which his mother still believes he has a share. In making his pronouncement Job overrules the cultural tenet that says that any white man stands above every black one:

> "I works to suit de man whut pays me Sat'dy night," he says. "When I does dat, it dont leave me a whole lot of time to please other folks."[6]

We applaud Job in this moment just as we laugh at Jason. At the same time that we applaud Job, however, we cannot help feeling anxious for him because Jason's earlier movements in the story have been so intensely acerbic that we are surprised that Jason is not outraged. Yet Job knows well that the tension is there, and he knows too that he has helped to quicken Jason's fire. He makes no obsequious attempts to clean up what he has said for he has said it all in full resolve. But he shifts the method of his response to a more imaginative level of folk idiom to counter Jason's scorn.

In Job's shift to the use of the folk idiom which allegorizes about the life of the boll weevil, Jason is eased into thinking that Job is becoming more amenable. But in talking about the boll weevil, who does not have a porch to sit on to watch others work and who never has Saturdays off, Job is obviously using the comic opportunity to set forth his criticism of the system of racial peonage. Moreover, in his use of the imaginative folk idiom, he manages to exert a control over Jason which Jason thinks he has quelled; for Jason, who leaves very little room for the fertile imagination, has to shift to the structure which Job provides in order to make his own hard-nosed reply. Job walks off and drives away from Jason, but all the anxiety the reader has undergone during these fragile exchanges is symbolized in the wobbling, insecure wheel which Old Job has been trying to bolt to his mule-drawn wagon.

Job brings a challenge to Jason's authority which resounds with stinging resentment. He defends himself and assails his antagonist in the same moment. Jason who would always be in control becomes the butt for our laughter. So preoccupied is Jason with himself, he overlooks the total reality. Rigidity is his vice. He ignores, as with his perception of Job, the possibility of distinctions between the actual people and the functions he wishes to give them. Job ultimately makes Jason comic by seizing, in his understated manner, the opportunity to make the presumptuous king of the feast become instead the main meal of the feast. By daring to be spontaneous, Job undercuts Jason's mechanical and illusory orientation of how the world should operate. Job helps us to see that in Faulkner's larger comic vision, the arrogant do arrange their own fall.

Whereas Job operates more by way of understatement to create comic effect, Old Het and Ned McCaslin operate mostly by exaggeration. Empirical minded, as are most truly comic characters, Old Het generally works to see how she can come out on the bright side of each situation. That is, like most comic characters she is very serious about the range of freedom she has for manipulating, though harmlessly, people and events. She moves about the town of Jefferson with a sense of revelry that disturbs the world order. We take delight in her machinations because not only does she usually triumph but she does so with impunity even after having broken some notable taboo. Old Het is an agent helping us to see life as Faulkner often saw it, that is, as a spectacle of human events reminiscent of a sideshow with one round of repetitious foibles after another.

Old Het has a clear sense of her situation and disposition, and she uses both to her advantage. She is a somewhat mechanized, but authentic and genuinely funny character in the overall comic framework of *The Town.* The vivacious old woman of unknown age, though thought to be anywhere between seventy and a hundred, lives in the Jefferson poorhouse. However, she spends most of her time on the square or on the road between the houses of the townspeople, occupying their time if she manages to catch them before they lock themselves in. She carries a shopping bag in which to collect her alms, and the hallmarks of her attire are tennis shoes and an ancient hat long worn and handed down from one of the long dead prominent townspeople. A lot of her time is spent at Mrs. Hait's who is a mutual joker. But Old Het also considers the white woman a good prospect for alms since Mrs. Hait was widowed and collected eight thousand dollars when her husband and five of I. O. Snopes's mules were killed on the railroad tracks. Of course, Old Het expects to get only the dribblings from Mrs. Hait's wealth. It is the Snopeses, as usual, who are after the big money.

Because we know the ways of the Snopeses, and have an adequate sense of the undaunted character of Old Het, we look, during the course of events, to see some form of confrontation in which Het will maneuver to hold her own with these key manipulators of the Yoknapatawpha world. We have a great deal of emotional investment in this old woman because she does confront and achieve superiority over people like I. O. Snopes who stand as objects of our own derision.

Old Het has such an affecting appreciation for a good laugh and is so genuinely lighthearted that she never seems to succumb to situations. For her, possessing an understanding of the whimsical nature of life is part of the basic equipment one needs to survive. Because she possesses this understanding, as Ned McCaslin also does, she has integrity as a human being and is not reduced to simple buffoonery. Thus, one is more inclined to laugh with her than at her. Moreover, the laughter that she generates is more social than racial in that even the whites in Jefferson perceive her as a master of her art.

It is Old Het who tells the story of the mule setting Mrs. Hait's house afire to Ratliff who in turn tells the story to Charles Mallison. The second and third tellers, Ratliff and Charles, relate her use of highly figurative language. Old Het has apparently enjoyed creating the language with which to narrate the episode. She is obviously quite conscious of her own humorous personality. She says that one incident between the chickens and the mule was just like something out of the Bible, but she meditatively revises her image to be a great deal more definite and provocative by suggesting that a "hoodoo witch's Bible" would be more probable.

A perpetual banana eater, Het is as comfortable in approaching the erudite Gavin Stevens with a crumpled ten dollar bill for his hire as Mrs. Hait's attorney as she is shrewd in managing to give the overcautious I. O. Snopes money for his errant mule which he has insisted he would not take. We marvel at the old woman's attempts to witness the total episode which is certain to ensue since a Snopes is involved. She is not one bit perturbed by the notorious I. O. Snopes, of the most ruthlessly scheming clan of all the county, who wants to insist that she leave their company when he is ready to talk business with Mrs. Hait. Snopes does not address Het directly, but she does speak directly to him as she sits in the makeshift kitchen of the barn, turning the ham in the skillet:

> "Lord, honey," old Het said. "If you talking at me. Dont you mind me. I done already had so much troubles myself that

> listening to other folks kind of rests me. You gawn talk what you wants to talk; I'll just set here and mind this ham."[7]

Highly skilled in the language of begging, Old Het has a special line of thanks ready for Gavin Stevens when she asks him for a dime to buy snuff and he gives her a quarter. She knows what appeals to people of his station. She has her own definition of what she means to the community of Jefferson, and has wittily concocted a logical explanation for her support at the hands of its people. Although they think of her as a beggar, Het says she is really a supreme servant to the community. In her own humorous terms, it is because of her needs that community people give; and according to the Bible, it is only through giving to her that they are blessed. She provides them with an opportunity for God's grace, she would say.

Old Het's agile manner of being able to reduce or raise all levels of life to the comic is aptly captured by the way she maneuvers about at seventy years old (or more) in tennis shoes. Her interactions demonstrate how the too serious king pin may be knocked over by a trifle of humor. As a force in Faulkner's comic vision Het suggests that the excessive leads to the tragic. Excess does not seem to leave one space enough to breathe independently, and it is essentially freedom from the excessive and restricting that Old Het always seems to be pursuing.

Faulkner's final book, *The Reivers*, is a comic novel in which the black man Ned McCaslin plays a major role. It is a fact that by Ned's comic manipulations and foibles the comic plot of the novel is sustained, including the more serious high comedy aspect of the plot which involves the initiation of the white boy Lucius Priest into adult life. Even though Ned may run into a number of pitfalls, one ultimately feels, however, that he is operating upon a logic of his own. And like all great comic characters he possesses enough of the quality of emotional disinterestedness not to become vanquished by his own folly.

We watch Ned as he becomes the first one to look at Boss Priest's new automobile when the car's caretaker, Boon Hogganbeck, opens the garage door. Ned's first move is to sit behind the steering wheel, the point of control, which he does without hesitation until Boon almost immediately runs him away. Like Old Het, Ned has a good sense of his own character, and therefore feels that he is entitled to a degree of privilege, also never allowing any to forget that he more than any is a direct male descendant of Lucius Quintus Corothers, the family founder. Ned believes that he will have a transfer of status from that of coachman to that of operator of the mechanized vehicle. But once he realizes that he has lost out in competition to Boon Hogganbeck, who would hardly let anybody else tamper with Boss Priest's machine anyway, he comes to an implicit agreement with Mr. Priest that he will desist from berating the machine if he is not asked to do any kind of service for it. Making the agreement is somewhat irritating to Ned, however, because he knows in actuality that Boon would not even permit him to wash the car if he wanted to. When he is extra-conscious of his comic manipulations of the people around him, Ned colors the situation with sarcasm and uses a brand of laughter, "Hee, hee, hee," which Faulkner reserves for him and which Boon sometimes mocks to show Ned that he does not always have the last word.

Ned is as much of a rascal as he is genuinely good-hearted. Both aspects of his character are reflected in his habit of carrying the Bible and a pint of whiskey in his attaché case. Since he watches everything that goes on around the Priest's place, he readily suspects that Boon and the young boy of the Priest family, Lucius, are going to take advantage of the absence of the heads of the family (who have gone to Lucius's maternal grandfather's funeral) to make a surreptitious trip to Memphis. Once he notices this, he turns all of his efforts towards joining the expedition. The boy and Boon are well on their way along the road to Memphis before Ned breaks wind and is discovered cramped beneath the seat with his attaché case. Naturally, Ned is ready with his justification of his right to travel, too. Although he is well aware that he lives in a society built upon racial exclusion, it is part of his comic genius to be able to maneuver his way into the heart of the party.

As we become involved in studying Ned's maneuverings, we see how he makes the point of his authority by arguing that the automobile belongs to Boss and that he is closer kin to the Boss than Lucius, the grandson, while Boon is not related to the family at all. Boon assumes that he is to make plans for accommodating Ned when they arrive in Memphis, but Ned ridicules his presumption and assures him that he has personal friends in the city and that he has his own plans for his stay there. Of course, in his self-assuredness, the first thing he does when he arrives in Memphis and leaves Boon and the boy Lucius is to swap old Boss Priest's automobile for a reputedly inept and stolen race horse. In doing so he sets the destiny of the trip and generates many of the circumstances of the novel's plot which lead to the initiation of Boss Priest's eleven year old grandson into the meaning of making choices in the adult world. But in Ned's own estimate, it is all done to rescue a friend in trouble, Bobo Beauchamp his black acquaintance from Jefferson, and to reestablish his reputation as a man who knows horses.

Ned is well aware when they leave home that they will have to return the car to Jefferson and give an account of their trip to Boss Priest and his son Maury. Later, in the town of Parsham where they hold the race, he thinks they might even have to take more than the automobile to Jefferson in order to "sugar back Boss Priest's nature."[8] Yet he feels that this great adventure is worth the risk of the old man's anger and is very comfortable in his expectations of total enjoyment until he learns about the muddy work he must become involved in with his Sunday clothes to get the automobile through the mudhole called Hell's Creek Bottom. He does his best to evade the work and to inject humor into their circumstance, and thus to have maximum control over the situation until he perceives that the true hell is not the slough itself but the sinister design of a man who plougs it purposely and efficiently in order to exploit travelers in automobiles who must hire his assistance at exorbitant rates in order to get through. In this moment of confrontation and recognition Ned's humor weakens, and we find ourselves in the midst of a comic void.

Ned sets up many of his schemes as if he is undertaking some great ceremony. Having this inclination toward the ceremonial he is a prime candidate for making a comic stumble. Like most human beings who become preoccupied with the ceremonial he loses sight of his identity as a dynamic rather than simply a formal or static being. Surely in comedy all that is required is one faulty move to set in motion a series of hilarious and negative effects as Ned does when he swaps the automobile for the horse. But since he possesses some of the daring qualities of the errant knave, Ned is prepared to take risks, believing that ultimately he will be able to talk and connive his way out of any bind. His is the true comic vision which asserts that situations are reversible. This is what is implied in his humorous and creative phrasing of what might have to be done to "sugar back Boss Priest's nature." Yet at some point confidence men in comedy such as Ned will have to be seen as helpless, no matter how much we might already have been assured of their resilience.

Ned thinks that he is a specialist in the psychology of animals and men. Filled with self-confidence, he believes that the horse he has traded for the car will run like the legendary mule which years back he contrived to have foaled from one of Zack McCaslin's prize mares and the farm jack. When Boon accuses him of having a stolen horse, he replies that the same is true of the automobile. He knows the advantage which he has over Boon in gaining his assistance to carry out his scheme. He knows the racial operations of the culture, too; therefore, he considers using the white boy Lucius to get the stolen horse across town while he follows on a mule, a role which he assumes the white people will deem to be in order. He also advertises the race as being run by the white man Boon Hogganbeck. Ned carries out the details of his operation so secretively and quickly that Lucius is amazed when a black youth walks easily and familiarly up to them in the town of Parsham where they have taken the horse by train through Boon's arrangements, and greets him, "Howdy, Mr. McCaslin."[9] The youth, Lycurgus, is the grandson of Uncle Parsham. It is Lycurgus who later comments to Lucius on Ned's determined nature. "When Mr. McCaslin make up his mind to do something, he gonter do it. . . . Aint you found out that about him yet?"[10]

Ned does have insight into the general manners of the public. As members of the crowd make their preparations for the race, he watches their actions and provides his own humorous assessment:

> "Folks is already kind of dropping by Possum's lot like they wasn't noticing themselves doing it, likely trying to find out who it is this time that still believes that horse can run a race. So likely we gonter have a nice crowd tomorrow."[11]

If Ned is taken for a simple fool, he certainly knows how to exploit such an occasion. That is, he knows the fool's province which, as Wylie Sypher points out, is all of life.[12] Thus, a comic but very serious effect is created when Ned encounters the law enforcement officers. Their roles are clearly reversed and Ned the designated offender and inferior demonstrates his superior insight into the true nature of the law. He exposes the sham in the logic peculiar to the law officers, thus rendering their rationale absurd. Ned holds a mirror up to them which a person of his station was not thought to have the intelligence nor the daring to do.

When Ned and Boon are arrested at the race track after running the first of their three projected races, Ned asks the officers for their reasons. He knows beforehand, however, that he probably will not get a direct answer since the representatives of the law hold the view that by sanction of the society he is of a group with no rights which have to be respected and that he should be kept that way. Nevertheless, Ned purposely asks to be given reasons. Faulkner has Ned do this so that he may expose Ned's and Boon's relationship as citizens to the law as the law is represented and carried out. Faulkner's additional intention is to use Ned to expose the particular racial dimension involved in a black man's encounter with the spokesmen of the law. The officers tell Ned that they will let him read the reasons. This is their way of seeking to intimidate and humiliate him for his illiteracy, but their actions lead humorously to their own greater degradation with an obvious indictment of their abuse of civil responsibilities. These representatives of the law are therefore depicted as being as intimidating as the sinister man with the mules back at the mudhole.

In the earlier encounter with the sheriff called Butch in the town of Parsham, Ned's outspokenness is thought by Butch to be out of place for a black man. For that reason he wants to know if Ned is familiar, not so much with the law, but with what the law specificially means in relation to a black man. Ned assures him that he is familiar with the law, and later presents an incisive psychological summation of the aberrant form of law which Butch stands for. His scathing summary is in line with Faulkner's long-held belief which he had articulated and represented very poignantly at least thirty years earlier in Percy Grimm, the deputy who leads the lynch mob in *Light in August*. The generally sadistic nature and character of scores of Southern sheriffs is vociferously indicated also in *The Wild Palms*. This type is rarely challenged except by the character significantly named Hope Hampton, the sheriff of *Intruder in the Dust* who has no one in the town who will accompany him into the vicious region of Beat Four to arrest one of the Gowries for two murders including the act of fratricide for which Lucas Beauchamp's life has been put in danger.

Along with Ned's there is also a challenge to the law as represented by the constable who recognizes, or at least gives consideration to, Ned's wise comment that there is somewhere that the law ends and just human beings begin. Ned makes his pronouncement upon officers like Butch to the venerable Uncle Parsham, who has watched Butch's display and briefly voiced his own contempt. According to Ned:

> "A man that never had nothing in it nohow, one of them little badges goes to his head so fast it makes yourn swim too. . . . Except it aint the badge so much as that pistol, that likely all the time he was a little boy, he wanted to tote, only he knowed all the time that soon as he got big enough to own one, the law wouldn't let him tote it. Now with that badge too, he dont run no risk of being throwed in jail and having it took away from him; he can still be a little boy in spite of he had to grow up. The risk is, that pistol gonter stay on that little boy mind just so long before some day it gonter shoot at something alive before he even knowed he aimed to."[13]

Ned, as we see, is more than antics. Beyond all of his mischief, he insists that the boy Lucius be courteous toward all. And even though he is amused by Lucius's sexual innocence he seeks to protect him from overexposure to the brothel and the sexually precocious boy Otis. Also, the motive behind his trading the automobile for the race horse was not simply to contrive a way to make himself some money at the race. Part of his undivulged motive has been to assist his friend Bobo Beauchamp in getting out of financial troubles. True to his comic nature, however, Ned never considers sacrificing his neck for Bobo Beauchamp if their racing plans do not follow through. Ned's final serious gesture is to give the boy Lucius the guidance, however whimsical, he feels the boy is yearning for regarding the decision the young morally conscious boy has to make about the money won gambling on the horse.

There is a very small but highly significant factor which makes the plot of this novel operative, if not always credible. This has to do with the way that Ned perceives Boon, and it is to some degree, a racial factor. Ned never refers to Boon as "mister," as the boy Lucius points out before they leave home and as Miss Reba confirms while they are in Memphis. Ned explains that he will not call Boon "mister" until he deserves it. But he follows this with his jeering laughter. The laughter suggests that Boon is too simple ever to come to deserve it, and Boon's simplicity of character is certainly emphasized throughout the story. That Boon is a mixed-breed of white and Chickasaw is also well established at the beginning of the novel, and Ned probably takes him as closer to his own caste, and therefore as less of a threat, than he would be if he were pure white. For this reason, Ned dares to pull many more of his stunts.

Ned is obviously an outgrowth of Simon who has appeared thirty-three years earlier in *Flags in the Dust*, but with regard to the artistic integrity of Faulkner's portrayal of him, Ned has greater affinity to Deacon who appears in *The Sound and the Fury*. Like Ned, Deacon has a trickster-type personality, but he is also a good friend and serviceable contact for the Southern aliens who come to study at Harvard. By manipulating the stereotype of himself as the black guardian, to which the Southerner like Quentin can identify and respond, he has created his own post as receiver of the young Southern gentlemen. Deacon would meet the train in his special patched suit and speak the language of the plantation until he conquered his new arrival. Like Ned he is mischievous but not malicious. Like Ned he is also very conscious of the racial myths whites have created and perpetuated about him. But unlike Ned, his love of protocol and ceremonial markings and his ambitious political plans bring to him an aura of pathos. Deacon is candid in presenting his view that Southern white folk are fine except that a black man finds it rather hard to live with them. But he is not so candid to reveal that the Northern white man must be somewhat similar, thus making for the nearly grotesque design of his life.

Highlighting the comic end of life is an essential part of Faulkner's vision concerning the outcome of the Yoknapatawpha world. This vision when articulated in its best form is certainly not free to exclude black being whether, as we have seen, the comic ramifications spring from particular black personalities or from situations directly related to the relationships between black and white being in this world. In certain situations, the blacks as underdogs must exploit their own comic ingenuity simply to endure the white presumption and arrogance. In these instances, as was demonstrated in the interchange between Old Job and Jason, the comic realm of the racial world hinges so closely upon the tragic that that which would be humorous often cauterizes the reader's emotions. In other instances, however, as with Old Het and Ned, Faulkner's comedy functions as it generally does throughout his works to pinpoint the irrational, ridiculous, vain, and unenlightened aspects of human behavior. When black characters are depicted with comic integrity they certainly promote this aspect of Faulkner's vision, and furthermore they definitely enhance his art.

ENDNOTES

1. Wylie Sypher, *Comedy* (New York: Doubleday Anchor Books, 1956), p. 245. I am deeply indebted in this discussion to the classic essays "Laughter" by Henri Bergson and "An Essay on Comedy" by George Meredith as well as Mr. Sypher's own essay "The Meanings of Comedy," all of which are collected in Sypher's *Comedy*.
2. Sypher, p. 111.
3. " . . . We see too many who content themselves as servants in white families" writes Ward L. Miner in "The Southern White-Negro Problem Through the Lens of Faulkner's Fiction." *Journal of Human Relations*, 14 (Fourth Quarter, 1966), p. 508; "The Negro character (in Faulkner's works) who is created with no social protest in mind is ultimately most satisfying as a human being," writes Elmo Howel. ". . . In the normal development of his saga he could not very well avoid the countless Negroes who live and work and play with no special grudge against the order of things," in "A Note on Faulkner's Negro Characters." *Mississippi Quarterly* (Fall, 1958).
4. Harry Modean Campbell and Ruel E. Foster, *William Faulkner: A Critical Appraisal (Norman: University of Oklahoma Press, 1951), p. 109.*
5. William Faulkner, *The Sound and the Fury* (New York: Vintage Books, 1963), pp. 311-312.
6. Ibid., p. 235.
7. William Faulkner, *The Town* (New York: Vintage Books, 1961), p. 237.
8. William Faulkner, *The Reivers* (New York: Vintage Books, 1966), p. 219.
9. Ibid., p. 165.
10. Ibid., p. 228.
11. Ibid., p. 205.
12. Sypher, p. 231.
13. Ibid., pp. 185-186.

IX.

Faulkner's Struggle With Racial Chaos and National Destiny

I began to see that though we may, as we acquire new knowledge, live through new experiences, examine old memories, gain the strength to tear the frame from us, yet we are stunted and warped and in our lifetime cannot grow straight again anymore than can a tree, put in a steel-like twisting frame when young, grow tall and straight when the frame is torn away at maturity.

–Lillian Smith
KILLERS OF THE DREAM[1]

One of William Faulkner's distinctions as an artist lies in the fact that he revealed through his act of writing and speaking, not only that he grieved for the human predicament and human weaknesses, but also that he felt a part of them. But by laying himself as naked in this acknowledgment as he could find the strength to, he evolved toward the belief that mankind, including his Southern homeland, doing likewise could redeem itself from its heritage of racial chaos.

The development of Faulkner's racial feelings as reflected in his extra-fictional statements appears to have three major phases. Aspects of these phases often run parallel to the general representations of black being in his fiction but are also sometimes different. His early period, up through the 1930s, provides the fewest public or extra-fictional statements. This period is clearly racist in some respects and just ambiguous in others. Yet it is also the period in his fiction from which emerge some of Faulkner's strongest black portraits: Dilsey, Rider, Christmas, and finally, Clytie. In his middle phase, the 1940s and early 1950s, the voice of Faulkner as a public speaker on racial issues becomes courageously straightforward and articulate. This is the period during which Faulkner's growing civil interests are also deeply tied up with his conviction that the United States, weakened by its arrogance and presumption with regard to its own dispossessed native black constituency, would not be able to stave off mounting world opposition to capitalistic democracy, especially from the Communists. He was also coming to view American racism as an absolute threat and cultural tragedy. His final phase, arising mostly as a result of pressure from both liberals and conservatives, culminated in a great deal of personal confusion. At moments Faulkner seems to have retreated into some of the old traditional ways of Southern thinking, the victim of what Lillian Smith called the old "stunted and warped" existence. It is the period marking the waning of his artistic and public voice.

In his late twenties Faulkner formed a literary friendship with the noted writer Sherwood Anderson. The relationship eventually ended in antagonism, with a tinge of envy on the part of the older artist Anderson for the younger Faulkner, but the association did prove to be very advantageous for Faulkner's literary career.[2] While friends, Faulkner and Anderson entertained each other with numerous tall tales. Out of the tension arising from their different class backgrounds, Anderson was quite susceptible to believing what must have been one of Faulkner's most absurd racial fables. According to Anderson, Faulkner not only stated but believed that sterility resulted from the first mixing of the African and Anglo-Saxon. In a character sketch of Faulkner, Anderson wrote:

> . . . there is in him also a lot of the same old bunk about the South. . . . He contended with entire seriousness that the cross between the white man and the Negro woman always resulted, after the first crossing, in sterility. He spoke of the cross between the jack and the mare that produced the mule and said that, as between the white man and the Negro woman, it was the same.[3]

In his biography of Faulkner, Joseph Blotner writes in response to Anderson's report that "it is not impossible that Faulkner, at twenty-seven, may have believed this, but it seems unlikely. Evidence to the contrary had been around all his life."[4] However, as Lillian Smith has pointed out, one peculiarity of the traditional Southern personality is that it is replete with contradiction, especially where race is concerned.[5]

Surely all Southerners did not wholeheartedly embrace the racial myths, but all, including Faulkner, had to face the fact that the world in which they lived was established upon highly imaginative notions of racial distinction. It is out of this frame of reference that Faulkner seems to be speaking in an interview published in the New York *Herald Tribune* in the Fall of 1931.[6] This is the first known printed interview of Faulkner's career. While some may claim that the traditionalist and reactionary statements printed in this interview are not exactly as Faulkner gave them (and they very well may not be), one cannot ignore the similarity to his most controversial interview, given during the initial desegregation efforts in Alabama in the mid-1950s.

If the words of the *Herald Tribune* article are indeed his, Faulkner rationalized paternalistically the refusal and irresponsibility on the part of the white man to release the blacks from peonage. Obviously geared toward sensationalism, the caption reads "'Slavery Better for the Negro,' says Faulkner." Slavery is not, however, the major subject of the interview. It is mainly about Faulkner, the young writer. Without doubt, the interviewer's questions about the South were capriciously designed to play up the Southerner's quaintness. Yet the language of the answers, the paradoxical phrasing, is characteristically Faulknerian.

While telling the interviewer that he did not care much for talking, Faulkner nevertheless responded with his own brand of curt self-assuredness, which appears as much an effort to present a posture as to present the truth. According to the interviewer,

> Mr. Faulkner thinks the Southern Negroes would be better off under the conditions of slavery than they are today. He pictures a kind of 'benevolent autocracy' as the ideal condition for the Negroes, though he admits such a system would not be sound theoretically. "Facts don't fit theories very often, but I never heard or read about a lynching in the slave days."[7]

In this assertion Faulkner embraced the typical paternalism of slavocracy. When asked if he thought slavery would soften the white slave owners, Faulkner said, "Most white men wouldn't need very much softening."[8] And yet the best way to protect the black man from lynching by white men is to put the black men back into slavery! "Negroes are childlike in many of their reactions," he is reported to have said.

There is a twenty year interim between Faulkner's New York *Herald Tribune* interview and his later public position on the racial situation in the South. In the meantime, he was a farmer, writer and occasional scriptwriter in Hollywood. In his everyday life Faulkner continued to be personally involved with blacks as he had been since his birth. He had a big farm in Mississippi and his tenants were black. In 1940 he delivered a funeral sermon in his parlor for his old nurse from childhood, Caroline Barr, called Mammy Callie. He referred to her in the sermon as "a fount of authority over my conduct and of security for my physical welfare."[9] Two years later he would memorialize her again in his dedication of *Go Down, Moses*.

Faulkner also corresponded with Richard Wright during this period, praising the great artistic potential shown in Wright's *Native Son*. He told Wright he thought his later book, *Black Boy*, was beneficial in that it said what needed to be said. But he thought that because *Black Boy* had not been executed with the artistic power which was apparent in *Native Son*, the book risked being not as influential as it could have been with people who were not already sympathetic with the current racial situation of the blacks.[10] These are the words of Faulkner's middle years. That he could give such implicit praise to highly forceful and racially indicting *Native Son* suggests a great deal of maturation on his part. The mature viewpoint which had begun to express itself through revelations of the intransigent and complex mental make-up of the Southern mind in such works as "Dry September," *Light in August* and *Absalom, Absalom!* was now preparing to articulate itself outside the fiction.

In the fall of 1940, Faulkner wrote to one of his agents about "the condition of this destruction bent world" with so-called democracies trying to destroy each other. He ended by saying, "Anyway it will make nice watching when the axis people start gutting one another."[11] In 1943, Faulkner expressed his feelings at length in a letter to his stepson, Malcolm Franklin, who was in military training in Arkansas, on the predicament of the black soldier. The letter reads somewhat like a manifesto:

> There is a squadron of negro pilots. They finally got congress to allow them to learn how to risk their lives in the air. They are in Africa now, under their own negro lt. colonel, did well at Pantelleria, on the same day a mob of white men and white policemen killed 20 negroes in Detroit. Suppose you and me and a few others of us lived in the Congo, freed seventy-seven years ago by ukase; of course we cant live in the same apartment hut with the black folks, nor always ride in the same car nor eat in the same restaurant, but we are free because the Great Black Father says so. Then the Congo is engaged in War with the Cameroon. At last we persuade the Great Black Father to let us fight too. You and Jim say are flyers. You have just spent the day trying to live long enough to learn how to do your part in saving the Congo. Then you come back down and are told that 20 of your people have just been killed by a mixed mob of civilians and cops at Little Poo Poo. What would you think?
>
> A change will come out of this war. If it doesn't, if the politicians and the people who run this country are not forced to make good the shibboleth they glibly talk about freedom, liberty, human rights, then you young men who don't live through it will have died in vain.[12]

In 1947 when the Veterans Club of Oxford, Mississippi, was discussing a memorial plaque to be placed in the courthouse yard for the dead veterans of the first and second world wars, some discussion arose among the citizenry as to whether the names of the dead black veterans should also be included on the plaque with the whites. Some of the citizens were outraged by the notion of their inclusion. Faulkner, advocating the inclusion of the names, also expressed himself on the issue in the town newspaper, *The Oxford Eagle*, with his own brand of rhetorical cynicism. He wrote that he was sure that the city fathers would not bow to the wishes of the white supremacists, even if the fathers reasoning would be that "the only time they're not niggers is when they're dead." The names of the blacks were indeed included but only after a compromise was reached. They were separated from the whites by a caption reading, "Of the Negro Race."[13]

As is evident in his letter to his stepson, Faulkner was moving into a new way of thinking, the distinguishing feature of which was a conviction that the black American must have equality. This equality was to be the same in definition for both the black and white audiences which he addressed. As he expressed it, he meant "equal right and opportunity to make the best one can of one's life within one's capacity and capability, without fear of injustice or oppression or threat of violence."[14] The blacks should be allowed to have a feeling of responsibility the same as the white members of the segregated Delta Council or any others who considered themselves Americans. Addressing the Delta Council in 1952, Faulkner reminded his fellow white citizens of "the duty of man to be responsible if he wishes to remain free."[15] This was the fundamental thesis of his public position, and with this he set out at the beginning of the 1950s to see what he could do in addition to his writing for the South's redemption and ultimately for the preservation of democratic ideals in America. Youth and the individual have the power to save Man,[16] he would say again and again to young audiences for the last decade or so of his life.

Beginning in 1950, Faulkner used the "Letters to the Editor" column of the Memphis *Commercial Appeal* as well as his addresses to various groups, as his primary platform to set forth his opinions about racial injustice. Especially in his letters to the *Commercial Appeal* he addressed the issues that became focal points for change: the state's legal system and educational policy. But behind all his arguments, there was always his fundamental concern with the Southern mode of thinking which he explored extensively in his writing. And although public school desegregation became his primary issue, there were other issues too which provoked his vehemence. His declarations appeared in the *Commercial Appeal*, for example, in protest against the sentence handed down by a jury upon three white men for the murder of three black children in Mississippi in January 1950. Most of the jurors had argued for the death penalty for one of the men, but the trial concluded with two life sentences and one ten year sentence.[17]

Some Mississippians were proud that the court had at least reached the point where they would convict a white person under such circumstances. But Faulkner felt that the verdict was not just and he used the occasion of his letter to the *Commercial Appeal* to give a warning:

> All native Mississippians will join in commending Attala County. But along with the pride and the hope we had better feel concern and grief because what we did was not enough; it was in effect only a little better than nothing, not for justice nor even punishment, just as you don't mete out justice or punishment to the mad dog or the rattlesnake; grief and shame because we have gone on record with the outland people who are so quick to show us our faults and tell us how to remedy them, as having put the price of murdering three children at the same as robbing three banks or stealing three automobiles.[18]

He went further to make a haunting pronouncement concerning the two jurors whom he referred to as having saved the lives of the murderers.

> It is to be hoped that whatever reasons they may have had for saving him, will be enough so that they can sleep at night free of nightmares about the ten or fifteen or so years from now when the murderer will be paroled or pardoned or freed again, and will of course murder another child, who it is to be hoped–and with grief and despair one says it–will this time at least be one of his own color.[19]

One year later Faulkner wrote again about the death sentence given to a black man, Willie McGee. McGee's sentence was the example of the dual legal system in which the death penalty in a case of rape was reserved for the black man. Faulkner did not believe that the white woman had been a rape victim, and he certainly did not believe that McGee should be executed.[20] His position was taken by the Southern reactionaries to be a betrayal of the cause of southern white womanhood and an indication that Faulkner had aligned himself with the Communists who had been accused of creating much of the publicity surrounding the case.[21] McGee was executed nevertheless.

In his lengthy essay, "Mississippi" (1954), in which he wrote of his love for his native locale, Faulkner also stated in unequivocal terms what there was about Mississippi that he hated most:

> But most of all he hated the intolerance and injustice: the lynching of Negroes not for the crimes they committed but because their skins were black (they were becoming fewer and fewer and soon there would be no more of them but the evil would have been done and irrevocable because there should never have been any); the inequality; the poor schools they had when they had any, the hovels they had to live in unless they wanted to live outdoors: who could worship the white man's God but not in the man's church; pay taxes in the white man's courthouse but couldn't vote in or for it; working by the white man's clock but having to take his pay by the white man's counting. . . .[22]

In his extra-fictional statements Faulkner consistently held that racial intolerance had its roots in economics. He played down the fears of race mixing. He said that it was not so much the economic dependency of white landowners upon black labor as it was the fear by the white that the black man whom he wanted to believe was his inferior was really his capable rival.[23] Faulkner argued that all the other arguments, like that of miscegenation, were really secondary factors used only to cloud the real issues which were economic.[24] He reinterated this point many times for nearly a dozen years, so much so that at times the point of view sounded monolithic.

Faulkner was in Rome at the end of the summer of 1955 when the fourteen-year-old black youth, Emmett Till, who had come to Mississippi on a vacation from Chicago, was murdered by two white men.[25] Faulkner reminded his fellow white citizens that the white man could no longer take unscrupulous advantage of power as he once had. No county in Mississippi was an entity unto itself, and neither was Mississippi. The county would not survive without the state, and in the same way Mississippi could not survive. America itself could not survive unless the whole white race acted responsibly. He feared that the white race had forgotten that it made up only one fourth of the earth's population. If the white man would not refrain from criminal acts for humane reasons, he should at least recognize that he could not afford to jeopardize himself by committing such crimes against a majority of colored peoples.[26] But again Faulkner's words were spoken to no avail. The two men were exonerated.

Before the larger body of the Southern community took an active stand on the issues involving desegregation of the public schools, Faulkner had already made his position clear. He voiced his opinions on the injustices in education and their origins just as he had done with the particular instances of illegality and criminality committed in Mississippi. By the fall of 1955, when he made his statement on the Emmett Till murder, he had spoken of racial injustices with confidence and conviction in the nations of Europe and in Japan. For the most part, the whole educational system in Mississippi was in very poor condition, he wrote in a public letter. It was virtually a "sort of community of state-supported baby sitters."[27] This made him "unable to sit quiet and watch it held subordinate in importance to an emotional state concerning the color of human skin."[28]

Faulkner argued that the educational system was not good enough to mitigate the educational thirst of whites who had always had more educational advantage than the blacks. If this were so then the system must have been substantially more inadequate for the blacks who had been denied educational opportunities for so long. He said that it was ridiculous for Mississippians to try to raise additional taxes to support a dual school system neither half of which would be "good enough for anybody."[29]

Four years before the Supreme Court ruling on school desegregation, Faulkner had been asked for his opinion on a statement published in *The Mississippian*, the University of Mississippi's school paper, in which the student editor commented that admission of blacks to the university was inevitable. His response was: "I think that young man stated something that sooner or later his papa will have to accept." Understanding very well the deep-seated nature of racial prejudice, however, Faulkner added that "papas throughout the South might have to die before it would really be accepted."[30]

The stand he took from the beginning over the controversial desegregation issue made the progressives and the liberals more inclined toward him and the conservatives and states' rights people more opposed. Ultimately, however, the force of opposition from both sides threw him into the midst of an even more heated controversy. His responses made not only his highly vulnerable position, but also his views with reference to the blacks, seem sometimes very similar to those held by the Southern papas he predicted would be most bound by tradition. It would even seem that what had been said with so much confidence from 1950 through 1955 had never truly crystallized in the depths of Faulkner's being. The position he wanted to hold, that of a moderate with convictions about racial equality, was undermined by his own language. The best that one can say is that the man who had wanted to be a moderate was, even more than the label itself denotes, caught rather disturbingly in the middle.

In his "Address to the Southern Historical Association" in Memphis, Tennessee, on November 10, 1955,[31] Faulkner focused on the pressing implications of segregation in America in light of what he saw as the encroachment of communism. Segregation in America was jeopardizing human freedom. He made an appeal for all people to do away with racial phobias and provincial myths. The American people needed to take note of worldwide developments and examine the imminent threat to any nation that wanted to secure within its cultural framework the tenets of "individual liberty, equality and freedom."[32] He called for an uncompromising concept of freedom with no hierarchies or caste system. The American people should confederate, forget about their distinctions, put the ideals of democracy into practice, and ally with other peoples around the world "if Americans wanted a world or even a part of a world in which individual man could be free, to continue to endure."[33]

Faulkner branded the articulate and outspoken black dissenters like Paul Robeson as misfits because they were not what he considered exemplary black Americans like Ralph Bunche, George Washington Carver, and Booker T. Washington.[34]

After his Memphis speech the Southern resentment to Faulkner mounted. Hostility and ridicule which so many had expressed in their replies to Faulkner's letters in the *Commercial Appeal* increased, and so did the menacing threats. Before the Supreme Court ruling on the schools in 1954, there had been strong opposition to Faulkner's views. But now he was seen as using his prestige to assist Federal encroachment upon Southern privileges and states' rights. The recalcitrant sector tried to scare him, and apparently succeeded. Faulkner wrote to a friend soon after the Memphis event, "I get so much threatening fan mail, so many nut angry telephone calls at 2 and 3 a.m. . . . "[35] Some of Faulkner's family were bitterly opposed to his progressive views. And it is reported that even his aging mother was upset by the way he was supposedly using his national and international influence "to stir people up."[36]

Faulkner's fear of what he called "the general emotional pitch"[37] of the adult world around him increased as the crisis grew. But as his personal fears grew, he nevertheless sought an even wider audience for the views he set forth in Memphis. He supplemented the "Address" with other material entitled, "On Fear: the South in Labor," and sent it to his agent in New York with specific instructions for a strategic placement in a national publication. The article was published in *Harper's* in June of 1956. By that time rioting had broken out at the University of Alabama over the admission of the young black woman Arthurine Lucy who had been forced away from the campus. Faulkner feared that if she returned she would be killed. He remembered that the Mississippians had bought all the guns and ammunition the local stores had in stock when the Supreme Court had handed down its decision on the schools two years earlier.[38] Chaos was close at hand. Faulkner feared that the Southern reaction would lead the nation into another civil war.

He was in New York at the time, and there he wrote what he called "Letter to the North" which he wanted to have released immediately by radio and the press.[39] In the "Letter" he advised the Northerners that there should be a momentary halting of the pace. Such would be the basic position that he would hold as a moderate from then on:

> Go slow now. Stop now for a time, a moment. . . . You have shown the Southerner what you can do and what you will do if necessary; give him a space in which to get his breath and assimilate that knowledge.[40]

During this period of crisis in his life Faulkner increased his drinking. He gave an interview, much of which he later repudiated, on the impending chaos which he saw growing out of the Northern effort to force integration upon the South. His "Letter to the North" had been mostly concerned with strategy, but this interview, as it was printed, threw all of his convictions into question. He was reported to have said that the 1954 decision of the Supreme Court had prolonged the struggle, although he did not disagree with the decree itself;[41] that "My Negro boys down on the plantation would fight against the north with me."[42] In another comment he even said that "if it came to fighting I'd fight for Mississippi against the Untied States even if it meant going out into the street and shooting Negroes. After all, I'm not going out to shoot Mississippians."[43] It was regarding this point of view of Faulkner that James Baldwin later responded: "the time Faulkner asks for does not exist."[44] Whether the interview was accurately reported or not, it precipitated a lot of controversy, and Faulkner duly repudiated.[45]

One statement of repudiation took the form of what he called "A Letter to the Leaders of the Negro Race," which proved to be about as provacative as the circumstance which had precipitated his need to write it. It was written at a point when the Civil Rights movement was just getting its footing. With the Supreme Court decision behind them and the Montgomery bus boycotts set in motion, the blacks were beginning to line up not only to test the decision of 1954, but also to challenge other existing discriminatory statutes.[46] With their energies rising, many black leaders were hardly impressed by words of moderation from a Nobel laureate or anyone else.

Faulkner began the letter, which *Ebony* printed under the title "If I Were a Negro," with repudiation of the statements about "shooting down Negroes in the streets:" He emphasized the danger and foolishness of such a position which he aptly said no "sane or sober man" would dare take. He had already outlined this in his letters to *Time* and *The Reporter.*[47] He also repeated what he had written in his *Life* article three months earlier: "Go slow now. Stop now for a time, a moment," explaining that what he meant by this advice was that the NAACP and other supporting organizations must "be flexible." He explained further that the *Life* article had been written at a time when he thought Authurine Lucy would be killed. Faulkner elaborated that he had no intention of suggesting that any individual black person "abandon or lower one jot his hope and will for equality," but that the leaders must always be "adaptable to circumstance and locality in their methods of gaining it."[48]

Unfortunately, however, as Faulkner elaborated further upon his suggested strategy, setting forth his proposals of what he would do if he were a black man, he victimized himself by using language shaped by Southern culture and its racial assumptions. This incensed the black readers more than his program for change, and revealed something about his personality reminiscent of the paternalistic attitude of his 1931 New York *Herald Tribune* interview. Likewise, in his earlier "Address to the Southern Historical Association" Faulkner had claimed that in all its existence, the continent of Africa had not developed one skilled craftsman until the coming of the Europeans.[49] Were one so inclined, one could still simply contend that the basic problem Faulkner had was simply one of misinformation. But in his speech, "A Word to Virginians," [50] the psychological implications of Faulkner's well entrenched past are so apparent as to appear pathetic.

The posture which Faulkner took in making his appeal to the Virginians is extraordinary, from a psychological perspective. Of course "A Word to the Virginians" was not intended for Sutpens or Snopeses, but for Virginians of the old line heritage, for the genteely bred. It was intended for those whom he thought retained the last vestiges of the more chivalric kind of honor and heroism. To a great extent the speech was an elaboration of what he had been saying all along, asserting the rights of the black man to equal opportunity and justice. But like the *Ebony* letter, it was also heavily undergirded with paternalistic jargon, containing an inept analogy comparing the disenfranchised blacks with "unbridled horses loose in the streets."[51] At this late date Faulkner even advanced the notion that perhaps it was the black man's tragedy that he was "competent for equality only in the ratio of his white blood."[52] Yet he stood firm in his convictions about the need to do away with injustices.

Obsequiously indulgent in the tone of his presentation, Faulkner appealed to the Virginian, the Southern model of so-called good breeding, to lead the South out of its backwardness. It was to Virginia that he appealed as,

> . . . the mother of all the rest of us of the South. Compared to you, my country–Mississippi, Alabama, Arkansas–is still frontier, still wilderness. . . . So let it be in Virginia toward whom the rest of us are already looking as a child looks toward the

> parent for a sign, a signal where to go and how to go. A hundred years ago the hot-heads of Mississippi and Georgia and South Carolina would not listen when the mother of us all tried to check our reckless headlong course. . . . But this time we will hear from you.[53]

However, the great mother, Virginia, also resisted desegregation of her schools by closing some of them for extended periods.[54]

This was Faulkner's final public statement. He retreated into silence to endure the confusion, but he could not live down the controversy. At an earlier, more triumphant time, he had been brave and wise enough to say what he thought he could live by during his lifetime: "Between grief and nothing I'll always take grief."[55] This was the testament he wanted to live up to, believing that the just life was worth the trouble though one might find that trouble hard to bear.

ENDNOTES

1. Lillian Smith, *Killers of the Dream* (New York: Anchor Books, 1949, 1961), p. 28.
2. Joseph Blotner, *Faulkner: A Biography*, two volumes (New York: Random House, 1974), vol. I, pp. 366-71.
3. Ibid., p. 498.
4. Ibid., pp. 498-499.
5. Smith, p. 130.
6. " 'Slavery Better for the Negro,' says Faulkner," New York *Herald Tribune*, November 14, 1931, p. 11.
7. Ibid.
8. Ibid.
9. William Faulkner, "Funeral Service for Mammy Caroline Barr" in *Essays, Speeches and Public Letters*, ed. James B. Meriwether (New York: Random House, 1965), p. 117.
10. Blotner, vol. II, p. 1190.
11. Ibid., p. 1061.
12. Ibid., pp. 1146-47.
13. Ibid., p. 1226.
14. William Faulkner, "Address to the Southern Historical Association," in Meriwether, op. cit., p. 150.
15. William Faulkner, "To The Delta Council," in Meriwether, op. cit., p. 129.
16. William Faulkner, "To the Graduating Class, University High School," (1951); "To the Graduating Class, Pine Manor Junior College," (1953); "To the Youth of Japan," (1955); and "Address to the English Club of the University of Virginia: A Word to Young Writers," (1958), in Meriwether, op. cit.
17. Charles D. Peavy, 'Go Slow Now': Faulkner and the Race Question (Eugene: University of Oregon Books, 1971), pp. 50-53.
18. William Faulkner, "To the Editor of the Memphis *Commercial Appeal*" (March 26, (1950); reprinted in Meriwether, op. cit., pp. 203-4.

19. Ibid., p. 204.
20. Blotner, p. 1378.
21. Ibid., p. 1377.
22. William Faulkner, "Mississippi," *Holiday Magazine* (April 1954); reprinted in Meriwether, p. 37.
23. Faulkner voiced this opinion on a number of occasions, including: "On Fear: Deep South in Labor: Mississippi" (1956); in Meriwether, p. 95; "Mississippi" (1954) in op. cit.; and Robert Jelliffe (ed.), *Faulkner at Nagano* (Tokyo, 1956), pp. 5, 77.
24. "On Fear: Deep South in Labor: Mississippi," in Meriwether, p. 105.
25. Blotner, vol. II, p. 1570.
26. William Faulkner, in the New York *Herald Tribune*, (September 9, 1955).
27. William Faulkner, "To the Editor of the *Memphis Commercial Appeal*" (April 10, 1955); reprinted in Meriwether, p. 220.
28. *Memphis Commercial Appeal* (April 3, 1955); reprinted Meriwether, p. 219.
29. *Memphis Commercial Appeal* (March 20, 1955); reprinted in Meriwether, pp. 215-16.
30. Blotner, vol. II, p. 1370.
31. Faulkner was one of three panelists including Cecil Sims, a Nashville attorney, and Benjamin E. Mays, President of Atlanta's Morehouse College. All three addresses were later collected in a pamphlet, *The Segregation Decisions* (Atlanta: Southern Regional Council, 1956).
32. William Faulkner, "Address to the Southern Historical Association" (November 10, 1955), in Meriwether, p. 147.
33. Ibid.
34. Ibid., p. 149.
35. Blotner, vol. II, p. 1585; originally stated in a letter to Jean Stein (November 1955).
36. Ibid., p. 1597; originally written in a letter to Else Jonsson (June, 1955).
37. *Memphis Commercial Appeal* (April 17, 1955); reprinted in Meriwether, p. 222.
38. Blotner, vol. II, p. 1591.
39. Ibid., p. 1589.
40. William Faulkner, "Letter to a Northern Editor," *Life Magazine* (March 5, 1956); reprinted in Meriwether, p. 91.
41. "Interview with Russel Howe" (1956), in Michael Millgate, ed., *Lion in the Garden: Interviews with William Faulkner, 1926-1962* (New York: Random House, 1968), p. 259; originally published in one version in the *London Sunday Times*, March 4, 1956, and in another version in *The Reporter*, March 22, 1956.
42. *Lion in the Garden*, p. 262.
43. Ibid., p. 261.
44. James Baldwin, "Faulkner and Desegregation," in *Nobody Knows My Name* (New York: Delta Books, 1961), p. 126.
45. William Faulkner, "To the Editor of *The Reporter*" (April 19, 1956); "To the Editor of *Time*" (April 23, 1956); "If I Were A Negro," *Ebony* (September 1956).
46. John Hope Franklin, *From Slavery to Freedom* (New York: Alfred A. Knopf, 1949, 1967), pp. 608-22.
47. See note 45.
48. William Faulkner, "A Letter to the Leaders of the Negro Race" *Ebony Magazine* (September, 1956); reprinted in Meriwether, pp. 107-12.
49. Meriwether, p. 104.
50. William Faulkner, "A Word to the Virginians," in *Faulkner in the University*, eds. Joseph Blotner and Frederick L. Gwynn (New York: Random House 1959), pp. 209-27.

51. Ibid., p. 209.
52. Ibid., p. 210.
53. Ibid., p. 212.
54. Franklin, p. 616.
55. Blotner, Vol. II, p. 1520.

X.

A Glossary of the Black Characters in William Faulkner's Works

Abe: Takes care of Doc Peabody's fishing pond, in *Sartoris* (1929), *Flags in the Dust* (1973).

Acey: A mourner at Mannie's funeral, in "Pantaloon in Black" (1940).

Alec (Uncle): Rider's uncle, in "Pantaloon in Black" (1940).

Alice: Maid to Miss Ballenbaugh who runs the rest stop at the Iron Bridge, in *The Reivers* (1962).

Ash (Old Man): Servant at Major de Spain's hunting camp, in "The Old People" (1940), "The Bear" (1942).

Aunt: Wife of Alec and the aunt who raised Rider, in "Pantaloon in Black" (1940).

Barger, (Sonny): Storekeeper in black section of town in "Uncle Willy" (1935).

Beauchamp, Amodeus McCaslin: Infant son of Tennie Beauchamp and Tomey's Turl (Terrel) who was born and died in 1859, in "The Bear" (1942).

Beauchamp, Bobo: Cousin of Ned McCaslin and groom for Mr. Van Tosch, in *The Reivers* (1962). It is his gambling which starts the chain of events involving the trade of the automobile for the old race horse.

Beauchamp, Callina: A daughter of Tennie Beauchamp and Tomey's Turl (Terrel) who was born and died in 1862, in "The Bear" (1942).

Beauchamp, Henry: Son of Molly and Lucas Beauchamp, in "The Fire and the Hearth" (1942).

Beauchamp, James Thucydus (Thucydides)–also known as Tennie's Jim: Hunting camp servant, in "The Old People" (1940), "The Bear" (1940). Runs away on his twenty-fifth birthday forfeiting the inheritance left in recompense for his white grandfather's evils. Grandfather to the mulatta cousin of Roth Edmonds who bears Roth's child, in "Delta Autumn" (1942). Also grandfather of Bobo Beauchamp, in *The Reivers*.

Beauchamp, Molly (Mollie) Worsham: Wife of Lucas and major character in "Go Down, Moses" (1941). Mentioned in "Delta Autumn" (1942). Object of contention between Zack Edmonds and Lucas, in "The Fire and the Hearth" (1942), when taken with small son Henry into Zack's house to be wet nurse for Zack's son whose mother dies in childbirth. Charles Mallison remembers her in *Intruder in the Dust* (1948), but she is deceased at the time of the major action.

Beauchamp (Mulatta): Roth Edmond's distant cousin by whom he had an infant son, granddaughter of James Beauchamp, in "Delta Autumn" (1942).

Beauchamp, Philip Manigault: Soldier from Mississippi who is involved in the killing of General Gragnou, the commander of a revolutionary division, later to become an undertaker, in *A Fable* (1954).

Beauchamp, Samuel Worsham (Butch): Pivotal character in "Go Down, Moses" (1941); grandson of Mollie Beauchamp electrocuted in Illinois for killing a policeman.

Beauchamp, Sophonsiba (Fonsiba): Lives in Arkansas with a man cast as a pseudo-intellectual, in "The Bear" (1942); sister of Lucas and James; mentioned in "The Fire and the Hearth" (1942).

Beauchamp, Tennie: A slave woman won from Hubert Beauchamp by Amodeus Beauchamp in a card game in 1859; married to

Tomey's Turl (Terrel Beauchamp); mother of Lucas, Sophonsiba, and James, mentioned in "Was" (1942), "The Bear" (1942), "The Fire and the Hearth" (1942), "Delta Autumn" (1942).

Beauchamp, Terrel (Turl) (Tomey's Turl): Husband of Tennie; father of James, Lucas, and Sophonsiba; mentioned in "Was" (1942), "The Bear" (1942), "The Fire and the Hearth" (1942), "Delta Autumn" (1942).

Bedenberry (Brother): Attacked by Joe Christmas in *Light in August* (1932), while Joe was being chased by the posse.

Benbow, Cassius Q. (Uncle Cash): Backed by the Burdens to run as U.S. Marshal of Jefferson; had been a Benbow coachman, in *The Unvanquished* (1938).

Big Top: Father of Little Top and Aleck Sander, and husband of Guster, in *The Town* (1957).

Bird, Tom Tom: Fireman at the power plant, in "Centaur in Brass" (1932). Reappears in *The Town* (1957), helping Flem Snopes steal the brass.

Bird (Uncle): One of the church members who comes to retrieve the money that Simon has taken from the church funds, in *Sartoris (1929), Flags in the Dust* (1973).

Bon, Charles: Son of Eulalia Bon of the West Indies and Thomas Sutpen, in *Absalom, Absalom!* (1936); major force in the shattering of Sutpen's dream when courting Sutpen's daughter; father of Charles Etienne Saint Velery Bon by an octoroon mistress.

Bon, Charles Etienne Saint Velery: Son of Charles Bon and his octoroon mistress, in *Absalom, Absalom!* (1936).

Bon, Eulalia: Haitian mother of Charles Bon who was married to Thomas Sutpen in 1827 and divorced from him in 1831, in *Absalom, Absalom!* (1936).

Bon (No first name given) (Octoroon): Mistress of Charles Bon in New Orleans and mother of St. Velery; travels to Sutpen's Hundred to mourn at Charles' graveside, in *Absalom, Absalom!* (1936).

Bond, Jim: Last living descendant of Thomas Sutpen; son of St. Velery Bon; designated an idiot, in *Absalom, Absalom!* (1936).

Briggins, Lycurgus: The grandson of Uncle Parsham Hood, in *The Reivers* (1962); involved with Ned and the boy Lucius in the race horse affairs.

Briggins, Mary: Daughter of Uncle Parsham Hood and Lycurgus' mother, in *The Reivers* (1962).

Brownlee, Percival (Spintrius): A slave sold by N. B. Forrest to the McCaslins; took up preaching and renamed himself Spintrius, in "The Bear" (1942).

Callie (Aunt): Longtime cook for Mrs. Priest, in *The Reivers* (1962).

Charley (Uncle): One of the servants at Cranston's Wells, Mississippi, in "Dr. Martino" (1931).

Chlory: House servant who mourns the death of her employer, Judge Allison, in "Beyond" (1933).

Christian, Walter: Janitor at Uncle Willy Christian's drugstore, in *The Town* (1957).

Christmas Hosts: The unnamed family in whose barn Young Bayard sleeps on Christmas Eve after getting lost on his way home from a hunting trip and at whose house he eats Christmas breakfast, in *Sartoris* (1929), *Flags in the Dust* (1973).

Christmas, Joe: Tormented and wandering protagonist of *Light in August* (1932). Orphaned as a child by his mother, Milly Hines, and later adopted by the McEacherns.

Cinthy: A servant of Gail Hightower's father, in *Light in August* (1932).

Clay, Sis Beulah: Friend whose death Dilsey mourned heavily, in *The Sound and the Fury* (1929).

Clefus: Office janitor for the attorney Gavin Stevens, in *The Town* (1957).

Daisy: Major de Spain's cook, in "The Bear" (1942).

Dan: Man who works for the Edmondses, in "The Fire and the Hearth" (1942).

Deacon: Southerner who migrated to Cambridge, Massachusetts and worked as a porter-envoi for the Southern boys at Harvard; made the acquaintance of Quentin Compson in *The Sound and the Fury* (1929).

de Montigny, Paul: Elly's boyfriend who causes the miscegenation stir, in "Elly" (1934).

Dicey: The midwife who delivers Milly Jones' baby, in "Wash" (1934).

Emmaline: Nurse for Louisa's baby, in "That Will Be Fine" (1935).

Ephraim: Father of Paralee and grandfather of Aleck Sander, in

Intruder in the Dust (1948). He divines where Mrs. Mallison's lost ring is.

Ephum: A worker at Miss Ballenbaugh's rest stop, in *The Reivers (1962).*

Eunice: Mother of Tomasina (Tomey) Beauchamp by her owner Lucius Quintus Carothers McCaslin, in "The Bear" (1942). Drowns herself on Christmas Day, 1832 after discovering that her lover-master has also fathered a child by their daughter.

Fathers, Sam (Had-Two-Fathers, Uncle Blue Gum): Son of a Chickasaw Indian and a black woman slave. Story told in "A Justice" (1931). Variation of his parentage given in "The Old People" (1940). Initiates Isaac McCaslin into the hunting ritual, in "The Bear" (1942). Mentioned in *Intruder in the Dust* (1948) and *The Reivers* (1962).

Gabe: Blacksmith, in *The Reivers* (1962).

Gatewood, Jabbo: Repairman for Manfred de Spain, in *The Town* (1957).

Gatewood, Noon (Uncle): Has blacksmith shop, in *The Town* (1957).

Gibson, Dilsey: Married to Roskus, the mother of Frony, T.P., and Versh; noted for her compassion for suffering humanity particularly in the crumbling Compson household, in *The Sound and the Fury* (1929); Compson cook, in "That Evening Sun" (1931).

Gibson, Frony: Dilsey and Roskus Gibson's daughter, mother of Luster, one of Benjy's caretakers, in *The Sound and the Fury* (1929); mentioned in "That Evening Sun" (1931); makes a home in Memphis with her pullman porter husband to which she carries her aging mother, in the appendix to *The Sound and the Fury* (1946).

Gibson, Roskus: Dilsey's husband, in *The Sound and the Fury* (1929); carriage driver, in "A Justice" (1931).

Gibson, T.P.: Son of Dilsey and Roskus, and one of Benjy's attendants in *The Sound and the Fury* (1929); mentioned in "That Evening Sun" (1931).

Gibson, Versh: Dilsey and Roskus' oldest son and one of Benjy's attendants in *The Sound and the Fury* (1929); mentioned in "That Evening Sun" (1931).

Guster: Wife of Big Top, cook for the Mallisons, and mother of

Aleck Sander and Little Top in *The Town* (1957).

Hatcher, Louis: He teaches Caddy to drive and hunts coons with the boy Quentin, in *The Sound and the Fury* (1929).

Hatcher, Martha: Wife of Louis, in *The Sound and the Fury* (1929).

Henry (I): Porter on the train, in *Soldiers' Pay* (1926).

Henry (II): Works for the bully Jack Houston, in *The Mansion* (1959).

Henry (Uncle): Mentioned as the man behind whose house the coon hunt begins, in *Sartoris* (1929), and *Flags in the Dust* (1973).

Het (Old): Comic character, in "Mule in the Yard" (1934), and *The Town* (1957).

Hood, Parsham (Uncle): Revered and respected old man, father of Mary Briggins and grandfather of Lycurgus, in *The Reivers* (1962).

Houston: A waiter, in *Sartoris* (1929), *Flags in the Dust* (1973).

Isham: Appears as the oldest servant on the hunting trip, in "Delta Autumn" (1942).

Isom: Son of Elnora Strother and grandson of Ned, in *Sartoris* (1929), *Flags in the Dust* (1973); also in *Sanctuary* (1931); mentioned in "All the Dead Pilots" (1931) and "There Was a Queen" (1933).

Jake: House servant to Judge Allison, in "Beyond" (1933).

Jesus: Nancy Mannigoe's husband and murderer and Aunt Rachel's son, in "That Evening Sun" (1931).

Jim: Adept groomsman who works with the hostler, Pat Stamper, in *The Hamlet* (1940).

Jingus: Servant to the Hawk family, in *The Unvanquished* (1938).

Job (Old): Old man who matches Jason Compson's wits, in *The Sound and the Fury* (1929).

Job (Uncle): Judge Dunkinfield's janitor, in "Smoke" (1932), and *The Town* (1957).

Joby (Old): Sartoris servant who is remembered, in *Sartoris* (1929), *Flags in the Dust* (1973). Colonel John Sartoris' body servant, in *The Unvanquished* (1938), and "My Grandmother Millard" (1943).

Jody: Son of Elnora Strother, who lives in Memphis, in "There Was a Queen" (1933).

Joe: Older boy who accompanies Charles Mallison and Aleck Sander on the hunting trip, in *Intruder in the Dust* (1948).

John Henry: Saves Young Bayard Sartoris from drowning, in *Sartoris* (1929), *Flags in the Dust* (1973).

John Henry's father (Unnamed): In *Sartoris* (1929), *Flags in the Dust* (1973).

John Paul: Hack driver, in "That Will Be Fine" (1935).

Jonas: A McCaslin slave, in "Was" (1942).

Jones (Doctor): A janitor at Colonel Sartoris' bank, in *Sartoris* (1929), *Flags in the Dust* (1973).

Jubal: Body servant to Saucier Weddel, in "Mountain Victory" (1932).

Jupe: Man who almost has a fight with Joe Christmas, in *Light in August* (1932).

Lena (Missy): A servant to the Hawk family, in *The Unvanquished* (1938).

Little Top: The oldest son of Guster and Big Top, in *The Town* (1957).

Louisa: A maid at a brothel in San Antonio, in *The Wild Palms* (1939).

Louvinia: Sartoris cook during the Civil War, in *Sartoris* (1929), *Flags in the Dust* (1973). Grandmother of Ringo, mother of Simon and Lucius, and wife of Jody, in *The Unvanquished (1938), "My* Grandmother Millard" (1943).

Lucius (Loosh): Philadelphia's husband and son of Jody and Louvinia, in *The Unvanquished* (1938), "My Grandmother Millard" (1943).

Ludus (I): Minnie's husband, in *The Mansion* (1959).

Ludus (II): Driver who squabbles with Boon Hogganbeck, in *The Reivers* (1962).

Luster (I): Son of Frony and grandson of Dilsey; Benjy's last attendant before he is sent off to the state asylum, in *The Sound and the Fury* (1929); mentioned in *Absalom, Absalom!* (1936).

Luster (II): Involved in the squabble between Boon Hogganbeck and Ludus, in *The Reivers* (1962).

Mandy (I): Cook for the McCallum family, in *Sartoris* (1929), *Flags in the Dust* (1973).

Mandy (II): Cook for Grandpa, in "That Will Be Fine" (1935).

Mannie: Young woman briefly married to Rider a few months before dying, in "Pantaloon in Black" (1940).

Mannigoe, Nancy: Prostitute killed by her husband Jesus, in "That Evening Sun" (1931). Nurse maid who kills the Stevens infant because she feels it is being wronged by the parents, in *Requiem for a Nun* (1951).

Marengo (Ringo): Childhood companion of the elder Bayard Sartoris, grandson of Joby and Louvinia and the son of Simon, in *The Unvanquished* (1938); mentioned in "My Grandmother Millard" (1943).

Mayes, Will: Ice plant watchman who becomes the victim of a lynching, in "Dry September" (1931).

McCaslin, Delphine: Sarah Priest's cook and Ned McCaslin's fourth wife, in *The Reivers* (1962).

McCaslin, Ned William (Ned William McCaslin Jefferson Mississippi): Coachman who swaps his boss' automobile for an old race horse, in *The Reivers* (1962).

McCaslin, Thucydus (Thucydides): Son of Roscius and Phoebe and husband of Eunice, in "The Bear" (1942).

McWillie: A jockey for the horse Acheron, in *The Reivers* (1962).

Minnie: Maid at Miss Reba's brothel, in *Sanctuary* (1931), *The Reivers* (1962), and *The Mansion* (1959) where she is married to Ludus.

Mitchell, Few (Uncle): Referred to as deranged, in *The Unvanquished* (1938).

Moore (Brother): Financial secretary for Simon Strother's church who comes to the Sartoris house with the delegation to try to retrieve the church money taken by Simon, in *Sartoris* (1929), *Flags in the Dust* (1973).

Mosby (Uncle Hogeye): Referred to as an epileptic pauper, in *Intruder in the Dust* (1948).

Mose (Uncle): A groom for Harrison Blair, in "Fox Hunt" (1931).

Mulberry: U.S. Marshal in Jefferson during Reconstruction; also known for bootlegging whiskey from a mulberry tree, in *Requiem for a Nun* (1951).

Nate: Man whose assistance was sought by lawyer Gavin Stevens as he started into the backwoods to investigate the Grinnup murder, in "Hand Upon the Waters" (1939).

Nelson, Callie (Aunt): Old nurse who shows great concern for the mortally wounded war veteran Donald Mahon, and grandmother of World War I veteran Loosh, in *Soldier's Pay* (1926).

Nelson, Loosh (Lucius): World War I Veteran and grandson of Aunt Callie, in *Soldier's Pay* (1926).

Oscar: A worker on the Edmonds' place, in "The Fire and the Hearth" (1942).

Philadelphia (Philadelphy): Loosh's (Lucius) wife, in *The Unvanquished* (1938); cook, in "My Grandmother Millard" (1943).

Phoebe: Mother of Thucydides, brought from Carolina with her husband Roscius by Lucius Quintus Carothers McCaslin, in "The Bear" (1942).

Pinkie: Slave of Gail Hightower, in *Light in August* (1932).

Powell, John: Hostler involved in the squabble between Boon Hogganbeck and Ludus, in *The Reivers* (1962).

Rachel: Cook for Belle Mitchell, in *Sartoris* (1929), *Flags in the Dust* (1973).

Rachel (Aunt): Jesus' mother, in "That Evening Sun" (1931).

Reno: Leader of the band hired by Young Bayard to serenade his sweethearts, in *Sartoris* (1929), *Flags in the Dust* (1973).

Richard: A helper in the McCallum kitchen, in *Sartoris* (1929), *Flags in the Dust* (1973).

Rider: Character who tragically agonized over his wife's death, in "Pantaloon in Black" (1940).

Roscius: Brought from Carolina by Lucius Qunitus Carothers McCaslin; Phoebe's husband and Thucydides' father, in "The Bear" (1942).

Rosie: Cook for Georgie's parents, in "That Will Be Fine" (1935).

Roxanne (Aunt): Mrs. Jason Compson II's servant, in "My Grandmother Millard" (1943).

Saddie: Elnora Strother's daughter, in "There Was a Queen" (1933).

Sam: Servant of the Varner family, in *The Hamlet* (1940).

Samson: Hotel porter, in *The Town* (1957).

Sander, Aleck: Son of Paralee and grandson of Old Ephram; together with Charles Mallison and Miss Habersham helps to investigate the Gowrie grave, in *Intruder in the Dust* (1948).

Sander, Paralee: Aleck Sander's mother, daughter of Ephraim and cook for the Mallisons, in *Intruder in the Dust* (1948).

Secretary: Chauffeur for Uncle Willy Christian's car and airplane, in

"Uncle Willy" (1935).

Shegog, (Rev.): Guest preacher from St. Louis who preached the Easter Sunday sermon at Dilsey's church, in *The Sound and the Fury* (1929).

Sickymo: Referred to as the former slave appointed U.S. Marshall of Jefferson during Reconstruction, also known for bootlegging liquor from a sycamore tree, in "The Bear" (1942).

Simon: Hunting camp cook, in "Race at Morning" (1935).

Sol: Railroad porter, in *Sartoris* (1929), *Flags in the Dust* (1973).

Strother, Caspey (I): World War I veteran son of Simon, Elnora's brother and Isom's uncle, in *Sartoris* (1929), *Flags in the Dust (1973).*

Strother, Caspey (II): Elnora's husband in the penetentiary, in "There Was a Queen" (1933).

Strother, Elnora: Daughter of Simon and Sartoris family cook and mother of Isom in *Sartoris* (1929), *Flags in the Dust* (1973). Mentioned in "All the Dead Pilots" (1931). Mother of Joby and Saddie, half-sister of Old Bayard Sartoris, and wife of Caspey in There Was a Queen" (1933).

Strother, Euphrony: Referred to as wife of Simon, in *Sartoris* (1929), *Flags in the Dust* (1973).

Strother, Simon: Father of Caspey and Elnora, Old Bayard's carriage driver and husband of Euphrony, in *Sartoris* (1929), *Flags in the Dust* (1973); referred to as Elnora's mother's husband, in "There Was a Queen" (1933); bodyguard of colonel John Sartoris during Civil War, in *The Unvanquished* (1938); also referred to as Ringo's father, in *The Unvanquished* (1938).

Sutpen, Clytemnestra (Clytie): Slave daughter of Thomas Sutpen, in *Absalom, Absalom!* (1936). She serves the Sutpen family and burns the house down in the end to protect the family privacy.

Sutterfield, Rev. Tobe (M. Tolleman): Appears in *Notes on a Horsethief* (1950) as the groom who helps with the three-legged race horse. Does the same job in *A Fable* (1954), but is also a leader of a society called Les Amis Myriades et Anonymes a la France de Tout le Monde.

Thisbe (Aunt): A servant in the Edmonds' household, in "The Fire and the Hearth" (1942).

Thomas (Son): A driver at the Priest's livery stable, in *The Reivers*

(1962).

Thompson (Pappy): Old churchman beaten by Joe Christmas when Joe enters the black church, running away from the posse, in *Light in August* (1932).

Tobe (I): Butler to the Saunders, in *Soldiers' Pay* (1926).

Tobe (II): Hostler, in *Sartoris* (1929), *Flags in the Dust* (1973).

Tobe (III): Servant of Miss Emily Grierson who disappears upon Miss Emily's death, in "A Rose for Emily" (1930).

Tomasina (Tomey): Daughter of Eunice by owner Lucius Quintus Carothers McCaslin, by whom Tomasina also has a child, Turl (Terrel), in "The Bear" (1942).

Tomey's Turl (Terrel): Son of Tomasina and Lucius Quintus Carothers McCaslin, in "The Bear" (1942). Married Tennie Beauchamp, in "Was" (1942); father of Lucas Beauchamp, in "The Fire and the Hearth" (1942); mentioned in "The Bear" (1942) as father of Lucas, James, and Sophonsiba; referred to in "Delta Autumn" (1942) as the greatgrandfather of the mulatta woman who has had a child by her distant white cousin, Roth.

Vines (Deacon): Member of the church upset by Joe Christmas as Joe flees from the posse, in *Light in August* (1932).

Walter (I): Butler of Mrs. Maurier, in *Mosquitoes* (1927).

Walter (II): Member of the crew of the tugboat in *Mosquitoes* (1927).

Wilkins, George: Married Natalie Beauchamp, the daughter of Molly and Lucas, in "The Fire and the Hearth" (1942).

Wilkins, Natalie Beauchamp: Youngest child of Molly and Lucas who marries George Wilkins, in "The Fire and the Hearth"(1942).

Worsham, Hamp: Molly Beauchamp's brother and servant of Miss Belle Worsham, in"Go Down, Moses" (1941).

Worsham, Mrs. Hamp: Wife of Hamp Worsham and servant of Miss Belle Worsham, in "Go Down, Moses" (1941).

Wylie, Ash (Old): Servant, in "A Bear Hunt" (1955).

Wylie, Job: Servant of Uncle Willy Christian, in "Uncle Willy" (1935).

Bibliography

Adamowski, T. H. "Joe Christmas: The Tyranny of Childhood." *Novel* 4 (1971): 240-251.

Adams, Richard P. "Faulkner and the Myth of the South." *Mississippi Quarterly* 14 (1961): 131-137.

Adams, Richard P. *Faulkner: Myth and Motion*. Princeton: Princeton University Press, 1968.

Akin, W. "Normal Human Feelings: An Interpretation of Faulkner's 'Pantaloon in Black.'" *Studies in Short Fiction* 15 (1978): 397-404.

Allen, Charles A. "William Faulkner's Comedy and the Purpose of Humor." *Arizona Quarterly* 16 (1960): 59-69.

Allport, Gordon. *The Nature of Prejudice*. New York: Anchor Books. 1958.

Ames, Jessie Daniel. *The Changing Character of Lynching: Review of Lynching, 1931-1941*. New York: AMS Press, 1973. Originally published by the Commission on Interracial Cooperation, Inc., Atlanta, Ga., 1942.

Anderson, Sherwood. *Dark Laughter*. N.Y.: Liveright, 1970. Originally published by Boni and Liveright, 1925.

Arthos, John. "Ritual and Humor in the Writing of William Faulkner." *Accent* 9 (1948): 17-30.

Bache, W. B. "Moral Awareness in 'Dry September.'" *Faulkner Studies* 3 (1954): 53-57.

Backman, Melvin. *Faulkner: The Major Years*. Bloomington: Indiana University Press, 1966.

Backman, Melvin. "Sickness and Primitivism: A Dominant Pattern in Faulkner's Works." *Accent* 14 (1954): 61-73.

Baldanza, Frank. "The Structure of *Light in August*." *Modern Fiction Studies* 13 (1967): 67-78.

Baldwin, James. *No Name in the Street*. N.Y.: Dell Publishing, Inc., 1973.

Bales, Robert F. *Personality and Interpersonal Behavior*. N.Y.: Holt, Rinehart, and Winston, 1970.

Barksdale, Richard. "White Tragedy–Black Comedy: A Literary Approach to Southern Race Relations." *Phylon* 22 (1961): 226-233.

Barth, J. Robert, S.J., ed. *Religious Perspectives in Faulkner's Fiction*. Notre Dame: University of Notre Dame Press, 1972.

Bassett, John. *William Faulkner: An Annotated Checklist of Criticism*. N.Y.: David Lewis, Inc., 1972.

Beach, Joseph Warren. *American Fiction, 1920-1940*. N.Y.: Macmillan, 1941.

Beck, Warren. "Faulkner and the South." *Antioch Review* 1 (1941): 82-94.

Bergson, Henri. *Time and Free Will*. London: G. Allen and Urwin, Ltd., 1921.

Bernberg, Raymond E. "*Light in August:* A Psychological View." *Mississippi Quarterly* 11 (1958): 173-76.

Billington, Monroe L., ed. *The South: A Central Theme*. N.Y.: Holt, Rinehart, Winston, 1969.

Blanchard, Margaret. "The Rhetoric of Communion: Voice in *The Sound and the Fury*." *American Literature*, January, 1970: 555-565.

Bleikasten, André. *The Most Splendid Failure: Faulkner's 'The Sound and the Fury.'* Bloomington: Indiana University Press, 1976.

Blotner, Joseph L. *Faulkner: A Biography*. 2 vols. N.Y.: Random

House, 1974.
Blotner, Joseph L., and Frederick L. Gwynn, eds. *Faulkner in the University*. N.Y.: Vintage Books, 1959.
Bogle, Donald. *Toms, Coons, Mulattoes, Mammies and Bucks: An Interpretive History of Blacks in American Films*. N.Y.: The Viking Press, 1978.
Boynton, Percy H. "The Retrospective South." In *America in Contemporary Fiction*. Chicago: University of Chicago Press, 1944.
Bradford, M. E. "Brother, Son, and Heir: The Structural Focus of Faulkner's *Absalom, Absalom!*" *Swanee Review* 78 (1970): 76-98.
Bradford, M. "Faulkner's Doctrine of Nature: A Study of the 'Endurance' Theme in the Yoknapatawpha Fiction." Ph.D. dissertation, Vanderbilt University, 1968.
Breit, Harvey. "A Sense of Faulkner." *Partisan Review* 18 (1951): 88-94.
Brooks, Cleanth. "Faulkner's Criticism of Modern America." *Virginia Quarterly Review* 51 (1975): 294-308.
Brooks, Cleanth. "The Community and the Pariah," *Virginia Quarterly Review* 39 (1963): 236-253.
Brooks, Cleanth. "History, Tragedy, and the Imagination in *Absalom, Absalom!*." *Yale Review* 52 (1963): 340-351.
Brooks, Cleanth. *William Faulkner: The Yoknapatawpha Country*. New Haven: Yale University Press, 1963.
Brooks, Cleanth. *William Faulkner: Toward Yoknapatawpha and Beyond*. New Haven: Yale University Press, 1978.
Broughton, Panthea Reid. *William Faulkner: The Abstract and the Actual*. Baton Rouge: Louisiana State University Press, 1974.
Brown, Sterling. "A Century of Negro Portraiture in American Literature." *Massachusetts Review* 7 (1966): 89-90.
Brown, Sterling. *The Negro in American Fiction*. Washington, D.C.: Association in Negro Folk Education, 1937.
Brylowski, Walter. *Faulkner's Olympian Laugh: Myth in the Novels*. Detroit: Wayne State University Press, 1968.
Cable, George Washington. *The Grandissimes*, 1880. Reprint ed. by Newton Arwin. N.Y.: Sagamore Press, Inc., 1957.
Cable, George Washington. *The Negro Question: A Selection of Writings on Civil Rights in the South*. Edited by Arlin Turner. N.Y.: W. W. Norton, 1968.

Campbell, Harry M. and Ruel E. Foster. *William Faulkner: A Critical Appraisal.* Norman: University of Oklahoma Press, 1951.

Cargill, Oscar. "The Primitivists." In *Intellectual America.* N.Y.: Macmillan, 1941.

Cassirer, Ernst. *The Philosophy of Symbolic Forms: Mythical Thought*. Vol. 2, New Haven: Yale University Press, 1955.

Cirlot, J. E. *A Dictionary of Symbols.* London: Routledge and Kegan Paul, 1971.

Coindreau, Maurice. "Preface to *The Sound and the Fury*." Translated by George M. Reeves, *Mississippi Quarterly* 19 (1966). Originally published in French, 1938.

Coindreau, Maurice. *The Time of William Faulkner.* Edited by George M. Reeves. Columbia: University of South Carolina Press, 1971.

Coles, Robert. *Flannery O'Connor's South*. Baton Rouge: Louisiana State University Press, 1980.

Collins, Carvel. "Faulkner and Certain Earlier Southern Fiction." *College English* 16 (1954): 92-97.

Collins, Carvel. *William Faulkner: Early Prose and Poetry*. Boston: Little Brown and Company, 1962.

Collins, Carvel. ed. *William Faulkner: New Orleans Sketches*. N.Y.: Random House, 1958.

Cooper, James Fenimore. *The Last of the Mohicans*. N.Y.: New American Library, 1962.

Corey, S. "Avengers in *Light in August* and *Native Son.*" *CLA Journal* 23 (1979): 200-212.

Cowley, Malcolm. ed. *The Faulkner-Cowley File: Letters and Memories, 1944-1962*. N.Y.: The Viking Press, 1966.

Cowley, Malcolm. "William Faulkner's Legend of the South." *Sewanee Review* 53 (1945): 343-361.

Cowley, Malcolm. ed. *Writers at Work: The Paris Review Interviews*. N.Y.: The Viking Press, 1959.

Cullen, John B. and Floyd C. Watkins. *Old Times in Faulkner Country*. Chapel Hill: The University of North Carolina Press, 1961.

Dabney, Lewis M. *The Indians of Yoknapatawpha: A Study in Literature and History*. Baton Rouge: Louisiana State University Press, 1974.

Daniels, Edgar F. and Ralph Wolfe. "Beneath the Dust of 'Dry September,' " *Studies in Short Fiction* 1 (1964): 158-159.

Davis, Arthur P. "The Tragic Mulatto in Six Works of Langston Hughes." *Phylon Quarterly* 16 (1955).

de Balzac, Honoré. *Père Goriot*. N.Y.: Signet Classics. 1962. Originally published, 1934.

de Beauvoir, Simone. *The Second Sex*. N.Y.: Alfred A. Knopf, Inc., 1952.

de Jovine, Anthony. *The Young Hero in American Fiction*. N.Y.: Appleton-Century-Crofts, 1971.

Doster, William C. "William Faulkner and the Negro." Ph.D. dissertation, University of Florida, 1955.

Early, James. *The Making of GO DOWN, MOSES*. Dallas: Southern Methodist University Press, 1972.

Eaton, Clement. *A History of the Old South*. N.Y.: Macmillan Publishing Company, Inc., 1949, 1975.

Eisinger, Chester E. "William Faulkner: Southern Archetype." In *Fiction of the Forties*. Chicago: University of Chicago Press, 1963.

Ellison, Ralph. "Twentieth-Century Fiction and the Black Mask of Humanity." In *Shadow and Act*. N.Y.: New American Library, 1966.

Everett, Walter K. *Faulkner's Art and Characters*. Woodbury: Barron's Educational Series, Inc., 1969.

Faulkner, William. *Absalom, Absalom!* N.Y.: Vintage Books, 1972. Originally published by Random House, 1936.

Faulkner, William. *As I Lay Dying*. N.Y.: Vintage Books, 1964. Originally published, 1930 by Jonathan Cape and Harrison Smith.

Faulkner, William. "Cathay," *The Mississippian*. November 12, 1919.

Faulkner, William. *Collected Stories of William Faulkner*. N.Y.: Random House, 1950.

Faulkner, William. *Essays, Speeches, and Public Letters*. Edited by James Meriwether. N.Y.: Random House, 1965.

Faulkner, William. *A Fable*. N.Y.: Random House, 1954.

Faulkner, William. *Flags in the Dust*. N.Y.: Random House, 1973. Originally published in 1929 by Harcourt, Brace as *Sartoris*.

Faulkner, William. *Go Down, Moses*. N.Y.: Modern Library, 1955. Originally published, 1942 by Random House.

Faulkner, William. *A Green Bough*. N.Y.: Harrison Smith and Robert Haas, 1933.

Faulkner, William. *The Hamlet*. N.Y.: Vintage Books, 1964. Originally published by Random House, 1940.

Faulkner, William. *Intruder in the Dust*. N.Y.: The Modern Library, 1964. Originally published by Random House, 1948.

Faulkner, William. "L'Aprės-midi d'une Faune." *The New Republic*, 6 August 1919.

Faulkner, William. *Light in August*. N.Y.: Modern Library, 1967. Originally published by Harrison Smith and Robert Haas, 1932.

Faulkner, William. *The Mansion*. N.Y.: Vintage Books, 1965. Originally published by Random House, 1959.

Faulkner, William. *The Marble Faun* and *A Green Bough* (combined edition). N.Y.: Random House, 1960. Originally published *The Marble Faun*, Boston: The Four Seas Co., 1924, and *A Green Bough*, N.Y.: Harrison Smith and Robert Haas, 1933.

Faulkner, William. *The Marionettes*. Charlottesville: Bibliographical Society of the University of Virginia, 1975.

Faulkner, William. *Mosquitoes*. N.Y.: Boni and Liveright, 1927.

Faulkner, William. *New Orleans Sketches*. New Brunswick: Rutgers University Press, 1958.

Faulkner, William. *Pylon*. N.Y.: Harrison Smith and Robert Haas, 1935.

Faulkner, William. *The Reivers: A Reminiscence*. N.Y.: Vintage Books, 1966. Originally published by Random House, 1962.

Faulkner, William. *Requiem for a Nun*. N.Y.: Random House, 1951.

Faulkner, William. *Sanctuary*. N.Y.: Jonathan Cape and Harrison Smith, 1931.

Faulkner, William. *Sartoris*. N.Y.: Harcourt, Brace, and Company, 1929.

Faulkner, William. *Soldier's Pay*. N.Y.: Boni and Liveright, 1926.

Faulkner, William. *The Sound and the Fury*. N.Y.: Vintage Books, 1963. Originally published by Jonathan Cape, 1929.

Faulkner, William. *The Town*. N.Y.: Vintage Books, 1961. Originally published by Random House, 1957.

Faulkner, William. *Uncollected Stories of William Faulkner*. Edited by Joseph Blotner. N.Y.: Random House, 1979.

Faulkner, William. *The Unvanquished*. N.Y.: Vintage Books, 1966. Originally published by Random House, 1939.

Fauset, Jessie. *Comedy American Style*. N.Y.: Frederick Stokes Company, 1933.

Fiedler, Leslie A. *Love and Death in the American Novel.* N.Y.: Criterion Books, 1960.

Fletcher, Angus. *Allegory: The Theory of a Symbolic Mode.* Ithaca: Cornell University Press, 1964.

Ford, Margaret P. and Suzanne Kinkaid. *Who's Who in Faulkner.* Baton Rouge: Louisiana State University Press, 1966.

Franklin, John Hope. *From Slavery to Freedom.* N.Y.: Alfred A. Knopf, 1961.

Frederickson, George M. *The Black Image in the White Mind: The Debate on Afro-American Character and Destiny, 1817-1914.* N.Y.: Harper and Row, 1971.

Friedman, Lawrence J. *The White Savage: Racial Fantasies in the Post-bellum South.* Englewood Cliffs, N.J.: Prentice-Hall, Inc., 1970.

Freud, Sigmund. *The Basic Writings.* Edited by E. A. Brill, N.Y.: Random House, 1965.

Frohock, W. M. "William Faulkner: The Private Versus the Public Vision." *Southwest Review* 34 (1949): 281-294.

Frye, Northrop. *Anatomy of Criticism.* Princeton: Princeton University Press, 1957.

Gaines, Ernest. *Bloodline.* N.Y.: W. W. Norton, Inc., 1976.

Gaines, Ernest. *Catherine Carmier.* N.Y.: Atheneum Press, 1964.

Gaines, Ernest. Interview with Charles Rowell. *Callaloo* 1, no. 3 (1978).

Geismer, Maxwell. "William Faulkner: The Negro and the Female." In *Writers in Crisis.* Boston: Houghton Mifflin, 1942.

Giles, Barbara. "The South of William Faulkner." *Masses and Mainstream,* 1950: 26-40.

Glicksberg, Charles I. "William Faulkner and the Negro Problem." *Phylon* 10 (1949): 153-160.

Gloster, Hugh M. *Negro Voices in American Fiction.* Chapel Hill: University of North Carolina Press, 1948.

Gloster, Hugh M. "Southern Justice." *Phylon* 10, no. 1 (1949): 93-95.

Godden, R. "Call Me Nigger!: Race and Speech in Faulkner's *Light in August.*" *Journal of American Studies* 14 (1980): 235-248.

Gold, Joseph. *William Faulkner: A Study in Humanism from Metaphor to Discourse.* Norman, Okla.: University of Oklahoma Press, 1966.

Greer, Dorothy D. "Dilsey and Lucas: Faulkner's Use of the Negro as a Gauge of Moral Character." *Emporia State Research Studies* 11, no. 1 (1962): 43-61.

Greer, Scott. "Joe Christmas and the 'Social Self.'" *Mississippi Quarterly* 11, no. 4. (1958).

Gresham, Jewell Handy. "The Fatal Illusions: Self, Sex, Race, and Religion in William Faulkner's World." Ph.D. dissertation, Columbia University, 1970.

Grimwood, James Michael. "Pastoral and Parody: The Making of Faulkner's Anthology Novels." Ph.D. dissertation, Princeton University, 1976.

Gross, Beverly. "Form and Fulfillment in *The Sound and the Fury*." *Modern Language Quarterly* 29, no. 4 (1968): 439-449.

Gross, Seymour, and John Edward Hardy eds. *Images of the Negro in American Literature*. Chicago: University of Chicago Press, 1966.

Guillaume, Paul, and Thomas Munro. *Primitive Negro Sculpture*. London: Jonathan Cape, Ltd., 1926.

Guthke, Karl S. *Modern Tragicomedy: An Investigation into the Nature of the Genre*. N.Y.: Random House, 1966.

Hagan, John. "Fact and Fancy in *Absalom, Absalom!*." *College English* 24 (1962): 215-218.

Hagopian, John V. "Comedy and Tragedy in William Faulkner." *American Studies Seminar*. Berlin: Amerika Haus, 1958.

Hagopian, John V. "Nihilism in Faulkner's *The Sound and the Fury*," *The Merrill Studies in THE SOUND AND THE FURY*. Edited by James Meriwether. Columbus, Ohio: Charles E. Merrill Publishing Co., 1970.

Harrington, Evans, and Ann J. Abadie eds. *The South and Faulkner's Yoknapatawpha: The Actual and the Apocryphal*. Jackson: University of Mississippi Press, 1977.

Hicks, Granville. "Faulkner's South: A Northern Interpretation." *Georgia Review* 5 (1951): 269-284.

Hill, A. A. "Three Examples of Unexpectedly Accurate Indian Lore." *Texas Studies in Literature and Language* 6 (1964): 80-83.

Hoadley, Frank M. "Folk Humor in the Novels of William Faulkner." *Tennessee Folklore Society Bulletin* 23 (1957): 75-82.

Hoffman, Frederick J. *William Faulkner*. N.Y.: Twayne Publishers, Inc., 1966.

Hooper, Vincent. "Faulkner's Paradise Lost." *Virginia Quarterly Review* 23 (1947).

Horney, Karen. *Our Inner Conflicts*. N.Y.: W. W. Norton, Inc., 1945.

Howe, Irving. "The Southern Myth and William Faulkner." *Arizona Quarterly* 3 (1951): 357-362.

Howe, Irving. *William Faulkner: A Critical Study*. N.Y.: Random House, 1952.

Howe, Irving. "William Faulkner and the Negroes." *Commentary* 12 (1951): 359-368.

Howell, Elmo. "A Note on Faulkner's Negro Characters." *Mississippi Quarterly* 11 (1958): 201-203.

Howell, Elmo. "Sam Fathers: A Note on Faulkner's 'A Justice.' " *Tennessee Studies in Literature* 12 (1967): 149-153.

Howell, Elmo. "William Faulkner and the Mississippi Indians." *Georgia Review* 21 (1962): 386-396.

Howell, Elmo. "William Faulkner's Chickasaw Legacy: A Note on 'Red Leaves.' " *Arizona Quarterly* 26 (1970): 293-303.

Howell, Elmo. "William Faulkner's 'Christmas Gift.' " *Kentucky Folklore Record* 13 (1967): 37-40.

Hughes, Langston. *Laughing to Keep from Crying*. N.Y.: Henry Holt and Co., 1952.

Hughes, Langston. "Mulatto." In *Five Plays by Langston Hughes*. Edited by Webster Smalley. Bloomington: Indiana University Press, 1963.

Hunt, John W. *William Faulkner: Art in Theological Tension*. Syracuse: Syracuse University Press, 1965.

Husserl, Edmund. *Ideas: General Introduction to Pure Phenomenology* Translated by W. R. B. Gibson. N.Y.: Macmillan Co., 1931.

Ingrasci, H. J. "Strategic Withdrawal or Retreat: Deliverance From Racial Oppression in Kelley's *A Different Drummer* and Faulkner's *Go Down, Moses*." *STUDIES IN BLACK LITERATURE* 6 (1975): 1-6.

Jackson, Blyden. "Faulkner's Depiction of the Negro." *Studies in English* 15 (1975): 33-47.

Jackson, Esther Merle. "The American Negro and the Image of the Absurd." *Phylon* 23 (1962): 359-371.

Jefferson, Thomas. *Notes on the State of Virginia,* 1784. Reprint: Philadelphia: H. C. Carey and I. Lea, 1825.

Jelliffe, Robert A. ed. *Faulkner at Nagano*. Tokyo: Kenkyusha, Ltd., 1956.

Jenkins, Lee. *Faulkner and Black-White Relations: A Psychoanalytic Approach*. New York: Columbia University Press, 1981.

Johnson, Beulah V. "The Treatment of the Negro Women as a Major Character in American Novels, 1900-1950." Ph.D. dissertation, New York University, 1955.

Johnson, James Weldon. *The Autobiography of an Ex-Colored Man.* In *Three Negro Classics.* Edited by John Hope Franklin. N.Y.: Avon Books, 1965. Originally published anonymously in 1912.

Johnson, Lemuel A. *The Devil, the Gargoyle, and the Buffoon: The Negro as Metaphor in Western Literature*. Port Washington: Kennikat Press, 1971.

Jones, Charles Colcock. *The Religious Instruction of the Negroes in the United States.* (1842) Reprint: N.Y.: Books for Libraries Press, 1971.

Jordan, Winthrop. *White Over Black: American Attitudes Toward the Negro, 1550-1812*. Chapel Hill: University of North Carolina Press, 1968.

Joyce, James. *A Portrait of the Artist as a Young Man*. N.Y.: Viking Press, Inc., 1964. Originally published, 1914.

Karcher, Carolyn L. *Shadow Over the Promised Land: Slavery, Race, and Violence in Melville's America.* Baton Rouge: Louisiana State University Press, 1979.

Kartiganer, Donald M. *The Fragile Thread: The Meaning of Form in Faulkner's Novels*. Amherst: University of Massachusetts Press, 1979.

Kartiganer, Donald M. "Faulkner's *Absalom, Absalom!*: The Discovery of Values." *American Literature* 37 (1965): 291-306.

Kazin, Alfred. "Faulkner: The Rhetoric and the Agony." In *On Native Grounds*. N.Y.: Reynal and Hitchcock, 1942.

Kazin, Alfred. "Faulkner's Vision of Human Integrity." In *The Inmost Leaf*. N.Y.: Harcourt, Brace, 1955.

Kent, George. *Blackness and the Adventure of Western Culture*. Chicago: Third World Press, 1972.

Kent, George. "The Black Woman in Faulkner's Works, With the Exclusion of Dilsey, Part I." *Phylon Quarterly* 35, no. 4 (1974).

Kent, George. "The Black Woman in Faulkner's Works, With the

Exclusion of Dilsey, Part II." *Phylon Quarterly* 36, no. 1 (1975).

Kerr, Elizabeth M. *William Faulkner's Gothic Domain*. Port Washington: Kennikat Press, 1979.

King, Richard H. *A Southern Renaissance: The Cultural Awakening of the American South*. N.Y.: Oxford University Press, 1980.

Kohler, Dayton. "William Faulkner and the Social Conscience." *College English* 11 (1949): 117-119.

Langer, Suzanne K. *Feeling and Form*. N.Y.: Scribner's, 1953.

Larsen, Nella. *Passing*. N.Y.: Alfred A. Knopf, 1929.

Larsen, Nella. *Quicksand*. N.Y.: Macmillan, 1971. Originally published by Alfred A. Knopf, 1928.

Leab, Daniel J. *From Sambo to Superspade: The Black Experience in Motion Pictures*. Boston: Houghton Mifflin Company, 1976.

Leary, Lewis. "William Faulkner and the Grace of Comedy." In *Southern Excursions: Essays on Mark Twain and Others*. Baton Rouge: Louisiana State University Press, 1971.

Lee, H. D. "Denial of Time and the Failure of Moral Choice: Camus' *The Stranger*, Faulkner's "Old Man," Wright's *The Man Who Lived Underground*." *CLA Journal* 23 (1980): 364-371.

Levin, Harry. *The Power of Blackness*. N.Y.: Vintage Books, 1958.

Lewis, R. W. B. *The Picaresque Saint*. N.Y.: J. B. Lippincott, 1956.

Litz, Walton. "William Faulkner's Moral Vision." *Southwest Review*, 37 (1952): 200-209.

Locke, Alain, "American Literary Tradition and the Negro." *Modern Quarterly* 3 (1926).

Longley, John L., Jr. *The Tragic Mask: A Study of Faulkner's Heroes*. Chapel Hill: The University of North Carolina Press, 1963.

Maclachlan, John M. "Southern Humor as a Vehicle of Social Education." *Mississippi Quarterly* 13 (1960): 152-162.

Maclachlan, John M. "William Faulkner and the Southern Folk." *Southern Folklore Quarterly* 9 (1945): 133-167.

Marshall, Paule. "The Negro Woman in American Literature." In *Keeping the Faith: Writings by Comtemporary Black American Women*. Edited by Pat Crutchfield Exum. Greenwich: Fawcett Publications, Inc., 1974.

Mather, Cotton. *The Negro Christianized, An Essay to Excite and Assist the Good Work, The Instruction of Negro Servants in Christianity*. Boston: B. Green, 1706; *Evans American Imprints*.

Matlack, J. H. "Voices of Time: Narrative Structure in *Absalom, Absalom!*" *Southern Review* 15 (1979): 333-354.

Matthews, J. T. "Marriage of Speaking and Hearing in *Absalom, Absalom!*" *English Literary History*, 47 (1980): 575-594.

McHaney, Thomas L. *William Faulkner: A Reference Guide*. Boston: G. K. Hall Company, 1976.

McPharlin, Paul. *The Puppet Theatre in America*. N.Y.: Harper and Row, 1949.

Meeker, Joseph W. *The Comedy of Survival*. N.Y.: Harper and Row, 1949.

Meriwether, James B. ed. *A Faulkner Miscellany*. Jackson: The University Press of Mississippi, 1974.

Meriwether, James B. *The Literary Career of William Faulkner: A Bibliographical Study*. Columbia: University of South Carolina Press, 1971. Originally published by Princeton University Library, 1961.

Meriwether, James B., and Michael Millgate. *Lion in the Garden: Interviews with William Faulkner*. N.Y.: Random House, 1968.

Merleau-Ponty, Maurice. *Phenomenology of Perception*. Translated by Colin Smith. London: Routledge, 1962. Originally published as *Phenomenologie de la perception*, Paris: Gallimard, 1945.

Millgate, Michael. *The Achievement of William Faulkner*. N.Y.: Random House, 1966.

Miner, Ward L. "The Southern White-Negro Problem Through the Lens of Faulkner's Fiction." *Jounal of Human Relations* 14 (1966): 507-517.

Momberger, P. "The Village and 'That Evening Sun': the Tale in Context." *Southern Literary Journal* 11 (1978): 20-31.

Moreland, Agnes Louise. "A Study of Faulkner's Presentation of Some Problems that Relate to Negroes." Ph.D. dissertation, Columbia University, 1960.

Mortimer, G. L. "Significant Absences: Faulkner's Rhetoric of Loss." *Novel* 14 (1981): 232-250.

Murray, Henry A. ed. *Myth and Myth Making*. Boston: Beacon Press, 1960.

Nash, Gary B., and Richard Weiss eds. *The Great Fear: Race in the Mind of America*. N.Y.: Holt, Rinehart, and Winston, Inc. 1970.

Nemerov, Howard. "Calculation Raised to Mystery: The Dialectic of *Light in August*." In *Poetry and Fiction: Essays*. New Brunswick:

Rutgers University Press, 1963.

Nicholson, Norman. "William Faulkner." In *Man and Literature*. London: S. C. M. Press, 1943.

Nilon, Charles H. *Faulkner and the Negro*. N.Y.: The Citadel Press, 1965.

O'Connor, Flannery. *The Complete Stories*. N.Y.: Sunburst Books, 1971.

O'Connor, Flannery. *Mystery and Manners*. Edited by Sally and Robert Fitzgerald. N.Y.: Farrar, Straus, and Giroux, 1961.

O'Faolin, Sean. *The Vanishing Hero: Studies in the Modern Novel*. Boston: Little, Brown & Co., 1957.

Osterweis, Rollin G. *The Myth of the Lost Cause, 1865-1900*. Hamden: Archon Books, 1973.

Osterweis, Rollin G. *Romanticism and Nationalism in the Old South*. Baton Rouge: Louisiana State University Press, 1949.

Owens, Leslie Howard. *This Species of Property*. N.Y.: Oxford University Press, 1976.

Page, Sally R. *Faulkner's Women: Characterization and Meaning*. Deland: Everett/Edwards, Inc., 1972.

Peavy, Charles D. "Faulkner's Use of Folklore in *The Sound and the Fury*." *Journal of American Folklore* 79 (1966): 437-447.

Peavy, Charles D. *Go Slow Now: Faulkner and the Race Question*. Eugene: University of Oregon Books, 1971.

Pitcher, E. W. "Motive and Metaphor in Faulkner's 'That Evening Sun.'" *Studies in Short Fiction* 18 (1981): 131-135.

Player, Raleigh P., Jr. "The Negro Character in the Fiction of William Faulkner." Ph.D. dissertation, University of Michigan, 1966.

Polek, F. "Tick-tocks, Whirs, and Broken Gears: Time and Identity in Faulkner." *Renascence* 29 (1977): 193-200.

Poulet, Georges. *Studies in Human Time*. Translated by Elliot Coleman. Baltimore: Johns Hopkins Press, 1956.

Powers, Lyall H. *Faulkner's Yoknapatawpha Comedy*. Ann Arbor: The University of Michigan Press, 1980.

Preminger, Alex, Frank J. Warnke and O. B. Harrison, Jr. *Princeton Encyclopedia of Poetry and Poetics*. Princeton: Princeton University Press, 1974.

Priestly, J. B. *Man and Time*. London: Aldus Books, 1964.

Pryse, Marjorie. *The Mark and the Knowledge: Social Stigma in Classic*

American Fiction. Athens: Ohio State University Press, 1979.
Raboteau, Albert J. *Slave Religion: The "Invisible Institution" in the Antebellum South*. N.Y.: Oxford University Press, 1978.
Ransom, Stanley A. ed. *Jupiter Hammon: America's First Negro Poet*. Port Washington: Kennikat Press, 1970.
Raper, Arthur. *The Tragedy of Lynching*. N.Y.: New York Universities Press, 1969. Originally published by University of North Carolina Press, 1933.
Reed, Joseph, W., Jr. *Faulkner's Narrative*. New Haven: Yale University Press, 1973.
Robinson, Evalyne Carter. "The Role of the Negro in William Faulkner's Public and Private Worlds." Ph.D. dissertation, Ohio State University, 1971.
Rose, Alan Henry. *Demonic Vision: Racial Fantasy and Southern Fiction*. Hamden: Anchor Books, 1976.
Rosenberg, Bruce A. "The Oral Quality of Reverend Shegog's Sermon in William Faulkner's *The Sound and the Fury*." *Literatur in Wissenschaft und Unterrich* 2 (1969).
Rosengarten, Theodore. *All God's Dangers: The Life of Nate Shaw*. N.Y.:Alfred A. Knopf, 1974.
Rubin, Louis D. "Notes on a Rear-Guard Action." In *The Curious Death of the Novel*. Baton Rouge: Louisiana State University Press, 1967.
Sachs, Viola ed. *Le blanc et le noir chex Melville et Faulkner*. Paris: Mouton and Cie, 1974.
Sand, Maurice. *History and the Harlequinade*. Vol. 1. London: Martin Secker, 1915.
Scheick, William J. *The Half-Blood: A Cultural Symbol in Nineteenth Century American Fiction*. Lexington: University of Kentucky Press, 1979.
Schwartz, Delmore. "The Fiction of William Faulkner." *Southern Review* 7 (1941): 145-160.
Seiden, Melvin. "Faulkner's Ambiguous Negro." *Massachusetts Review* 4 (1963): 675-690.
Seyppel, Joachim. *William Faulkner*. N.Y.: Frederick Ungar Publishing Co., 1971.
Shaw, Joe C. "Sociological Aspects of Faulkner's Writing." *Mississippi Quarterly* 14 (1961).

Slabey, Robert M. "Joe Christmas: Faulkner's Marginal Man." *Phylon* 21 (1960): 266-277.

Slatoff, Walter J. *Quest for Failure: A Study of William Faulkner.* Ithaca: Cornell University Press, 1960.

New York Herald Tribune. "'Slavery Better for the Negro,' says Faulkner." 14 November 1931.

Smith, Lillian. *Killers of the Dream.* N.Y.: Anchor Books, 1949, 1961.

Sowder, William J. "Lucas Beauchamp as Existential Hero." *College English* 25 (1963): 115-127.

Spencer, Benjamin. "Wherefore This Southern Fiction?" *Sewanee Review* 47 (1939): 500-513.

Starke, Catherine J. *Black Portraiture in American Fiction: Stock Characters, Archetypes, and Individuals.* N.Y.: Basic Books, 1971.

Stein, Bysshe. "Faulkner's Devil" *Modern Language Notes* 76 (1961): 731-32.

Stein, Gertrude. "Melanctha." In *Three Lives.* N.Y.: Vintage Books, 1958.

Steinberg, Aaron. "William Faulkner and the Negro." Ph.D. dissertation, New York University, 1963.

Stonum, Gary Lee. *Faulkner's Career: An Internal Literary History.* Cornell University Press, 1979.

Straumann, H. "Black and White in Faulkner's Fiction." *English Studies,* 60 (1979): 462-470.

Stuckey, C. F. "Bill de Kooning and Joe Christmas." *Art in America.* 68 (1980): 66-79.

Swiggart, Peter. *The Art of Faulkner's Novels.* Austin: University of Texas Press, 1962.

Sypher, Wylie. *Comedy.* New York: Doubleday, 1956.

Taylor, C. A. "*Light in August*: the Epistemology of Tragic Paradox." *Texas Studies in Literature and Language* 22 (1980): 48-68.

Taylor, Walter Fuller. "The Roles of the Negro in William Faulkner's Fiction." Ph.D. dissertation, Emory University, 1964.

Taylor, William R. *Cavalier and Yankee: The Old South and American National Character.* N.Y.: Holt, Rinehart, and Winston, 1967.

Thrall, Willard F., Addison Hibbard and C. Hugh Holman. *A Handbook to Literature.* New York: The Odyssey Press, 1960.

Tischler, Nancy. "William Faulkner and the Southern Negro." *Susquehanna University Studies* 7 (1965): 261-265. Incorporated into Tischler, *Black Masks: Negro Characters in Modern Southern Fiction.* University Park: Pennsylvania State University Press, 1969.

Turner, Arlin. "William Faulkner, Southern Novelist." *Mississippi Quarterly* 14 (1961): 117-130.

Twelve Southerners, *I'll Take My Stand*. N.Y.: Harper and Brothers, 1930.

Twombly, Robert C., and Robert H. Moore. "Black Puritan: The Negro in Seventeenth-Century Massachusetts." *William and Mary Quarterly* 24, no. 2 (1967).

Underhill, Evelyn. *Worship*. London: Nisbet and Co., 1937.

Underwood, Henry J., Jr. "Sartre on *The Sound and the Fury:* Some Errors," *Modern Fiction Studies* 12, no. 4, 1966-1967.

Vickery, John B. "Ritual and Theme in Faulkner's 'Dry September.'" *Arizona Quarterly* 18 (1962): 5-14.

Vickery, Olga. *The Novels of William Faulkner*. Baton Rouge: Louisiana State University Press, 1964.

Volpe, Edmond L. "Character Types and Themes." In *A Reader's Guide to William Faulkner*. N.Y.: Farrar, Straus, 1964.

Waggoner, Hyatt H. *William Faulkner: From Jefferson to the World*. Lexington: University of Kentucky Press, 1959.

Wagner, Linda W. ed. *William Faulkner: Four Decades of Criticism*. East Lansing: Michigan State University Press, 1973.

Wallace, Ronald. *The Last Laugh: Form and Affirmation in the Contemporary American Comic Novel*. Columbia: University of Missouri Press, 1979.

Warren, Robert Penn. *Band of Angels*. N.Y.: Signet Books, 1956.

Warren, Robert Penn. *Brother to Dragons*. N.Y.: Random House, 1953.

Warren, Robert Penn, ed. *Faulkner: A Collection of Critical Essays*. Englewood Cliffs, N.J.: Prentice-Hall, 1966.

Warren, Robert Penn. "Faulkner: The South and the Negro." *Southern Review* 1 (1965): 501-529 .

Warren, Robert Penn. *Segregation: The Inner Conflict in the South*. N.Y.: Random House, 1965.

Watson, J. G. "If Was Existed: Faulkner's Prophets and the Patterns of History." *Modern Fiction Studies* 21 (1976): 499-507.

Weisgerber. *Faulkner and Dostoyevsky: Influence and Confluence*. Translated by Dean McWilliams. Athens: Ohio State University

Press, 1974. Originally published in French, 1968.

Whicher, Stephen E. "The Compson's Nancies: A Note on *The Sound and the Fury* and 'That Evening Sun.'" *American Literature* 26 (1954): 253-255.

White, Walter. *Flight*. N.Y.: Alfred A. Knopf, Inc., 1926.

White, Walter. *Rope and Faggot*. N.Y.: Alfred A. Knopf, 1929.

Williams, David. *Faulkner's Women: The Myth and the Muse*. Montreal: McGill-Queens University Press, 1977.

Wilson, Robert N. *The Writer as Social Seer*. Chapel Hill: University of North Carolina Press, 1979.

Wittenberg, Judith Bryant. *Faulkner: The Transfiguration of Biography*. Lincoln: University of Nebraska Press, 1980.

Wolfe, Ralph Haven and Edgar F. Daniels. "Beneath the Dust of 'Dry September.'" *Studies in Short Fiction* 1 (1964): 158-159.

Woodward, C. Vann. *The Burden of Southern History*. 2nd ed., rev. Baton Rouge: Louisiana State University Press, 1960, 1968.

Woodward, C. Vann. *The Strange Career of Jim Crow*. N.Y.: Oxford University Press, 1974.

Yellin, Jean Fagan. *The Intricate Knot: Black Figures in American Literature, 1776-1863*. N.Y.: New York University Press, 1972.

Zink, Karl. "Faulkner's Garden: Woman and the Immemorial Earth." *Modern Fiction Studies* 2 (1956): 139-149.

Zink, Karl. "Flux and the Frozen Moment: The Imagery of Stasis in Faulkner's Prose." *PMLA* 71 (1956).

Index

INDEX

INDEX